CW01457432

Using Theories for Second Language Teaching and Learning

BLOOMSBURY GUIDEBOOKS FOR LANGUAGE TEACHERS

This series brings together books that enhance language educators' teaching practice. The books provide practical advice and applications, suitable for use in a range of contexts and for different learning styles, which are evidence-based and research-informed. The series appeals to practitioners looking to develop their skills and practice and is also suitable for use on a variety of language teacher education courses. The books feature a range of topics and themes, from critical pedagogy, to using drama, poetry or literature in the language classroom, to supporting language learners who have anxiety.

Forthcoming in the series:

Critical Pedagogies for Modern Languages Education, edited by Derek Hird
    Psychology-Based Activities for Supporting Anxious Language Learners,
    Neil Curry and Kate Maher
Teaching Beginner Level English Language Learners, Lesley Painter-Farrell
    and Gabriel Díaz-Maggioli

Using Theories for Second Language Teaching and Learning

DALE T. GRIFFEE AND GRETA GORSUCH

BLOOMSBURY ACADEMIC

LONDON • NEW YORK • OXFORD • NEW DELHI • SYDNEY

BLOOMSBURY ACADEMIC
Bloomsbury Publishing Plc
50 Bedford Square, London, WC1B 3DP, UK
1385 Broadway, New York, NY 10018, USA
29 Earlsfort Terrace, Dublin 2, Ireland

BLOOMSBURY, BLOOMSBURY ACADEMIC and the Diana logo are trademarks of
Bloomsbury Publishing Plc

First published in Great Britain 2024

Copyright © Dale T. Griffee and Greta Gorsuch, 2024

Dale T. Griffee and Greta Gorsuch have asserted their right under the Copyright, Designs
and Patents Act, 1988, to be identified as Authors of this work.

For legal purposes the Acknowledgments on p. xi constitute an extension
of this copyright page.

Series design: Grace Ridge
Cover image © Eugene Mymrin/Getty Images
Series logo © warmworld/Adobe Stock

All rights reserved. No part of this publication may be reproduced or transmitted
in any form or by any means, electronic or mechanical, including photocopying,
recording, or any information storage or retrieval system, without prior
permission in writing from the publishers.

Bloomsbury Publishing Plc does not have any control over, or responsibility for, any
third-party websites referred to or in this book. All internet addresses given in this
book were correct at the time of going to press. The author and publisher regret any
inconvenience caused if addresses have changed or sites have ceased to exist,
but can accept no responsibility for any such changes.

A catalogue record for this book is available from the British Library.

A catalog record for this book is available from the Library of Congress.

ISBN: HB: 978-1-3502-5891-4
PB: 978-1-3502-5890-7
ePDF: 978-1-3502-5892-1
eBook: 978-1-3502-5893-8

Series: Bloomsbury Guidebooks for Language Teachers

Typeset by Newgen KnowledgeWorks Pvt. Ltd., Chennai, India
Printed and bound in Great Britain

To find out more about our authors and books visit www.bloomsbury.com
and sign up for our newsletters.

CONTENTS

FIGURES

TABLES

PREFACE

The title for this preface might well be "Off Balance: Why Theory Is Being Given a Second Look." Books do not appear in a vacuum. They are products of a time and a circumstance. *Using Theories for Second Language Teaching and Learning* is no exception. It is a book by second language educators and applied linguists, for second language educators and applied linguists, at a particular time. Our field, particularly applied linguistics, sometimes feels ahistorical, as if it exists out of time. But we have come to think we are very much in time. To be clearer, we live in a wobbly balance between the last half of the twentieth century and the early twenty-first century.

We think many readers of this book were born, and became educators, during this time period. We swam in this wobbly time and swim in it now, like fish not noticing the water. But something is happening in our field. We suspect the balance, such as it has been, is being upset by a transition from a traditional way of thinking about theory to a newer and less traditional way of theorizing. The first way of theorizing is drawn to confirmatory experimental research, friendly to academic discourse communities, and dominated by second language acquisition scholars. The second and less traditional way of theorizing is drawn to discovery through action research and grounded theory designs, friendly to multiple discourse communities (including those of educators), and not dominated by any particular branch of the field of applied linguistics or second language education. This shift necessitates a reconsideration of the role of theory as a topic in its own right.

+++++

We note that in the course of our long collaboration as authors, we have exchanged the order of our names even though our contribution of effort has been equal. In our 2016 *Evaluating Second Language Courses*, we appeared as Dale T. Griffee and Greta Gorsuch. In our 2018 *Second Language Testing for Student Evaluation and Classroom Research*, we appeared as Greta Gorsuch and Dale T. Griffee. Now, in *Using Theories for Second Language Teaching and Learning*, we return to Dale T. Griffee and Greta Gorsuch.

ACKNOWLEDGMENTS

We wish to thank the following individuals for their assistance, both direct and indirect:

Kevin Andia, Ghadi Matouq, Anna Morton, Mirai Nagasawa, and Adolfo Villanueva for being our muses.

Larissa Caye for putting the *Common European Framework of Reference* so firmly on our radar.

Diane Larsen-Freeman, Shawn Loewen, and Harold Palmer for helping us understand so much, so persistently, about our field.

Kevin Andia, Junli Chen, Nena Choi, Joseph Garcia, Ginny Hsiao, Sarah Huang, Jinsol Kong, Angela Pineda, Jude Mensah, Daiki Suematsu, and Katie Weiss for studying Communicative Competence and asking probing questions about it.

Nena Choi and Jinsol Kong for their timely help on Korean language questions.

Kristen Michelson for our collegial conversations on a key topic we could not agree on the name of. Her name: Multiliteracies; my name: Multiple Literacies.

Jim Lee for his collegiality and friendship.

And finally, Etsuo Taguchi for his friendship and wholehearted support for over two decades.

CHAPTER ONE

An Introduction to Theory

Why This Book?

Theory has a key role in second language teaching. Teachers make plans and decisions based on theories, some overtly known to them and some less overtly so, to respond to second language learners' needs. In this book, we make the case that theories can be published and abstract, but also private and very localized. Teachers may use multiple theories at the same time as they solve the "problem" of working with learners in schools and other settings (Breen 1991; Borg 2003). Yet, teachers knowing which theories they tap into, or even identifying theories made from their own experiences and priorities (Alamarza 1996), is rarely a stated outcome in second language teacher education programs. Rather, teachers knowing more theories on a conscious level, often defined by faculty members and their own research interests, is the usual outcome. The theories typically are abstract and come from fields such as education, linguistics, organizational learning, psychology, and second language acquisition (SLA), with SLA theories typically occupying center stage.

Theories taught in teacher programs may also primarily focus on learners. Yet, it is an obvious fact that there are multiple actors in second language education, namely learners *and* teachers *and* institutions (Ahmadian and Tavakoli 2011; Alamarza 1996; Borg 1999). These actors interact, and any number of recognized and unrecognized theories, assumptions, principles, and practices come into play concerning learning, teaching, and language itself. When we talk of a group of learners or teachers or a school having a "culture," we think that the interactions between actors and theories of learning, teaching, and language may account for some of that culture.

How We Theorize the Interactions

Our understanding of how we theorize is simply one way of presenting what we theorize, but it is important because it is how we organize our book chapters. We imagine classrooms with three primary actors: teachers, learners, and the institution. We also imagine three theories present in any given classroom: theories of teaching, theories of learning, and theories of language. This 3x3 gives us a structure for nine chapters, in our case Chapters 2 through 9 for how teachers, learners, and institutions interact with theories of teaching, learning, and language.

For instance, Chapter 4 portrays the interaction between teachers and theories of language, with language being construed as course content. It describes Communicative Competence and Proficiency, two public, well-known, abstract (nonlocalized) theories. But it also portrays a French teacher's private, local theories as he teaches and writes quizzes. His dilemma is what to make of the language as use ethos promoted by the theories of Communicative Competence and Proficiency, and his own time-honored, powerful, yet nearly unconscious theory of language as form (Borg 1999).

Using Theories for Second Language Teaching and Learning balances the end goal of teachers "knowing more theories" with teachers knowing theory. We define "knowing theory" as knowing what theory is, what theory types there are, and what theory is useful for; and being able to recognize and evaluate theories in classrooms, at institutions, and in publications and conference presentations. Thus, this book is about helping teachers understand and constructively use theory.

Theory seems abstract and hard to grasp. Nevertheless, in this book, we want to say something about theory that is concrete and helpful to teachers. This chapter sets the stage for the remaining eight chapters of the book. We ask the question: In terms of theory, what do teachers need to know? We approach this question by assuming that to understand and critique how particular theories operate in our field of second language education, teachers need to know about theory in general. Theory operates in many academic disciplines and institutional settings, and accordingly, we cast our net wide. What results is a rich and varied picture of intellectual and practical choices and decisions.

Why This Chapter?

We begin by presenting a Model of Theory (Figure 1.1), which helps to relate different ways of thinking about theory. The model sets the structure for this chapter, and the six sections below in turn bring context to the model. First, we describe teachers' attitudes to theory. Second, we offer a comparison of theory to similar concepts, including prejudice, bias, and ideology. Third, we define theory and offer specific characteristics of theory. Fourth, we describe parts of theory, including those that form a backdrop for theory (zeitgeist and metatheory) and those that commonly appear as theory in published papers and conferences (construct, hypothesis, model, and metaphor). Fifth, we outline variations (types) of theories that are defined not only by disciplines in which they are found (hard sciences, social sciences, etc.) but also by their purpose and use (to describe, to show causality, etc.). Sixth and finally, we describe levels of theory from high (very abstract) to middle (abstract) to low (specific) to public (published and discussed and used by many) to private (unpublished and used by single individuals). We end the chapter with reflective projects for readers to probe the concepts.

A Model of Theory

To understand theory, teachers need to know about ways of looking at theory as seen in Figure 1.1. As mentioned earlier, we propose six lenses (teacher attitudes, etc.) through which to view theory. The model has a top to bottom orientation. The top half begins wide and then narrows down at the center in order to bring theory into ever-sharper definition using the broadest category (attitudes) to the narrowest (definition). The bottom half shows that once we have defined theory, we can elaborate how theory operates. Thus, from the center, the model begins narrow (parts of theory) and becomes wider as we move downwards to a broad elaboration of theory (levels). See Figure 1.1.

Teachers' Attitudes toward Theory

It is our experience that classroom teachers tend to be atheoretical (Stern 1983), either because they do not think about theories at all or because they somewhat reject theories. Theories do not seem useful. Perhaps teachers were introduced to theories in a surface way in their training, but in subsequent daily life, they did not concern themselves with theories.

We think there may be at least six reasons classroom teachers tend to disregard theory (Gorsuch and Griffee 2018). The first is the many terms used to describe theory, which creates confusion. Theory is referred to in teacher education resources and in research literature variously as frames of reference, frames of interpretation, hunches, conceptual schemes, normative principles, coherent views, hypotheses, models, metaphors, frameworks, theoretical claims, persuasions, perspectives, concepts, pedagogic intuitions, and schemes (see, for example, Long 1993: 225; Rossi, Freeman, and Lipsey 1999: 63). Do they all mean the same thing? Or are they subtly different?

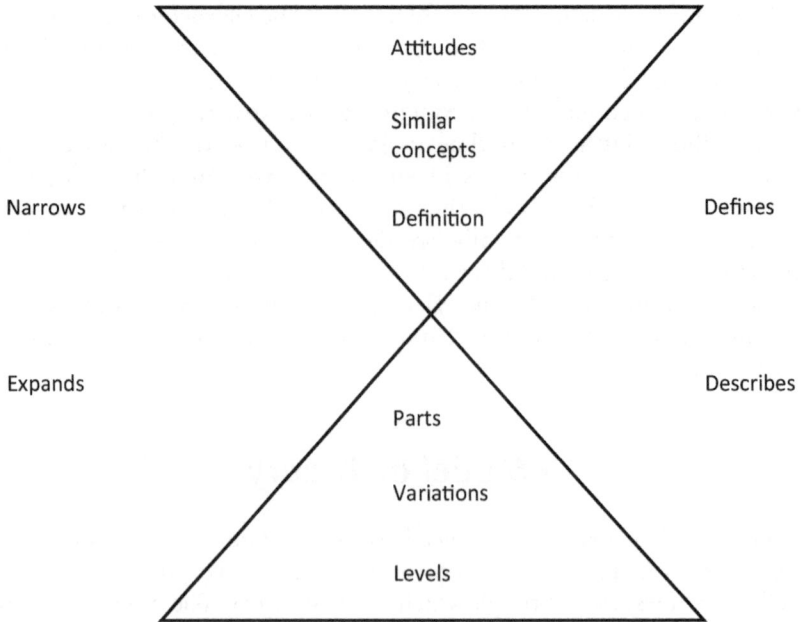

FIGURE 1.1 A model of theory.
Source: Authors.

Teachers may wonder, as they read some resource on, say, vocabulary teaching, whether the author's self-described "framework" was even presenting a theory. Is not "framework" just a collection of best practices? That the framework is a theory that guides the design and methodology of vocabulary teaching practice might be missed.

The second reason is the large number of theories available to second language teachers (Beretta 1991). Presented in the many journals, resource books, and newsletters that pass by teachers' notice in their working lives, the theories appear chaotic, random, and contradictory (Beretta 1991). Theories differ in what they attempt to explain, in their form, and what traditions they emerge from (Long 1993; Ravitch and Riggan 2017: 26), adding to the seeming chaos.

The third reason is that teachers do not perceive published theories as written for them. Ellis (1997), citing Gee (1990), points out that the different communities of researchers and teachers produce different discourses, or ways of thinking and communicating, that are mutually unappealing (Montgomery and Smith 2015). The two discourse communities (researchers and teachers) have different modes of expression and different values. Their goals are different (MacDonald, Badger, and White 2001; Rankin and Becker 2006). Thus, the research concerns of classroom teachers are not valued by researchers, and the theories produced and used by researchers are not made useful in an enduring way to classroom teachers (MacDonald, Badger, and White 2001). Note that teachers here are described as having research concerns (things they want research to do) but perhaps not the same research concerns as, say, SLA researchers or large-scale proficiency test developers (Burgin and Daniel 2021; Montgomery and Smith 2015).

The fourth reason is that while in training programs, teachers commonly study subjects such as teaching methods, materials, phonology, linguistic description, teaching grammar, and language learning (Bartels 2005; Tedick and Walker 1994, 1995). The course offerings likely reflected the interests and abilities of the program faculty members at that time. However, theory is seldom if ever directly or consistently taught as a concept or a tool (Griffee and Gorsuch 2016: 74).

The fifth reason is that many teachers worldwide do not have extensive or continuing professional training. As a result, they do not have even a minimum of exposure to commentary or discussion on the role of theory in teaching and learning (Gorsuch and Taguchi 2009: 252).

The sixth and final reason is that many teachers experience a hidden curriculum generated by their institutions that theory and practice are different and that learning the "norms" of practice is what is valued (Burgin and Daniel 2021; Dupuy and Willis Allen 2012). Even graduate students employed as teaching assistants in education, English, or foreign language departments may get little assistance or clarification on theory and practice (Griffee 2012a; see also Chapter 7 in this book). For all these reasons, we believe that working second language teachers tend to find themselves somewhere on a continuum between not thinking about theories at all or rejecting theories as irrelevant to them.

How Theory Is Related to Similar Concepts—Prejudice, Bias, Ideology

Here we compare the term "theory" to related terms. On one hand, comparing theory to these may help clarify what theory is. On the other hand, these terms are related to theory, but they are not precisely the same thing. This can be a problem because what is called "theory" by one person may be judged as "prejudice" by another and thus not taken seriously. Therefore, we need to know the differences between these terms. In what follows, we arrive at working definitions of prejudice, bias, and ideology. We assume the following: (1) Each term must stand alone and not be defined by using the other terms; and (2) each term must nonetheless be shown to have an interrelationship. We would like to show, for example, how ideology is like a theory or shares some characteristics of a theory but yet is not entirely the same thing. For each term, we offer a brief context, a list of characteristics of the term, and finally a definition for the term.

Table 1.1 Characteristics of Prejudice

1. Prejudice is a feeling (Allport 1979), an attitude, or a judgment (Auestad 2015: xix).

2. Prejudice tends to be unconscious and is often hidden because it is a socially nondesirable term. This characteristic of unconsciousness is a similarity between prejudice and bias.

3. Prejudice is usually negative but can be positive (Auestad 2015). When prejudice presents in a positive way, it is often expressed by an expert in a field as a way of expressing a preference.

4. Prejudice can be toward anything: a person, a place, a thing, a methodology, a practice, a theory, or an action.

5. Prejudice is resistant to change because it selectively focuses attention to evidence that supports it while disregarding evidence that does not (Auestad 2015: xxi). This selective attention is called confirmation bias and reveals another similarity between prejudice and bias.

Source: Authors.

Prejudice

Allport (1979: 6) defined "prejudice" as a "feeling, favorable or unfavorable, toward a person or thing, prior to, or not based on, actual experience" (see also Auestad 2015: xix; Brandt and Crawford 2016: 884; *Webster's* 1999). See Table 1.1.

Thus, prejudice is defined as a (usually negative) feeling transferred from a dispreferred category toward a perceived example of that category. For example, if you do not use songs and music in teaching because you believe they are not a serious use of time and then someone offers you a lesson plan that includes the use of songs and music, you reject it without trying it. That is prejudice. If, on the other hand, you try the lesson plan and still do not like it after a time or two, that is a judgment.

Bias

A dictionary definition of "bias" is strong opinion in one direction (*Webster's* 1999) that is systematic and action oriented. See Table 1.2.

An example from second language testing is the case of a hypothetical teacher. Cassandra is a native speaker of Mandarin who is employed as an English as a Second Language (ESL) teacher in the United States. In addition to teaching, part of the course involves listening to student presentations and then rating their performances. Cassandra's scores are similar to those of the other ESL instructors except for female students who are native speakers of Mandarin. For only those learners, Cassandra's ratings are very

Table 1.2 Characteristics of Bias

1. There are many kinds of bias.
2. According to Phillips (2000), bias is unconscious. This means we are usually unaware of a bias in ourselves although bias in others is often apparent to us.
3. Bias is not an immediate feeling (as is prejudice) but an action. This implies that we can correct for it or take actions to mitigate against it.
4. There is a certain systematicity to bias. It is not a specific action but a kind or class of actions.

Source: Authors.

harsh. When shown her ratings, Cassandra expresses true surprise but then also denies the apparent bias. To paraphrase Phillips (2000: 152), bias is a potential influence that we fail to take into account. In second language education research, bias may be present during the collection and subsequent interpretation of data. Our definition for bias, then, is an unconscious but systematic set of actions toward something.

Ideology

The makeup of the word (idea + logy) points to its meaning as the study of ideas. In this sense, "ideology" can be understood as a form of theory or a philosophy (*Webster's* 1999). For Erikson and Tedin (2003: 64), a general definition of ideology is a "set of beliefs about the proper order of society and how it can be achieved" (see also Kerlinger 1984). Parsons (1951: 24) emphasizes group membership in saying that "ideologies are the shared framework of mental models that groups of individuals possess that provide both an interpretation of the environment and a prescription as to how that environment should be structured" (see also Denzau and North ([1994] 2000: 24). Keller (2007: 93) offers what he believes is a modern, current definition: "a coherent set of ideas brought together not for strictly intellectual purposes but, rather in the service of some strongly held communal beliefs or values." In this definition, purpose seems paramount. Finally, Jost, Federico, and Napier (2009: 309) note that "ideologies crystallize and communicates the widely (but not unanimously) shared beliefs, opinions, and values of an identifiable group, class, constituency, or society . . . by making assertions or assumptions about human nature, historical events, present realities, and future possibilities—and to envision the world as it should be, specifying acceptable means of attaining social, economic, and political ideals." In this last definition, the implications are that values and opinions can be seen as facts and that action can be taken to form the world according to those values. See Table 1.3.

Table 1.3 Characteristics of Ideology

1. Ideologies are concerned with thoughts and ideas that fit together to form a coherent whole. Thus, on one hand, this is a characteristic ideology shares with theory and philosophy.
2. On the other hand, a characteristic of ideology that separates it from theory or philosophy is its tendency to consider values as facts. By confusing values and facts, ideology insulates itself from the attack of empirical data. Any fact that might challenge an ideology is absorbed as a value that can be rejected as "fake news."
3. Thoughts and ideas of ideologies are shared by individuals and unite them into groups.
4. Ideologies identify beliefs, opinions, and values of the group and tell persons who hold the ideology what the world is like and what it should be like.
5. Ideologies contain a call for action. Minar (1961) says that an ideology helps organize an individual's life, justifies what they are doing, and calls for action. This is a difference between an ideology and a theory: if an idea prompts action, the belief system that holds that idea is an ideology.

Source: Authors.

A real-life example comes from a not-long-ago job search. On invited campus visits, a job candidate was asked to guest teach in a regularly scheduled foreign language course. In nearly every case, a syntax or word morphology lesson was requested, regardless of the ordinary course content. The assumption seemed to be "teaching sentence-level grammar is a foundational skill for a teacher" suggesting a language as form orientation in those institutions (see Chapters 4, 7, 9). Where this became an ideology is when alternate topics for guest teaching such as pronunciation or culture were offered by the job candidate but were then rejected by the hosting search committee. The various schools would not consider a job candidate who did not share the same values or expertise as their own. Thus, we define "ideology" as a set of beliefs that unite individuals into groups, describes a vision of society, and based on that vision prescribes how things should be, resulting in a call for action. People fight for or prescribe an ideology; they do not fight for or prescribe a prejudice, a bias, or a theory.

Theory

In the second language education field, theory is at times more defined by what it is contrasted to, in our case, "practice," as in "theory and practice" (Richards and Schmidt 2002; see also, for example, Coombe 2022: 6). We will make a number of arguments about what theory is by beginning with this basic premise: Theory is composed of general principles based on reasoned argument and supported by evidence. Further, we agree that theory is a set of logically connected statements about how something works and why (Vogt, Gardner, and Haeffele 2012: 11). Within our own field, there is no shortage of useful definitions for theory. Noting that there are about as many definitions of theory as there are second language researchers who work with theory, Snow (1973: 78) declares that "a theory is essentially a symbolic construction that is designed to bring generalizable facts (or laws) into systematic connection" (see also Prabhu 1990: 166; VanPatten and Williams 2007). Most comprehensive is Mitchell, Myles, and Marsden (2013: 2), who state that "a theory is a more or less abstract set of claims about the entities which are significant within the phenomenon under study, the relationships which exist between them, and the processes which bring about change." In this case, "abstract" does not mean vague or inapplicable, for, according to Graves (1996: 2), theory can be personal and fitted to one's immediate situation. See Table 1.4.

We define "theory" here as a set of explicit, connected beliefs that explains how and why something works, that is based on reasoned argument, and which can be probed by evidence. It is this last part ("reasoned argument" and "probed by evidence") that inspires our use, throughout this book, of the term "posit." To posit an idea is to put forward or propose an idea that can be tested. We look to examples of theory in all the remaining eight chapters of this book. In Chapter 6, we argue that Metacognition in part posits that language learners have potential awareness of and control over their thought processes. In the same chapter, we portray a teacher who posits that his students may find his descriptions of his own language learning strategies useful. Neither of these statements comprises all that a given theory has to say; hence our belief that most theories are sets of connected beliefs (Table 1.4).

Parts of Theory

We now pass from the part of the model that narrows and defines to the part that expands and describes theory, namely the parts of theory (Figure 1.1). By "part," we mean identifiable aspects of theory. We believe that most theories can and will have some of these aspects or characteristics. We do not believe that all the parts of theory described here will be explicitly stated by those who develop or use a theory. Nor do we believe that the parts of theory named here will appear in the order given. Either way, readers of theory need to know these parts so when they encounter them, either explicitly by name (say, hypothesis) or implicitly by function (say, zeitgeist), they are familiar with them. We list and discuss six components: Zeitgeist, metaphor, metatheory, hypothesis, model, and construct.

Table 1.4 Characteristics of Theory

1. A theory is a (relatively) simple explanation of something that is more complex.

2. A theory has internal coherence, meaning that its various parts fit together.

3. A theory is an explanation. If we do not have a theory, we do not have an explanation for what we are doing. We cannot effectively communicate what we are doing to another person.

4. Whenever we explain what we believe or why we are doing something, we are explaining our theory whether we call it a theory or not.

5. A theory is contrasted with an action, a technique, or more generally a practice. Practice is what we do, and theory is our understanding of what we are doing.

6. Teachers have theories that sometimes they can clearly articulate.

7. Theories may be strongly held (similar to ideology) or weakly held (similar to prejudice).

8. All theories rely on data of some kind, from some source.

9. When a theory is personal, teacher identity may be in play. Disconfirming evidence (data) from the classroom is ignored or discounted (similar to bias) or the theory is modified to accommodate the new evidence. This latter process is exciting and is experienced by teachers as growth and discovery (Prabhu 1992: 238).

10. Like prejudice and ideology, theories cannot be proved right or wrong. Unlike prejudice and ideology, theories can be challenged by research, the results of which can be used to confirm or disconfirm theories.

Source: Authors.

Zeitgeist

Zeitgeist was first used by the German writer Goethe in 1827 (see Goethe 1902; Boring 1955). "Zeit" is usually translated into English as "time" and "geist" as "spirit." Thus, zeitgeist, which is now an English loan word, is taken to mean the spirit of the times. Edwin Boring (1955), an American psychologist, gave three definitions for zeitgeist: (1) "The climate of opinion as it affects thinking" (101); (2) "the sum total of social interaction as it is common to a particular period and a particular location" (102); and (3) "the total body of knowledge and opinion available at any time to a person living within a given culture" (106). Thus, zeitgeist is current knowledge plus all past knowledge as seen through the lens of current knowledge. Another way to understand zeitgeist is the taken-for-granted background and assumptions of a certain group of people (say, second language teachers and researchers), in a certain place (say, the country in which you live), at a certain time (say, now). Certain times and places in the past have had a zeitgeist such as "the Roaring 20s" in the 1920s United States, a time of modernization, social change, and licentiousness. Our own zeitgeist might be seen as affordable international travel, personal computers, the internet, satellite communication, artificial intelligence, robotics, and more recently living with a virus in a world pandemic (Zakaria 2020). The zeitgeist of contemporary foreign language teachers might include Communicative Language Teaching (CLT), a concern for identity, a reexamination of the "native speaker," more value placed on qualitative data, online computer searches, email, online videos, virtual professional conferences, online teaching, and electronic professional journals and newsletters.

The Role Zeitgeist Plays in Theory

For Goethe and his eighteenth- and nineteenth-century colleagues, zeitgeist was considered "a superorganic soul, an immortal consciousness undergoing maturation with the centuries" (Boring 1955: 102). For twentieth-century writers Snow (1973), Kuhn (1970), and Boring (1963), their zeitgeist involved major theoretical advances in a science, for example, Einstein and the theory of relativity. To our early twenty-first-century ears, zeitgeist sounds like a general context, a worldview, or a paradigm. Zeitgeist, by whatever name, is relevant to theory because it is the context in which theory exists and in which theorizing take place. It has three functions that can impact theory. First, it is the cradle of much of what we call knowledge, and the totality of what we know and believe to be true. We know it is relative, but it feels absolute. Second, zeitgeist restricts, or conserves. It restricts by limiting the possibilities of theory and theorizing, and thus research agendas and the resulting knowledge research generates (Boring 1955: 104). Seen in a more positive light, zeitgeist is conservative in that it demands that research be responsible by being grounded in available evidence and knowledge. Third and finally, zeitgeist sets the agenda for theorizing because it is the source for new ideas.

Metaphor

According to Nash (1963: 336), metaphor is a link between an experience that is new or not well-understood experience, and a familiar experience. It offers an explanation by suggesting a relationship between what one is trying to explain and that one expects one's interactants will also know. This understanding of metaphor, termed interactional, is derived from Richards (1936) and Black (1962) and represents a more modern understanding of metaphor than Aristotle's comparative understanding of metaphor as simply a poetic device. McGlone (2007: 109) defines "metaphor" thus: "A metaphor is a figure of speech in which a word or phrase is used to describe something it does not literally denote, e.g., This journal is a gem." Another definition comes from Lakoff and Johnson (1980: 5) who say that a word or phrase is being used metaphorically when one thing is being understood in terms of another thing. A metaphor from our field might be, "Communicative Language Teaching is a puzzle."

There is a tradition of antagonism toward the use of metaphor in scientific writing and thus theory. Nash (1963) lists five objections to the use of metaphors: (1) they are not relevant to scientific explanation, (2) they lack parsimony (too much unintended baggage), (3) they are vague and not believable, (4) their comparisons are imprecise, and, as a result, (5) they are prone to error. A major objection is that metaphors are not true. Plato objected to the use of metaphor as a component of theory because metaphors are aligned with poetry and are, therefore, in opposition to truth. In other words, as Dooremalen and Borsboom (2010: 122) state, metaphors are always untrue. Objectivism holds that there is an objective world and truth is the extent to which statements about the world correspond to the world as it really is. If you hold to what Lakoff and Johnson (1980) term the myth of objectivity, you believe that the world is made up of objects that are independent of how we experience them. Thus, if a tree fell in a forest and there was no one around, the falling tree would still make a sound. To describe reality, we need words that are capable of being defined in a clear and objective way. And for some, metaphor is not capable of that. "Poetry and figurative language such as metaphors are not precise and do not fit reality in any obvious way and should be avoided" (187). Taking the metaphor above, you might argue that CLT is difficult to implement in many foreign language settings. You may believe that CLT indeed presents a puzzle to curriculum designers and teachers. Yet, CLT as such is not impenetrable. It can be understood if studied, and if understood, it might be implemented. It is not a puzzle for everyone. Or, some might agree that CLT is a puzzle, but that a puzzle is a good thing and that one should try to solve the puzzle.

The Role Metaphor Plays in Theory

A well-known example of a metaphor used in theory is David Hume's ([1772] 2004: 23) billiard ball. You need some familiarity with the game of billiards, and you need to know what a billiard table is and how billiard balls operate. Hume could assume that in the eighteenth century his readers had that knowledge. The metaphor is one billiard ball moving and hitting another ball with the result that the second ball moves. Hume uses this metaphor to explain cause and effect, as will be seen below and throughout this book, as a highly significant goal of many theories and of science in general.

In explicating the role metaphor plays in theory, we rely on five sources: Nash (1963); Lakoff (1987, 1992); Bohleber (2018); Thibodeau, Matlock, and Flusberg (2019). Metaphors in theory have a primary and a secondary function. The primary role is to explain a theory or aspects of a theory. Metaphors do this by using the known, familiar, simple, concrete, and easy to grasp to illuminate the unknown, unfamiliar, complex, abstract, or difficult. In our field, the metaphor of "down the garden path" is used by Ellis, Rosszell, and Takashima (1994) to describe the process by which a particular theory is thought to work—a form of cause and effect. "Down the garden path" means to wander down a path that might be a dubious path with no clear end in sight. Yet the path is so pretty. The process Ellis and his colleagues wished to describe has to do with a grammar teaching practice (Tomasello and Herron 1988) where "learners were induced to make [an overgeneralization] error, which was then written on the board and corrected . . . followed by an oral recitation of the correct form and a brief explanation" (Ellis, Rosszell, and Takashima 1994: 11). The idea was that learners would engage in lengthy form-focused sessions in which they had opportunities to make mistakes, notice the mistakes, and then use the correct grammatical forms the teacher wished to focus on. This intense cognitive experience would ostensibly cause learners to notice a "gap" between what they knew and the correct form (see Chapter 6 on the Noticing Hypothesis). Thus, the pedagogical practice, and the theoretical motivation for it, is likened to leading learners down a garden path.

The secondary function of metaphors in theories is heuristic. "Heuristic" means that metaphors suggest things about the theory that can be investigated. As Nash (1963) puts it, a metaphor can generate and elaborate the basic idea in the theory. His example is John Locke's idea of the mind at birth as a blank slate (tabula rasa) upon which others (family, culture, and others) are free to write. This concept directs our attention to the role of the environment and its influence on human development and the course of peoples' lives, which continues to be an object of research to the present day. Even Dooremalen and Borsboom (2010), who believe metaphors are untrue and do not belong in theory, allow for this heuristic function of metaphors. In the Ellis, Rosszell, and Takashima (1994) study mentioned earlier, the metaphor of leading learners down a garden path might suggest two avenues among many to investigate—can the garden path (the pedagogical treatment) be changed to some different effect? And do the persons who are walking down the path (the learners and their characteristics) have an effect?

Metatheory

"Metatheory" is a term that is seldom commented on (Hjørland 1998; Snow 1973; Sousa 2010) by those who develop, investigate, or use theories. It is, however, significant to theory because metatheory is a combination of philosophic assumptions, including ontological, epistemological, subjective, and methodological assumptions, consisting of individual values and beliefs (Allana and Clark 2018; Dervin 2003: 136). "Meta" means "beyond" or "outside." Thus, metatheory is what lies behind any particular theory. Those who work with theory are subject to these assumptions, sometimes without knowing it. The question is not whether people have such beliefs, but rather are they aware of them? For many of us, our first contact with theory would be courses we take. When we read about theory, whether in textbooks or articles, we might see terms such as experimental study, grounded theory, qualitative data, critical realism, postmodernism, or constructivism (see, for example, Allana and Clark 2018). These, and others, are metatheoretic ideas. Significant authors in our fields, such as J. D. Brown, Christopher Brumfit, Marianne Celce-Murcia, Rod Ellis, Glenn Fulcher, Aline Godfroid, Joan Jamieson, Diane Larsen-Freeman, Shawn Loewen, Michael Long, Rosamund Mitchell, David Nunan, Teresa Pica, Masatoshi Sato, Henry Widdowson, and others, come to mind. Their work and writings, and the assumptions behind them, form the fabric of current metatheory.

Metatheory and Theory

Metatheory contextualizes theory. If we accept the insight from Allana and Clark (2018: 2) that "meta-theory addresses fundamental beliefs about the world that guide an individual's actions and can be termed to be paradigms or world views," then metatheory is inescapable and functions as a framework for theory use and/or theory construction. We think it helps to understand a theory by knowing the metatheory that lies behind it. This would be true whether one is reading about a theory, working out a personal teaching theory, or working to adapt a theory to practice. A case in point would be Aisha, the subject of our teacher case study in Chapter 9. She sees language as texts and choices, and plans what she asks learners to do accordingly. Aisha reads articles and books by Dell Hymes and Janet Swaffar, who see language as use and the world as something that is constructed. Nonetheless, Aisha's colleagues pressure her to "cover" a certain number of pages in a textbook per lesson. The textbook leads learners to learn sentence patterns and the correct ways to manipulate syntax and word forms. Their prevailing belief seems to be that language exists outside of individuals and that it is a collection of immutable forms. Aisha and her colleagues operate in different metatheoretic worlds. Likely, they read different authors and consult different sources for problems they wish to solve.

Metatheory accounts for some of the political adversity second language educators and scholars experience in their professional lives. "Advocates of different metatheories can be intolerant of and harsh toward alternative perspectives" (Abrams and Hogg 2004: 99). Relative to Aisha's struggles (Chapter 9), Abrams and Hogg also note that it is helpful to know what metatheory you subscribe to so you can consult with others who hold the same view. They also recommend consulting with colleagues who hold contrary metatheories to learn how to deal with criticism.

Hypothesis

According to McLeod (2018), a hypothesis is a precise, testable statement of what the researcher(s) predict will be the outcome of the study. Creswell (2009: 134) describes the process: "The investigator makes a prediction about the expected outcome, basing this prediction on prior literature . . . that suggest a potential outcome" (see also Cozby and Bates 2018). With the term "hypothesis," there is general agreement as to its meaning and function, but its application is more complex. The more common types of hypotheses one will encounter in the literature are simple/complex, directional/nondirectional, null, primary/secondary, and exploratory. None of these are mutually exclusive. A simple hypothesis involves only two variables posed in an "if X then Y" relationship. For example, if students attend more classes, they will achieve better grades. A complex hypothesis has more than one set of variables (if X then Y then Z), as in: "If students attend more classes, they are more likely to complete the course content, and will thus receive higher grades." Both simple/complex hypotheses are causal hypotheses because they imply that some manipulation of one thing will cause a change in another thing (see, for example, Figure 1.2).

A directional hypothesis is where a positive or negative difference is predicted. One group of learners gets one kind of instruction. Another group gets another kind. Setting aside the different kinds of instruction as a causal agent, a directional hypothesis would simply state that the average test score of the first group will be higher than the average test score of the second group. A nondirectional hypothesis states that the average scores of the groups might differ, but the researcher does not know which group may or may not have gotten higher scores. The null hypothesis (H_0) states that there is no predicted relationship between group membership and average test scores (or number of books read per month or number of absences or whatever). An alternative hypothesis, then, written as H_1, states that the average test scores (or whatever is being counted) will be higher for one group over another.

Finally, the American Psychological Association (APA) *Publication Manual* (2020: 86) describes primary, secondary, and exploratory hypotheses as quantitative analytic strategies. Exploratory hypotheses are suggested by the data collected in the study being reported, while primary and secondary hypotheses are generated by prior theoretical considerations or previously reported empirical studies. Schmidt (1990) offers both a primary hypothesis ("I will claim that conscious processing is a necessary condition for one step in the language learning process") (131) and a secondary hypothesis (among others) that follows after additional argumentation ("intake is that part of the input that the learner notices") (139). See Chapter 6 for more on Schmidt and the Noticing Hypothesis (1990).

Hypotheses and Theory

Teachers will encounter the term "hypothesis," or statements or proposals standing in for a hypothesis, while reading or hearing accounts of research. There is agreement that a hypothesis is an informed guess as to predicted patterns and events, based either in theory or on data. Research reports follow a predictable pattern, namely a literature review followed by a statement of the purpose followed by a hypothesis or research question. This arrangement suggests that the hypothesis is a link between theory (the literature review) and research (the research purpose, the data, and the findings). In other words, hypotheses set an agenda for research either in an immediate sense (in the same report in which the hypothesis appears) or in future research by the original author and by others (see Chapters 6 and 7 for historical accounts of hypotheses/proposals forming research agendas).

Models

These have various forms: physical (a model airplane), mathematical (factor analysis results, structural equation model results, or printed equations), or pictorial (printed lines, arrows, circles, and squares). Models we typically see with theory are in a pictorial, or iconic, form. Thus, a model is a reduced or simplified explanation of a process being theorized, usually depicting key variables (arrows, circles, and squares) in graphic form (Snow 1973). In some cases, a model can be used to describe a process, not theorize it (Achinstein 1965). In our field, Griffee and Gorsuch (2016: 17) state that a course evaluation model is a plan, or a theory, that has the specific function of guiding teachers and administrators through a course evaluation. They point to the SOAC Course Evaluation Model (Griffee and Gervara 2011) as an example of a pictorial model that links course outcomes, assessments, curriculum, and stakeholders (see Figure 8.3, Chapter 8). Csizer and Kontra (2012) offer a structural equation model, comprised of both a visual model and confirming data from 239 language learners that depicts learners' perceptions of whether and how their conceptualizations of English as a lingua franca, English for specific purposes, and English as a native language contribute more, or less, to their professional and life communication aims. Figure 1.1 in this chapter is a visual model that organizes the present chapter.

Models and Theory

Models describe and explain a theory by creating images of variables and the relationships among them. This makes clear the theorists' underlying assumptions about what is important to consider in a theory. Lor (2019: 104) notes that models have a heuristic function, meaning that they suggest possible relationships that can be investigated. As Hjørland (2000: 521) pointed out, models help us "visualize how some things might work and what variables should be taken into account." As a result, models change over time as more thought and research is done. A classic example is that of language use in tests as modeled by Bachman and Palmer in 1996 (63) and then once again in 2010 (36 and 38) when they added cognitive strategy and language use situation input and output components. It is possible to have two (or more) correct models of the same theory, but it would not be possible to have two correct theories of the same phenomenon (Achinstein 1965: 105). A case in point from our field is the theory of Communicative

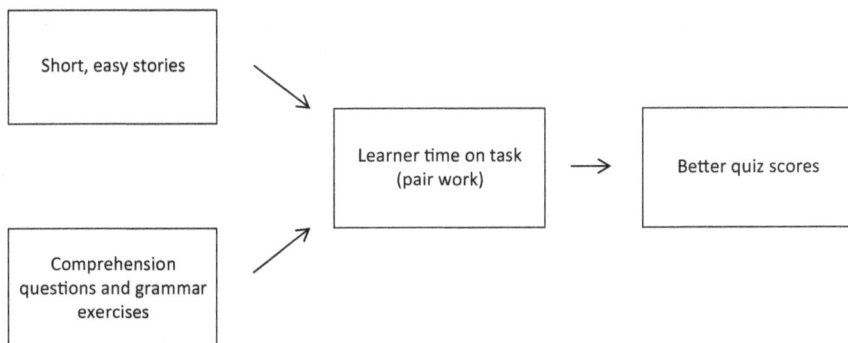

FIGURE 1.2 Visual model of a teacher's theory.
Source: Authors.

Competence (Chapter 4), which has been modeled many times by multiple scholars (for an account, see Fulcher and Davidson 2007). When teachers are explaining their teaching innovations or their research, a model that describes the phenomenon, the variables, and their relationships can be illuminating. The model becomes a visual representation of the teacher's theory. As an example, see Figure 1.2.

Figure 1.2 depicts a teacher's theory, which assumes causation. Most models have a general top-to-bottom or left-to-right orientation. Figure 1.2 has a left-to-right orientation and shows the teacher having learners read short easy stories in the L2. Learners also do work on comprehension and grammar based on the stories. The teacher's theory is that if he can have learners spend a substantial time working on stories and comprehension during class in pairs, their quiz grades will increase. The unidirectional arrows from one variable to the other show that the teacher believes one thing causes another.

Constructs

As understood by Mouton (1996: 181), a construct is "the most elementary symbolic construction by means of which people classify or categorize reality." Over time, we have experiences that come to seem patterned. From these we form concepts that are a general label for what we experience. Thus, concepts act as sorting bins for our experiences. We make sense of life through concepts. Simple concepts can become highly abstract and multidimensional through study and experience. At that point, we call them "constructs." Some well-known constructs are nation, intelligence, and identity. In applied linguistics, constructs include fluency (Chapter 5), reading comprehension, teacher and learner expectancy (Chapter 5), language teacher assessment literacy, learner knowledge about language (Chapter 7), and learner attention and noticing (Chapter 6).

Constructs, then, are abstract definitions or interpretations of observed behavior. Researchers must provide evidence for their definitions and interpretations (Riazi 2016: 55). Defining a construct and then gathering empirical data to support the definition is known as construct validation. When a test or questionnaire or interview is used for research, the constructs they are based on must be validated using data and supporting evidence. An ever-present danger of constructs is the Reification Fallacy, which is treating a construct as if it were real, or somehow set in stone. A common example of reification is the construct of intelligence. As a reified entity, intelligence is misunderstood and simplistically considered to be something that one has or does not have—an inborn trait. This belief minimizes the need for diligence and persistence in learning knowledge, and learning to use knowledge (Metacognition, Chapter 6). And, in fact, the construct of intelligence is undergoing constant elaboration, theorization, and revision (Harari 2015; Kahneman 2011), much like the construct of Communicative Competence in our field of second language education (Celce-Murcia, Dornyei, and Thurrell 1995; Fulcher and Davidson 2007).

Constructs and Theory

There is little consensus as to whether constructs come from theories, or theories come from constructs. In the constructs-come-from-theory camp, Riazi (2016: 55) defines "constructs" as hypothetical representations of human abilities and behaviors based on theory and research. Further, Gravetter and Forzano (2003) posit constructs as variables that are assumed to exist and that are created from theory. Other commentators argue a more subtle relationship between constructs and theory. Gelso (2006) says a theory is a statement of the suspected relationship between and among constructs. Thus, theory does not explain the constructs, theory *is* the constructs. In this view, what some might think of as the construct of intelligence ought to be thought of as a theory of intelligence with multiple dimensions (constructs) in interactive relationship (Kahneman 2011). Similarly Creswell (2009: 51) cites Kerlinger's (1979: 64) definition of theory as still valid today: a theory is "a set of interrelated constructs (variables), definitions, and propositions that presents a systematic view of phenomena by specifying relations among variables." An example of the latter view from our field is the theory Communicative Competence (Chapter 4), which is comprised of multiple constructs in relation to each other, including language knowledge, the ability to use language knowledge, and the characteristics of the language use situation (Bachman and Palmer 1996; Fulcher and Davidson 2007; Council of Europe 2018; Gorsuch 2019a).

Variations of Theory

Variations refers to how a theory can be classified, constructed, or used in practice. In this section, we will list and define theory variations, or types, as put forth by Snow (1973), an education researcher, and John (1980) and

Abend (2008), both sociologists. We present these in chronological order of publication, as these three sets seem not conceptually related to each other. The authors do not cite antecedents for their typologies, and we wonder if the authors were unaware of each other. However, we agree with Abend (2008) that what is meant by theory may be unclear. Abend notes that when we assume that one understanding of theory is correct and others are not, serious misunderstandings can occur (186). Our purpose in this next section is to show that theory can be typed in different ways. Theories that we take on one hand as "truth" or on the other hand as "worthless" may not be shown to be so. The different variations of theories shown here also show that theory can be used for different purposes in promoting knowledge growth in a field.

Snow's (1973) theory variations: Snow divides his theory variations into upper-level variations (A–C) and lower-level variations (D–F).

A. Axiomatic Theory: A theory that has concepts from which hypotheses can be formed. The hypotheses are tested using data, and positive results validate the theory. Axiomatic means an interlocking set of "rules" taken to be true as in *If A, then B, and then therefore C.*

B. Broken Axiomatic Theory: A theory that is "broken by continuing research" (84). They lack sufficient validation (vestiges of a dying theory) or evidence (proto theory not yet born).

C. Conceptual Theory and Constructs: Theories that may have missing constructs and are thus as yet incomplete. Theorists are engaged in defining and validate constructs to complete gaps in a theory.

D. Descriptive Theory: A theory that systematically describes phenomena but does not introduce new constructs—a building block of future theory building.

E. Elementisms: Theories that identify elementary units of analysis that may be developed into constructs or variables.

F. Formative Hypotheses: Theories engaged in early hypothesis formation. Whether testable or untestable, such early hypotheses can help develop theory.

Theories A–F represent more- to less-developed theories. Thus, types D, E, and F are lower-level types "characterized by relatively simple summarization of empirical relationships without substantial inferences or deductive logic" (Snow 1973: 87). We note that all theory types are necessary for theory building and that all theory types are present in general society and in our field. The theory of intelligence is a notable C-type theory that is always, and necessarily, under construction. Bloom's taxonomy of educational objectives (Bloom et al. 2001) would, under this system of categorization, be a D-type theory. From our field, the CEFR *Qualitative Aspects of Spoken*

Language Use (Council of Europe 2021), a set of scaled descriptions of spoken language, would be a D-type theory.

Next is John's (1980) theory typology who posits three theory types: propositional theory, grounded theory, and exact theory. Propositional theories are generalizations based on patterns in empirical data. They are assumed to be generalizations reflective of a real world and having an external reality. They are developed through deduction: hypotheses, then models, then tested with evidence. They are "default" theories because they are the most familiar.

Grounded theories are generalizations built through an inductive process relying on deepening insights and repeated analyses of data. They produce clear categories and hypotheses to be validated by future research. Exact theories shape perceptions of phenomena and are based on rational argument and constructed models, as opposed to observing regularities or patterns and then arriving at theory. Exact theory allows insight through rational thought.

An example of a "default" type of propositional theory from our field would be the Noticing Hypothesis (Schmidt 1990; see also Chapter 6) or the theory of Comprehensible Output (Swain and Lapkin 1995). Grounded theory is used to explain phenomena and change in social/educational settings. These theories are quite rare, in fact, in that they require very specific developmental steps with confirmations and disconfirmations of evolving theorizations. Henry (2018) describes this methodology while theorizing online media creation and L2 learners'/creators' motivation. Finally, exact theories are more often found in the hard sciences where mathematical modeling is used in fluid dynamics in aeronautics or artificial hearts, for example.

Our last variation of theory is Abend (2008), who has seven categories he calls T1 through T7. T1 is a theory that establishes a relationship between two or more well-defined, replicable variables. This results in general theoretical statements or generalizable principles. T2 is a theory that creates a causal explanation that can be tested, although there is not necessarily an attempt to make a generalizable statement. T3 is a theory with a hermeneutical function, which is to generate further questions and arrive at possibly novel interpretations of phenomena. There may be no attempt at a causal explanation. T4 is not a theory per se but a systematic study of major theorists with the goal of creating analyses or critiques or reconstructions of concepts and theory relevant to topics of interest in a field. T5 is a theory that is very broadly applied as a means of understanding the world, a paradigm. Examples: Postmodern Theory, Critical Theory. T6 is a theory with a contemplative, political flavor that seeks to create a reasoned account of a path to a new reality. And finally, T7 is a theory that uses a conceptual analysis to reflect and comment on problems facing a field of study. For example, how to categorize theories or how to think about knowledge.

Examples from our field for some of these theory variations would include Swan's (2005) reasoned critique and reframing of Task-Based Language Teaching (T3). For T6, examples would be Canagarajah (1999), who discusses the role and status of native speaker and non-native language teachers in a postcolonial world; and also Lee and Canagarajah (2018), who argue for an expanded view of literacy in academic writing. Examples of T7 are published discussions of what defines a native speaker of a language (Ortheguy, Garcia, and Reid 2015). As might be seen in previous sections, there are preferences in second language education for certain theory types. As illustration we note: VanPatten and Williams (2007), a theory that does not include generalized principles, would not be acceptable by some researchers as a theory at all. In Abend's typology, this would be a T1 theory. These apparent preferences are one of the reasons we wrote this book.

Levels of Theory

Our sixth and final category for discussing theory in general is level: the idea that theories can be classified by the range or scope of their coverage. For example, Newman (2000: 49) divides theories into three broad groups: micro-level, which deals with small amounts of time and space; macro-level, which deals with overall social processes; and meso-level, which attempts to link micro- and macro-level theories; while Glazier and Grover (2002) distinguish between substantive, formal, and grand theory.

The High Middle Low Theory Model

In this final section, we describe the High Middle Low Theory Model to which we refer throughout the rest of this book. Thus, when we refer to Communicative Competence as a high-level theory, we are describing where we believe this theory belongs in the model. We believe that thinking of theories in terms of their level (or range or scope) is a compelling means of identifying a theory in terms of what it seeks to explain, or do, and what it does not seek to explain, or do. High-level theories such as Communicative Competence seek to explain important phenomena, language use in this case, across all spheres of existence. High-level theories do not explain pedagogical application in micro-settings such as classrooms, again, in the case of Communicative Competence.

In Griffee (2012b) and then later in Gorsuch and Griffee (2018), we postulated the HML (High-Middle-Low) model, which divides theories into high-level theories, middle-level theories, and low-level theories. Each of these three are further subdivided into public theories and private theories. See Figure 1.3.

What makes a theory public is that the theory has been published and/ or presented and is freely discussed or known outside of an individual who posited the theory. What makes a theory private is that it is known to, or used

(Public) High-level theory	(Private) High-level theory
(Public) Middle-level theory	(Private) Middle-level theory
(Public) Low-level theory	(Private) Low-level theory

FIGURE 1.3 Griffee's (2012b) High Middle Low Theory Model.
Source: Authors.

by, the individual who posited it. It is neither widely known nor published. It is not discussed. High-level theories, sometimes called grand theories, are comprehensive and very wide ranging. Such theories, if public, have become what most would agree on as a kind of objective reality. Outside our field, this would be Einstein's Theory of Relativity, or the Theory of Plate Tectonics (Winchester 2004). Within our field, examples would be Communicative Competence, Kunnan's test validation quadrants (Kunnan 1998), and second language Proficiency models (Hulstijn 2011). High-level theories can be private in that before Einstein published his Theory of Relativity, he worked on his theory over many years of private introspection and in discussion with a circle of close colleagues (Isaacson 2007).

Middle-level theories, sometimes called domain theories, are articulated, reasoned out over time, and written down. They are used to motivate and focus research agendas. They are designed to be abstract so they can apply generally to many situations. If public, as many are, these are the theories we read about in research journals and hear about at professional conferences. They are discussed, argued over, and tested, and over time either supported or left unsupported. Such theories come from specific academic disciplines such as Communication Studies, Education, Applied Linguistics, and Psychology. Outside our field, an example would be Working Memory Theory (Psychology). Within our field, examples would be any of the Second Language Acquisition theories, such as the Comprehensible Input Hypothesis (Krashen 1982), Practice (DeKeyser 2007), or models of second language reading text readability (Newnham 2013). Like high-level theories, middle-level theories can be private. The individual or research team creating the theory may be preparing the theory for publication or presentation.

Low-level theories, sometimes called teacher theory, are overwhelmingly private. These are the intuitive and efficient working theories of practitioners based on experience. Their purpose is to solve the "problem" of classroom instruction for specific groups of learners in specific schools or learning contexts. "Low" here simply means "local," "specific," "individualized." In this sense, "low" in low-level theory does not mean poor or somehow less than middle-level theories. Most low-level teacher theories are not articulated, which means they are not necessarily open to introspection or discussion. If pressed, however, a teacher might state a low-level theory in terms of "What works for me and why," and "This is how my students learn."

A few final notes about the High Middle Low Theory Model: One interesting aspect of the HML model of theories is that it divides all three levels into public and private. This invites investigation into the origins of all theories, especially low-level or teacher theory. In other words, how does a private teacher theory become public? Or, how does high- or middle-level public theory become incorporated into teachers' private low-level theorizing practices as they plan lessons?

Reflective Projects

1. What theories did you already know before you read the chapter? Can you explain them to another person? Can you apply them to your teaching in some way? If yes, explain how. What might be some challenges to applying the theory to your teaching?

2. We would guess that some of the theories we mentioned in this chapter are new to you. What are they? Choosing just one of the theories, what is it about this theory that interested you?

3. The authors of this chapter posit quite a few things in this chapter. Make a list. What do the authors posit about theory? What do they posit about teachers? How might these proposals or statements be tested?

4. How could you use the High Middle Low Theory Model in Figure 1.3 to focus on questions you might pose about theory? You might, for example, add arrows or lines, or draw question marks next to components that do not seem clear. For instance, what could you add or change in Figure 1.3 to pose the question of how a teacher's low-level private theory becomes low-level public theory? How else might Figure 1.3 be used for your own purposes?

PART ONE

Teachers

CHAPTER TWO

Theories of Teaching and Teachers

Why This Chapter?

This chapter focuses on the interaction between theories of teaching and second language teachers. By "theories of teaching," we mean any middle- or low-level theory that explains how teachers instill knowledge or skills in learners. As we noted in Chapter 1, teachers make plans and decisions based on theories, some overtly known to them and some less overtly so, to respond to second language learners' needs. Hence our mention of middle-level teaching theories, which might be consciously known to teachers, and low-level teaching theories, which may be harder for teachers to pin down and talk about (see the High Middle Low Theory Model; Figure 1.3). Given this duality of middle- and low-level teaching theories, we argue that a theory of teaching is a way of looking at or conceptualizing what a teacher is doing, or should be doing, in a classroom. We agree with Rupley, Blair, and Nichols that "teachers have profound influence on how much students learn" (2009: 125). Clearly, taking the time to conceptualize second language teachers' theories is time well spent.

This chapter is foundational in that we establish the nature of teaching theories, which manifest in both public middle-level theory and private low-level theory (see Figures 1.3, 8.4, and 8.5). This shifting and complex quality of teaching theories sometimes makes them difficult to discern in workplace life and in one's own teaching. It is our hope that in this chapter, readers can begin the significant process of recognizing teaching theories when they see them and become aware of them in their own teaching. To begin, we describe the ways second language education has historically theorized teaching using terms such as "tradition," "method," and "approach." We also set out a series of nine implications of teaching theory. We then briefly describe the high-level theory of language, Communicative Competence (CC), which sets a context for the intellectual world (the zeitgeist) in which we find ourselves, and Roger, a teacher we get to know in this chapter. Together, we hope these steps get readers started at recognizing and seeking out teaching theories.

Then, we set a pattern for Chapters 2 through 9 by outlining how the High Middle Low Theory Model (Figure 1.3) applies to teachers and theories of teaching. We offer a table after our middle-level theory description suggesting what the theory posits, or proposes, about teachers and teaching. The middle-level theory we focus on in this chapter is the Direct Instruction Model, from the field of education. While this may not be well known in second language education, we believe the unremarked-upon outlines of it are in common use in second language classrooms. In other words, we think it makes an appearance as a low-level theory of teaching. It is even possible that the teachers using practices implied by the Direct Instruction Model are not aware that this model is a theory. We note that the Direct Instruction Model is not the same as the Direct Method, which was more well known in twentieth-century second language teaching (Kelly 1976; Richards and Rodgers 2014).

After this, we highlight low-level teacher theories by portraying classroom artifacts through a teacher case study. Artifacts are focal points or products or practices. Through artifacts, a theory might be seen more clearly. The practices or artifacts for this chapter are assignments, syllabuses, and the classroom management of an English as a second language teacher in an intensive language program in the United States. Our teacher, Roger, sits in a pool of ambivalence as he struggles to interpret an indistinct institutional and professional culture (see also Chapter 8) where there is a general theory that learners are supposed to communicate, but where there is no clear theory of how this is to be done. Roger does not have a theory of how to do it, either. Finally, we offer reflective projects for readers to probe important concepts from the chapter.

Ways to Theorize Teaching

It would be usual in a teacher resource book such as this to offer two or three citations for middle-level theories of second language teaching and then to launch into a description of what the theories posit (propose) teachers should be doing. We do not take this route. Instead, we concluded that there is an *is* to what teachers do and that there is also a *should* to what teachers do. The *is* is not better than the *should*, and the *should* is not better than the *is*. Both ought to be open to teachers, indeed necessary. Teachers ought to have resources, whether self- or other-observations or lesson plan reviews or journals, to know the *is* of their intellectual work. What middle- and low-level teaching theories are in play? Teachers ought to have resources—books or websites or internet groups or conferences or courses or mentors—to explore the options of the world of *should*. What public low- and middle-level theories are on offer, and what do they mean in terms of both *is* and *should*? But, as Larsen-Freeman (1990) points out, there is as yet no theory of teaching for second language teaching (see, however, Borg 2003; Celce-Murcia, Dornyei, and Thurrell 1997; Richards 1990). Apparently, we do not theorize what we do, or we rely on other disciplines such as linguistics and psychology, or education (Nunan 1999) for our main sources of middle-level teaching theories. We believe this is still largely the case.

Nevertheless, there are ways to discern theory in our field. In second language education, there are historically many terms used to conceptualize what a teacher does in the classroom. These terms include "approach," "image," "method," "philosophy," and "tradition." See Table 2.1.

It is our contention that these terms are stand-ins for theory. Descriptions (the *is*) or explanations or prescriptions (the *should*) for teaching such as these function as theories. As seen in Chapter 1, a theory is a proposal that describes, explains, and predicts some phenomenon of interest. In this

Table 2.1 Terms Used to Conceptualize What Teachers Do

Term	Source	Example
Approach	Richards and Rodgers (2014: 22)	"*Approach* [original emphasis] refers to theories about the nature of language and language learning that serve as the source of practices and principles in language teaching."
Image (Metaphor)	Griffee (2018: 326)	"A metaphor is an image that holds values and actions about our teaching … popular metaphors of teaching include that of gardener (growing) and coaching (directing)."
Method	Larsen-Freeman and Anderson (2011: xi)	"Methods serve as a foil for reflection that can aid teachers in bringing to conscious awareness the thinking that underlies their actions."
Philosophy	Griffee (2018: 326)	"What I believe about teaching."
Tradition	Thomas (2013: 26); Larsen-Freeman (2015); Jin and Cortazzi (2011)	"Grammarians and teachers gradually adapted the received pedagogical tradition for students who needed to learn both an analytic metalanguage and [the language] itself."

Source: Authors.

chapter, the phenomenon of interest is teaching. Thus, we think approaches and methods of teaching, such as Communicative Language Teaching (CLT), Task-Based Language Teaching, and Grammar Translation, are ways of thinking about actions done by teachers in second language classrooms.

To further illustrate this stand-in function, we consider what Gebhard and Oprandy (1999: xiii), second language education specialists, call two approaches to the enhancement of teaching: a developmental approach and an exploratory approach. For a developmental approach, the goal is to improve teaching, it is prescriptive, it wants to solve problems, it is seen as a product, and a typical activity would be a teaching methods study. For an exploratory approach, the goal is to increase awareness, it is descriptive, it wants to investigate possibilities, it is seen as a process, and a typical activity would be a teaching diary.

A developmental approach deals with what to teach and how to teach it (the *should*). If you, the reader, are a practicing second language teacher and graduated from a teacher education program, you likely studied teaching methods, materials, pronunciation, grammar, and language acquisition (American Council on the Teaching of Foreign Languages and Council for the Accreditation of Educator Preparation 2015; Bartels 2005). The idea is to give teachers a kind of database or a supply of knowledge that would enable them to do the work of teaching, such as managing a class, writing and using assignments, and writing and using a syllabus. This implementation, as noted by Fanselow (1988, 2019), is a product and the desired product is improved teaching.

In contrast, an exploratory approach emphasizes reflection that increases teacher awareness (the *is*). Awareness enables teachers to see what is happening when he or she is teaching and thus to consider alternatives, what Fanselow (1988, 2019) calls a process (see also Bartels 2005). This requires description, rather than prescription. Description of what someone does while teaching can be enabled by another person observing the teacher conduct lessons or do reviews of lesson plans, assignments, and syllabuses for purposes of coaching. Teachers can also do descriptions of themselves by video-recording their lessons and then taking the time to review them in a focused way. Fanselow (2019) and Bellarmine (2019) offer clearly written and effective inventories for teachers to use for self-assessment.

Implications of a Teaching Theory

A theory of teaching is an explanation of how teachers teach knowledge or skills to learners. We offer some implications of teaching theories:

1. If you observe a teacher in a classroom, you might be able to get an idea of his or her assumptions or principles. These assumptions or principles are derived from his or her teaching theory. In other

words, we can observe classroom activity and based on our observations, guess or approximate the teaching theory that informs the activity.

For example, if we observe a teacher showing a picture or a map and posing repetitive yet slightly different questions and statements, we can eventually guess the teacher was influenced by the Direct Method. This method posits that language is primarily oral, that students learn a second language by speaking in the language (Nunan 1999), that there is direct reference to some visual input, and that verbal exchanges are often teacher-directed, resulting in repetitive, yet slightly different, questions and statements (Larsen-Freeman and Anderson 2011).

2. There are several approaches and methods that we can identify by name. For example, Richards and Rodgers (2014), in their table of contents, list the Oral Approach, Situational Language Teaching, the Audio-Lingual Method, Total Physical Response, the Silent Way, Community Language Learning, the Natural Approach, and Suggestopedia. These can be taken as second language teaching theories.

3. We can study these teaching theories (point 2 above) and as a result have guidance to create assignments and a class syllabus and to model class management based on the theories (the *should* of teaching).

4. We as teachers have implicit (hidden, private) teaching theories whether we know it or not (the *is* of teaching). In terms of the High Middle Low Theory Model, this implicit teacher theory is low-level theory (Chapter 1).

5. Our implicit teacher theory may correspond closely with one of the recognizable, historical teaching traditions or methods named in point 2 or it may be a mix of several.

6. Our implicit teacher theory may not be derived from any recognizable, historical teaching tradition or method, but rather may be a kind of default pattern of doing things, such as having learners stand up to answer a question or having learners copy paragraphs from the board. These defaults may come from a need to control large classes or to assert a teacher's authority.

7. One of our primary sources for teacher theory is our experience as learners in classrooms. As learners, we watched our teachers and acquired over time a sense of what teaching is and what teachers do (Borg 2003; Nunan 1999).

8. A certain theory of teaching may arouse in us an emotional as well as a cognitive response. We may be very fond of and attracted to a theory of teaching or we may be repelled by one.

We have encountered teachers who like using the Audio-Lingual Method (Larsen-Freeman and Anderson 2011) because they think it is predictable, and this predictability makes learners more relaxed. We have encountered other teachers who hate the Audio-Lingual Method because they are overwhelmed by having to stage a barrage of statements for learners to repeat and fast-paced dialog rehearsals for learners to do.

9. Certain individuals are associated with certain theories or philosophies. It is likely that we have heard of these persons although we may not know exactly what theory or philosophy they posit. For example, B. F. Skinner is associated with behaviorism or Reinforcement Theory (Audio-Lingualism); Vygotsky with constructivism or Social Development Theory (related also to Multiple Literacies; see Chapter 9); Asher (Total Physical Response) with humanism; and John Dewey and Boyd Bode with pragmatism (Project Work).

Communicative Competence as a Context

While we describe Communicative Competence (CC) in more detail in Chapter 4, we touch on this significant high-level theory here. If we wish to understand the ambivalence and reactions of Roger, our case study teacher, we need to know about the zeitgeist (the overall intellectual environment) in which Roger and his teacher colleagues do their work (see Chapter 1 about zeitgeist). CC is a theory of language that takes the perspective of language as use (see Chapter 4). It focuses on the phenomenon of language users making and interpreting meanings of both spoken and written language. In terms of CLT (Chapter 3), developing learners' CC is seen as the aim, where learners are assisted to accomplish social or cognitive goals using language, not simply learn the vocabulary and sentence-level forms of a language. CLT is thus a theory of teaching, and CC is a theory of language and language ability.

In the High Middle Low Theory Model (Figure 1.3), high-level theory refers to the scope of a theory, not to its quality or superiority over middle- or low-level theory. CC has a very broad scope in that it applies to every language user in a general way. Further, just about everyone who is a second language teacher has heard the term, even if, like Roger, they are unaware of the extent and direction of the theorizing that has been done over the years with CC (Bachman and Palmer 2010; Canale and Swain 1980; Celce-Murcia, Dornyei, and Thurrell 1995; Council of Europe 2001, 2018; Fulcher and Davidson 2007; Hymes 1972). Generally, high-level theories, once they are public, are associated with multiple researchers who have contributed to the theory, tested it, refined it, and commented on it. In contrast, low-level theories, which are overwhelmingly private, usually have single authors. They are personal or implicit, even though many teachers may have the same or similar low-level theories, such as "Students need more practice" and "Students should use the grammar and vocabulary I teach them" and "It is OK for learners to use some first language when they are figuring out a second language problem—it helps them think."

CC has multiple constructs (classifications or categorizations of phenomena; see Chapter 1). One useful yet lesser-known model comes from Celce Murcia, Dornei, and Thurrell (1995) and illustrates very well a theorization of CC's constructs (components). See Table 2.2 (see also Table 4.3, Chapter 4, for a more detailed description).

Table 2.2 One Theorization of the Constructs of Communicative Competence

Component	Definition
Discourse competence	"Discourse competence concerns the selection, sequencing, and arrangement of words, structures, sentences and utterances to achieve a unified spoken or written text" (Celce-Murcia, Dornyei, and Thurrell 1995: 13)
Linguistic competence	"It comprises the basic elements of communication: the sentence patterns, the constituent structure, the morphological inflections ... lexical resources ... phonological and orthographic systems needed to realize communication as speech or writing" (Celce-Murcia, Dornyei, and Thurrell 1995: 16–17)
Sociocultural competence	"The speaker's knowledge of how to express messages within the overall social and cultural context of communication" (Celce-Murcia, Dornyei, and Thurrell 1995: 23)
Strategic competence	"Knowledge of communication strategies and how to use them" (Celce-Murcia, Dornyei, and Thurrell 1995: 26)
Actional competence	"Competence in conveying and understanding communicative intent" (Celce-Murcia, Dornyei, and Thurrell 1995: 17) (knowledge of communicative functions and speech acts; see also Austin 1975; Searle 1969; Chapter 3)

Source: Table original to this book; information sourced from Celce-Murcia, Dornyei, and Thurrell (1995).

While discourse competence, linguistic competence, and sociocultural competence are seen as knowledge, strategic competence and actional competence are seen more as ability, a kind of *doing*. All constructs here, including strategic competence, interact in the service of actional competence. All five constructs in Table 2.2 are necessary for learners to ask someone to do something, or read and respond to emails, or listen to and interpret announcements, or whatever social and cognitive goals learners have that require language use. It is interesting that the idea of learners having social and cognitive goals implies a different kind of classroom management than teachers standing at the front and being the center of attention for extended periods (Nunan 1999). While there may be good reasons for teachers to judge that certain concepts require a whole-class explanation, it is supposed that generally learners pursue social and cognitive goals by interacting with other language users and with other language sources such as course books, books, films, and websites (Council of Europe 2018; see also Chapters 6 and 9). As our case study teacher Roger will find, the second language education field in some respects interprets learners' social goals in terms of communicative functions (actional competence in the Celce-Murcia, Dornyei, and Thurrell [1995] model; Table 2.2).

The main point we wish to convey is that the constructs in Table 2.2, if viewed as single components, can be separated from the others, resulting in a "narrow" interpretation of CC that tends to focus primarily on grammar and vocabulary as knowledge (linguistic competence in Table 2.2; see also Gorsuch 2012, 2019a). This is a view of language as form (Chapters 4 and 9). For many educators operating out of this orientation, language forms comprise course content and thus the course syllabus. They use their efficient, goal-directed, implicit low-level theory to do the business of teaching. The same teachers or administrators may think that by focusing on language forms they are serving the aim of developing learners' CC and thus engaging in CLT.

CLT may be ill-defined, which might contribute to a narrow treatment of CC. Nunan describes CLT as "less a [teaching] method than a broad philosophical approach to language" (2015: 10). There are few actual classroom activities or techniques that can be rigidly labeled as those of CLT, resulting in perhaps a "fuzzy" idea of CLT (Larsen-Freeman and Anderson 2011: 115). This allows for flexibility in teaching, as Larsen-Freeman and Anderson (2011) rightly point out, but at the same time this "fuzziness" allows teachers like our French teacher Rick (Chapter 4) to think learners are communicating, and that he is teaching communicatively, when in fact learners are just practicing in pairs the spoken sentences and dialogs that Rick has assigned. Within this muddle and conceptual crossover, CC and CLT together approach being zeitgeist, a prevailing spirit of the time. Roger, the teacher in our current chapter, is aware that he should do CLT. He knows that somewhere in the background there is something called "Communicative Competence," but with two very similar acronyms for the two areas (CC versus CLT), is it not the same as CLT?

How the High Middle Low Theory Model Applies to Theories of Teachers and Teaching

In this section, we describe a middle-level theory called the Direct Instruction Model. Because our case study teacher, Roger, comes from a background in education, he has come across this model. Like any well-defined middle-level theory, the Direct Instruction Model makes overt, stated assumptions of the internal logic developed over time by those who research the theory (Tarver 1985). These assumptions are statements of what a theory posits or proposes. One function of the "posits" of a theory is to guide action for further thought and research. Another function can be more applied, in that the proposals made by the theory may guide practical actions. That said, the Direct Instruction Model is an applied teaching theory that is meant to be both researched and applied to a teacher's actions (Rupley, Blair, and Nichols 2009; Stein, Carnine, and Dixon 1998; Tarver 1985). Just like teaching approaches or methods familiar to us in second language education, what is posited by the Direct Instruction Model guides teachers' actions. See Larsen-Freeman and Anderson (2011) for portrayals of different second language teaching methods in terms of their principles (what they propose or assume) and resulting actions (what a teacher does). There is a caveat: What a teaching theory or method proposes does not necessarily rigidly prescribe specific teacher actions (the *should*). Proposals from multiple, independently developed theories with very different purposes and bases may seem to result in similar teacher actions, for instance, the verbal repetitions of the Audio-Lingual Method and the seeming learner repetition in Community Language Learning (Richards and Rodgers 2014; Stevick 1986). Rather, the posits of theories are meant to be interpreted. As we will see, Roger was not led to interpret this particular theoretical model that he learned about in his education coursework (Stein, Carnine, and Dixon 1998). In other words, he read about or saw some demonstrated techniques, but he did not become even moderately conversant in the posits or principles of the Direct Instruction Model, a common problem in teacher education (Stevick 1982). He did not develop the ability to interpret or apply the Direct Instruction Model.

The Direct Instruction Model

We focus here on the Direct Instruction Model, a theory of teaching concepts developed by Siegfried Engelmann to teach his own children mathematics in the 1960s (K. Engelmann 2020). Engelmann worked out "scripts" of extended verbal interaction of teachers with small groups of children to master small parts of well-defined larger concepts such as telling time, getting meaning from reading texts, algebraic reasoning, and fractions. One hallmark of the Direct Instruction Model was the importance of immediately helping struggling child learners through verbal scripts, coaching, teacher modeling of strategic thinking, and review (Engelmann and Carnine 2016; Gersten, Woodward, and Darch 1986; Stein, Carnine, and Dixon 1998). Thus, an early goal of the model was to ensure that all children learned and that they had "opportunities to learn" through direct interaction with teachers and peers (Rupley, Blair, and Nichols 2009: 129).

Engelmann later worked with Douglas Carnine, an education researcher specializing in working with underperforming and struggling learners. Both theorists concluded that children are innately capable of learning what teachers have to offer (Engelmann and Carnine 2016; Tarver 1985). Therefore, it is up to teachers to engineer what they want students to learn in such a way as to make that possible (Engelmann and Carnine 2016: 464). This is accomplished by (1) carefully choosing significant "large" concepts and breaking them down into teachable and learnable pieces (Botts et al. 2014; S. Engelmann and Carnine 2016; Gersten, Woodward, and Darch 1986); (2) scripting the verbal interactions between teacher and learners according to the learnable pieces (Engelmann and Carnine 2016; Rupley, Blair, and Nichols 2009; Tarver 1985); and (3) scaffolding learners by modeling the thought processes useful to learning the concepts (Rupley, Blair, and Nichols 2009).

For (1), examples of "large" concepts are reading and comprehending narrative texts (Rupley, Blair, and Nichols 2009) and "problems and solutions" found in historical events (Stein, Carnine, and Dixon 1998). When broken down into smaller learnable pieces, reading and comprehending narrative texts become a series of lessons on "recognizing sequential development, fact versus opinion, and a stated main idea" (Rupley, Blair, and Nichols 2009: 127). For (2) and (3), an example for reading would be the teacher doing a think-aloud as he or she reads through a small part of a text, demonstrating how to find evidence of sequential development (Rupley, Blair, and Nichols 2009: 128), for instance,

> First I look for any "number" words … oh look … here's "first" and "after that" … and I then keep going down a few more lines … I'm using my finger to keep my place … oh there's "finally." So, tell me what I saw? Point and say them. Did I miss anything? So then I go back to "first" and I read just before and just after that word. So then I decide "first" belongs to "Billy first went to his friend's house."

While the Direct Instruction Model is a teacher-directed model of instruction (Goeke 2009; Stein, Carnine, and Dixon 1998), teachers are to incrementally reduce their part in the scripts and practice activities until learners can show they have mastered the knowledge and skills set as goals (Botts et al. 2014; Hollingsworth and Ybarra 2009; Rupley, Blair, and Nichols 2009). Learners show their mastery through classroom tests and through their interaction with teachers and peers in small group coaching sessions. No new knowledge or skills are introduced until the "old" content is reviewed and then connected to the new content. For this reason and for other reasons, the Direct Instruction Model has a strong tradition of evaluation (Tarver 1985; see also Chapter 8), not only of learners (Rupley, Blair, and Nichols 2009) but also of the outcomes of Direct Instruction Model programs (e.g., see Botts et al. 2014; Tobin and Calhoon 2009). The importance and tradition of evaluations of instructional programs (the teaching itself), plus the provision in the Direct Instruction Model for timely and extensive mastery-focused interventions with struggling learners, has captured the attention of many educators specializing in disadvantaged or at-risk or struggling learners (Al-Shammari, Al-Sharougi, and Yawkey 2008).

Sensitivity of Direct Instruction Model to Content and Curriculum

Several researchers (Archer and Hughes 2011: 29; Engelmann and Carnine 2016: vi; Stein, Carnine, and Dixon 1998) insist that Direct Instruction Model teaching be placed in the context of Standards, Curriculum, Teaching, and Testing. As we will learn in Chapter 9, Curriculum is a significant high-level theory area involving ongoing practical reasoning and inquiry (Bobbitt 1924; Reid 1999) about tests, instruction, and materials and textbooks. In the context of the Direct Instruction Model, Standards specifies the decisions made by teachers and administrators as to which key concepts are to be taught and then what goals arise from these choices (Hollingsworth and Ybarra 2009). Curriculum is based on Standards and thus identifies instructional strategies, scaffolding instruction, and specifies the order in which items will be taught and the lesson scripts themselves. Thus, Standards and Curriculum together comprise a syllabus, an artifact we may be more familiar with in second language education. Stein, Carnine, and Dixon (1998) note that the Direct Instruction Model is unique in that as a teaching theory, much importance is placed in integrating instruction (Teaching) and Curriculum. A teaching theory might be thought of as a teaching procedure that can be applied to any content: "many educators today consider any systematic instruction that includes teacher modeling to be Direct Instruction" (227). However, Stein, Carnine, and Dixon (1998) point out that the Direct Instruction Model places great importance on identifying which "big ideas" or significant concepts (Standards) will be attempted to begin with. Rather than choosing many topics ("teaching for exposure") to work on with learners lightly, few topics or concepts should be chosen so that learners work on them intensively ("teaching for mastery") (229; see also Botts et al. 2014; Tarver 1985). And, whatever subtopics or sub-concepts are identified for a syllabus (Curriculum), they are related strongly, through teacher explanation, demonstration, and review, to the big concepts (Standards). As Rupley, Blair, and Nichols (2009: 131–2) note, "What really set the teachers ... apart ... was their use of coaching children in how to apply the word identification skills they were learning in phonics while they were reading everyday texts." In this case, a subtopic (Curriculum) was phonics. The "big concept" (Standards) was comprehending everyday texts.

Goals are derived from decisions on which big ideas to work with learners on (Standards and Curriculum), and this very much changes the instruction (Teaching) a teacher will do with learners. Teaching, as noted above, includes three broad strategies: modeling strategic thinking, guided practice, and independent practice. For small component-type skills and knowledge, such as teaching sound to symbol correspondence in reading, teachers may elect to use modeling and guided practice for a longer period of time and then transition learners to independent work. But for comprehension strategies in reading, a more "macro" concept, teacher may engage in modeling and guided practice but then turn to more extensive independent practice (Rupley, Blair, and Nichols 2009). Thus, the Direct Instruction Method is sensitive to content (Al-Shammari, Al-Sharoufi, and Yawkey 2008; Rupley, Blair, and Nichols 2009).

Finally, Testing is feedback given to learners, and to programs, with direct relation to Standards, Curriculum, and Teaching (Engelmann and Carnine 2016: vi). Tests document the extent to which students have met the goals that have been set. In general, teachers will not continue to new goals or new knowledge until learners show the ability to work with current knowledge and skills independently (Hollingsworth and Ibarra 2009). If tests, quizzes, or assignments show that learners have not achieved mastery, the teacher reviews for programmatic reasons. He or she reviews with a particular focus on the scripts used in extensive interaction with learners in small groups. Was a step missed? Was there a problem with the script (Brown 1985; Engelmann and Carnine 2016)? See also Stein, Carnine, and Dixon (1998) on the use of script checklists for good scaffolding practices. As will be seen in our case study, our teacher Roger does not know about the way Curriculum and Teaching are theorized as interdependent in the Direct Instruction Model. Thus, he teaches every small or large concept the same way and emphasizes teacher-to-whole class talk and explanations. To him, Direct Instruction is any teacher-fronted talk on whatever topic is stipulated in the syllabus for that day, but not the scaffolding, the guided practice, and extensive teacher-to-learner and learner-to-learner interaction in small groups implicated in our theory of teaching in this chapter.

The Direct Instruction Model and Second Language Teaching

The Direct Instruction Model, a product of K-12 Education in the United States, is not much mentioned in the second language teaching literature. In the 1990s, second language education commentators Richards (1990) and Celce-Murcia, Dornyei, and Thurrell (1997) compared "indirect" and "direct" teaching methods for speaking. With commentaries such as these, the main issue at hand was whether learners could learn how to do conversation by picking up conversational rules implicitly through interaction. In this view, learners learn conversation by doing conversation. In direct instruction, however, "new linguistic information is passed on and practiced explicitly" (Celce-Murcia, Dornyei, and Thurrell 1997: 141). This linguistic information would be the "main rules of conversational or discourse-level grammar" such as "politeness strategies" and "communication strategies" and "openings, closings, and the turn-taking system" of conversation (141). Celce-Murcia Dornyei, and Thurrell note that direct instruction of this kind might remind second language educators uncomfortably of traditional sentence-level grammar teaching. Neither Celce-Murcia, Dornyei, and Thurrell (1997) nor Richards (1990) seem to take notice of the Direct Instruction Model (Engelmann and Carnine 2016) per se. Neither work cites any of the research or commentary associated with the Direct Instruction Model familiar to US K-12 commentators. Yet Celce-Murcia, Dornyei, and Thurrell (1995) show great sensitivity to teachers' ability to pick out key concepts for the teaching of speaking in their CC model (see Table 2.3), from which they draw their arguments in favor of direct teaching of discourse-level conversation rules in their 1997 work. Richards (1990), himself a second language Curriculum and materials specialist, suggests key concepts (turn-taking, topic control, repair, conversational routines, fluency, pronunciation, and register) and suggests teaching them as strategies, similar to what the Direct Instruction Model stipulates.

More recent mention of the Direct Instruction Model in second language education does directly invoke elements of the US model dating from the 1960s and 1970s. Al-Shammari, Al-Sharoufi, and Yawkey (2008) evaluate an English language program in Kuwait for elementary school children based on Engelmann's Direct Instruction Model. Due to research methodology problems with the project, it is not possible to know what knowledge growth was studied in learners. The authors merely claim that learners in Direct Instruction Model–inspired lessons did "better." But the real value of the research is in the detailed description of how ordinary Kuwaiti teachers in the study were taught how to carry out Direct Instruction Model–type instruction at the level of individual lessons. The authors argue effectively that participating teachers gained insights into improving learners' reading comprehension using principles of the Direct Instruction Model. See Table 2.3 for what the Direct Instruction Model posits.

Low-Level Theories Concerning Teaching and Teachers: A Teacher of English

This chapter identifies and describes low-level theories about teaching and teachers held by an entry-level English as a second language teacher in the

Table 2.3 What the Direct Instruction Model Posits

1. Teaching is extended, structured verbal interactions between teachers and learners.
2. The verbal interactions are worked out beforehand, and these are called scripts.
3. The scripts themselves are the focus of evaluation of the teaching.
4. Teaching is working with learners in small groups.
5. All learners can learn if the concepts and sub-concepts are well chosen and if scripts are well designed.
6. Struggling learners get immediate help.
7. The goal of teaching is mastery of well-defined, predetermined, significant concepts.
8. Choosing significant concepts requires careful thought.
9. Larger, significant major concepts will be cut up into smaller teachable and learnable parts.
10. Teaching scripts depend on the smaller, teachable parts chosen for a lesson.
11. Teaching is the scripted verbal interactions (#1 above), coaching, teacher modeling of strategic thinking, review, and guided and independent learner practice.
12. Teachers scaffold learners intensively at first and then reduce help until learners demonstrate independent mastery of knowledge or skills.
13. Teaching and evaluation coexist equally. Evaluation and tests are used for knowing whether learners need review or further help but also for evaluating the teaching (the scripts) and the concepts and sub-concepts chosen for instruction.

Source: Authors.

United States. First, we describe Roger's background, including his first and second language status, and his graduate-level bilingual education degree. Second, we describe Roger's school, its mission, and the assignments and syllabuses that are shaped by the school's purpose. Indeed, Roger has little say on the syllabus. Third, we describe two classes Roger teaches: one on grammar, and the other on speaking. We see details of Roger's classroom management. We will be privy to Roger's thoughts after he notices the lead teacher at the school standing in the hall outside his classroom, apparently listening to him teach. Finally, Roger's low-level theories about teaching and teachers will be identified.

Roger's Background and Education

Roger is an American male in his late twenties. This is his first full-time teaching job. He comes from a bilingual family speaking both Spanish and English. His family maintains close contact with their family and friends in South America, and Roger has spent extended periods there. In fact, at one time, Roger considered Spanish his native language, and when he returned to the United States in his mid-to-late teens, he studied English as a second language. As a learner of English in school, his studies mainly concentrated on grammar and vocabulary with the idea that these areas of knowledge would help him read his school textbooks on history, art, math, and science. He learned quickly in those areas, and since his pronunciation and fluency in English had been set from childhood and was already very native-like, he was soon taken as a native speaker. Roger is friendly, and people like talking to him.

Roger has a recent MA in bilingual education. In the state where he lives, "bilingual" means Spanish and English. He was employed as a research assistant during his MA and thus did not teach except for some student practica where he observed fourth and fifth grade teachers work with "limited English" students from China, Estonia, Mexico, and Ukraine on English letters, sounds, and word identification. Roger was much taken with how the teachers kept up a steady flow of questions and talk with the children. Their answers to the children's utterances were long and encouraging in tone. The teachers and the learners seemed to have a warm sort of rapport that Roger liked.

Roger's MA-level classes were large with twenty to thirty-five students. Many of the students were full-time K-12 teachers during the day, and thus most of the courses were held at night. One-third of the classes were held online. He did not get to know many of his classmates, and there was little cooperation among classmates to work on projects together or to form study groups. Roger's MA coursework was on K-12 teaching methods, bilingual teaching methods, teaching reading, instructional design, instructional technology, and child first and second language acquisition. It was in his instructional design course that he had a basic introduction to two or three theories, including the Direct Instruction Model and something called Backward Design. The emphasis in the course was reading about the teaching theories and then watching videos where the theory was discussed and perhaps briefly demonstrated. The instructional design course was held a year before Roger did his classroom observations, and so even if he had thought of it, he had no way to connect what he learned about the teaching theories to the teaching he observed. Roger's education was of the developmental approach. Nonetheless, when he completed the MA he felt he had a future as a teacher. Whatever job he took in future, his job was to teach, and this meant talking to students, having a warm rapport with them, explaining things to them, and making them feel that he cared.

Roger's Work

After graduation, Roger finds a full-time job in the same town where he got his degree. The job is at a newly opened intensive English as a second language school. It is a local branch school, part of a large international chain. It is not a job to keep in the long-term, but it is good enough for him to support himself until he figures out his next step. The chain, and the local branch school, has made some big marketing promises to attract paying students. The school claims that in a fairly short time, its curriculum, teaching, and intensity together will qualify an international student for English-medium university classes. All teachers in the school are either native English speakers or non-native speakers judged to have a native-like ability. Many of the instructors as well as the school branch business manager and the teaching director are graduates from the same education college Roger went to, or from an applied linguistics MA program in another college at the university.

Each month-long term, Roger teaches two classes—one in the morning, meeting for three hours; and another in the afternoon, meeting for two and a half hours. Up to two ten-minute breaks can be taken in any one class. This term, Roger is teaching "Structures and Grammar" to low-level learners who are newly arrived and "Speaking" to middle-level learners who have been at the school for about six months. Roger is told by the teaching director that the goal of the "Structures and Grammar" class is getting students to use certain predetermined grammatical structures in both speaking and writing. The goal of "Speaking" is to work with students so they can engage in everyday conversations. The teaching director also says something about "communicative functions" and working with learners to think through what they wish to communicate and figuring out how they can express those intentions more easily in speech (see actional competence in Table 2.2). Roger does not know what the teaching director means by "functions," and he asks about it. She answers, "Communicative functions have to do with what learners intend to say and how they interpret what other speakers mean to say. Like, expressing regret, or making a request." Roger is still unclear on the "function" part, but he does hear the word "communicative." He comes to accept—as does every teacher in the school—that he is to teach communicatively. Because he lacks further information, he assumes a commonsense definition of communication, namely where information is passed from one person to another verbally.

Several months ago, someone had come from the regional office for an afternoon training seminar where she talked about CC (Chapter 4) and CLT (Chapter 3). To Roger and most of the other teachers there, the trainer had seemed to use "Communicative Competence" and "Communicative Language Teaching" interchangeably. The trainer had given two teaching demonstrations in the form of Presentation, Practice, and Production (PPP, Chapter 3). One had been a dialog (Presentation), a worksheet (Practice), and then a role play (Production) taking place in the school on an academic topic. Another had been a dialog, a worksheet, and then a role play, but this time in the "real world," at a bank. Both teaching demonstrations involved learner speaking but not listening, reading, or writing. She had asked the teachers at the meeting to identify from the dialog the communicative functions in the bank role play, and one teacher, Marianne, had said "Making a request, and making a complaint?" "Yes, that's right," the lady from the regional office had said. She did not expand on "functions," however. Instead, she had gone on to tell the teachers about the grammatical structures that could be practiced from the dialogs, and how they could encourage learners to use them. As a result, Roger never connected the "functions" of the seminar to the "communicative functions" mentioned by the lead teacher at the beginning of the speaking course as there were several months in between.

Roger is given a textbook for each class. The class syllabus, also given to him by the teaching director, specifies that he must cover the first three chapters in each book for this term. By habit, Roger consults only the required pages. He generally likes what he sees. There is plenty for students to do. Roger could read the introduction of each textbook. Also, teachers' manuals for all required textbooks are there in the teachers' break room for consultation. These resources might offer information so Roger could understand more fully what the authors intended, but he has never consulted them. The teaching is intensive, and as much as he enjoys engaging with the learners in class, he is worn out at the end of the day. And he still has to take assignments home at night to grade!

Roger is more ambivalent about the syllabuses he is given to use. On one hand, he appreciates the work that has gone into making them. The content for each course is spelled out. Grammatical structures are to be covered and practiced for the "Structures and Grammar" course. Academic and social speaking situations are to be covered for the "Speaking" course. Then, the sequence is given for the content, day by day. The syllabus also shows that daily assignments are requested, particularly in the "Structures and Grammar" course, which is writing intensive. On the other hand, Roger feels the syllabuses are too full. He wonders if the regional marketing department claims more than learners can achieve in a given time frame. Thus, Roger has no choice as to the curriculum categories (grammatical structures and speaking situations named in the syllabus), but assignments and class management are largely up to him. As long as students do well on a school-administered end-of-term test, and move up a "level," Roger can give assignments and teach as he likes. Roger's colleagues share assignment ideas freely in a central folder. They are mostly worksheets with grammatical structures, vocabulary, and expressions for learners to practice, ending with a more open-ended assignment such as writing a paragraph or a dialog. Roger also likes the creativity of making his own assignments, although making assignments for the "Speaking" class has always been a problem.

Roger's Teaching—"Structures and Grammar"

Roger has twelve students in his morning "Structures and Grammar" class. He starts by taking roll. By the third session he knows students' names. He arranges his students in a semi-circle facing the board. Although Roger's desk is off to the left, he places a chair in the center of the circle in front of the board where he spends most of his time sitting or standing. He assigns an exercise from the textbook by directing the students to the page in the text he wants to cover. He also writes the page and exercise number on the board. The page is mostly taken up with a major assignment that looks like a paragraph from an essay about natural cures for sickness. Learners are to find the grammatical mistakes in the paragraph and write the correct forms underneath. For example: "Garlic is a natural medicine, it is a very safe antibiotic." Learners are to supply a "causal connection" between the two clauses, as in "Because garlic is a natural medicine, it is a very safe antibiotic" (example from Wajnryb 2012: 32). The textbook authors intend, as they state in the teacher's manual, for the learners to notice patterns in the mistakes, in this case omissions of causal connectors and conjunctions. Then, learners are to come up with grammatical rules that are suggested by the patterns, but Roger does not know that. He does see a small note at the bottom of the page that learners can talk to each other about the rules, making the note a minor assignment in his eyes. Roger thus slightly dismisses this and does not see learners' talk as the point of the exercise. After all, it involves speaking and this is not a speaking class. The point of the exercise, to him, is to write the correct causal connectors where appropriate.

Roger reads the paragraph exercise instructions in the textbook slowly and clearly, and assigns a time on the clock by which the assignment is to be completed. He then asks the students to work in pairs. The students turn to each other and start discussing the assignment. Roger hears this and reminds them that they must use only English. This is school policy and is strongly enforced. Roger sits in his chair and waits for the students to complete the exercise. After a few minutes, he feels restless and that he ought to be teaching. He begins walking around the class listening to learners talk. He sees one pair of students simply making two sentences by removing the comma instead of using causal connection words. Roger goes to the board and starts writing examples of what the exercise requires. The examples come from Roger's own mind and are drawn from spoken language, not written, as in: "I'm late because the bus didn't come," "because" being the connector. He reads his examples in a slow, clear voice. He then explains where the causal connectors can go. He gives another example from his own mind and repeats his initial explanation. Students listen carefully but ask no questions even when Roger asks if they have any.

There are two or three more sequences like this—learners working from the textbook and then Roger circulating, and when he senses learners having trouble, he goes up to talk at the board. The class period is finished, and Roger is still at the board talking. He notices learners are restless and looking at the clock. He asks students for their own examples, but he does not wait for an answer. His voice is now slightly raised in pitch and volume, and he is determined that his students understand the last detail of the lesson. As a result, he goes several minutes past the time the class should have ended. Finally, after repeating his point for the third time, he dismisses the class. The lead teacher is standing outside the classroom door. "Everything OK?" she asks. She has heard Roger's voice all the way down the hall. "Oh sure," says Roger. He feels a little nervous. Why was she listening? Was his explanation of causal connectors not good? Maybe his examples were not good? It does not occur to him that the lead teacher hears a lot of teacher talk coming from Roger's class and that he sounds strained. The lead teacher is concerned. Is Roger admonishing students about something? Is there some topic learners are having trouble with? Perhaps she can help. At any rate, should not learners be asking questions or offering their own examples? Or, perhaps Roger could be asking questions and waiting for answers?

The "Speaking" Class

Roger has fifteen students in his afternoon "Speaking" class. The conversation situations for the day are: (1) finding "ethnic food" in the supermarket for a dinner you want to make for a friend (functions: asking for information, making suggestions); and (2) getting help from your friend in the kitchen to make the dinner (function: requesting help). Roger loves to cook, and so he is excited about the topics for the day. And he has had a lot of experience finding the ingredients for the food he likes to make at various specialty shops around town. Roger begins class by taking roll. Learners are sitting at their desks in rows. Roger writes one of the speaking situations for the day on the board: "Finding ingredients for a dish you want to make for a friend." Using the required textbook as a cue, he asks learners to tell him about some dish from their country they would like to make for a friend. He writes what they say on the board. He talks for several minutes about what he wants to make, a tasty dish called *ajiaco*. He explains that it is a kind of meat soup, and he then talks about the ingredients and the different shops where he likes to get them from. He underlines "ingredients" on the board. He puts students into groups of three and tells them they are supposed to write up a list of ingredients they will need. A few groups are done within minutes, and since they have not been told what to do, they look at each other's lists and talk haltingly about where they can find the things on the list, mainly using their cell phones and a map application as a means of communication, as in "It's here," and then showing the name of a shop and its location in town on their cell phone screens.

Roger sees the groups with the cell phones, but he has his hands full with two groups who are having trouble and who insist on using a bilingual dictionary to find their ingredients, which renders words like *terasi* (a Javanese word) into "shrimp paste," which no store, even a large supermarket with international customers, is likely to have. Roger's talk with them consists of encouraging them to know when to ask a relative back home to send certain foods. He models some modal forms such as "Could you send me _____?" And then one student wants to know when to use "some" versus the indefinite article "a" or a number word such as "two pieces of." Roger talks to one of the groups for quite a while on this topic. It is never a waste of time to review grammar, he thinks, as the school-mandated test at the end of the term is oriented to grammar, even the speaking test for the course he is teaching now.

When Roger gets back to the textbook, forty-five minutes have gone by. They have a short break, as much for getting the two slow groups to finish up as for anything else. When learners return to class, Roger tells them to look in the textbook at the dialog for "finding food in a supermarket." An international student is visiting the store and talking to a series of store clerks in different departments in the supermarket. Students read the dialog aloud after Roger for each line. Then Roger puts the students in pairs, and the students read the dialog aloud to each other. He then asks learners to rewrite the dialog using their list of ingredients.

What the learners did earlier in the course is partly helpful in that they now have a list of ingredients they want. There is a note at the bottom of the textbook page on "functional talk" that says "asking for information" with sample structures such as "Do you have any _____?" and also "making suggestions" with sample structures such as "You might look in _____" and "I think it might be _____." Roger does not really see the note about communicative functions, which might have been helpful with the early finishing groups from the first part of class. Those groups could have used the functions and structures to have the clerk say, "We don't have that. I think it might be at another store." A few learners might have done just that, but Roger, circulating around the classroom, insisted learners stick with something that closely resembled the original dialog. Instead of coaching individual learners to go beyond the dialog and yet explore the communicative functions, he emphasized he wanted students' scripted speech to be "accurate" and "grammatically good."

To finish up, Roger has the class members perform their dialogs for the rest of the class. He corrects students immediately after each performance and turns each correction into a mini grammar lesson with him doing all the talking. He is still talking when he realizes class is over and he has not gotten to the second speaking situation. So, he quickly gives it as an assignment to

Table 2.4 What Roger's Low-Level Theory Posits about Teaching and Teachers

---

1. Language teaching means to teach the forms of the second language.

2. Teaching means maintaining steady verbal engagement with learners. Verbal engagement leads to rapport.

3. Learning students' names creates rapport.

4. Teaching means to explain things. Explanations are done at the front of the room, at the board.

5. "Real" teaching theories are read about but not necessarily practiced in real life.

6. It is okay to attune teaching and content coverage to mandatory tests.

7. If a learner is speaking to another person, that is communicating.

8. Communicative Competence and Communicative Language Teaching mean the same thing. They imply some kind of action on the parts of learners that the teacher initiates.

9. It is better to run out of time in a class than to not have enough to do.

10. Teachers having students listen to and read at the same time activity directions, key words, and dialogs is important to classroom management. This practice is also a simple and quick way to ensure comprehension.

11. It is okay to intervene if learners have difficulties, and it is okay to do the intervention with the whole class if it improves learners' understanding of grammar.

12. Communicative functions are not useful for language teaching, whereas language forms are.

13. Learners' L2 talk outside of the language presented by the activity at hand is not valued.

Source: Authors.

write a dialog of the learner cooking the dish at home with a friend. He does not mention the communicative functions that might be useful to know for expression as well as interpretation, such as: making a request, giving an instruction, or making a suggestion. See Table 2.4 for what Roger's low-level teaching theory posits.

Roger is in a curious position. He has a graduate degree but little job experience. What he read about and heard in lectures were middle-level teaching theories. But he had no concurrent or previous teaching experience to relate to what he was learning formally for his degree. Middle-level theory was never actualized or experimented with in his teaching. We are not arguing that middle-level teaching theories are better than low-level teaching theories. But we do think that it is worthwhile to learn about theories new to us, whether high, middle, or low. We do this to keep up professionally and keep fresh intellectually and not be ground down by daily routines and busy schedules. We argue that to learn a middle-level theory such as the Direct Instruction Model, the theory must be interpreted. By "interpreted," we mean the proposals a theory makes (the posits) need to be picked out and thought about. Part of interpretation is also thinking about what a theory posits and applying this to perhaps one thing in one's classroom practice, beyond the level of "No, that won't work in my class." Rather, "How would I decide which concept to focus on?" and "How would I split that up into learnable parts?" and "What would I actually say to learners?" and "Where can I find out more about these 'scripts?' "

Roger's interpretation of the Direct Instruction Model (Table 2.3) is pretty impressionistic and basic. What he saw in his observations of a reading class with children was extended verbal interactions between the teacher and the learners. He saw teachers working with learners in small groups. He likely saw struggling learners get help. He believed these actions created rapport between the teacher and learners, a personal quality Roger valued. But what Roger saw was only some set of activities while not being privy to the teacher's planning and thoughts. If the teacher Roger observed had been using the Direct Instruction Model, it may not have been made clear by his MA course instructor. If the elementary school teacher had been consciously using the theory, and Roger had had more time to closely observe and engage in an exploratory approach to learning teaching, he would also have seen that the teacher was using repeated questions and leading statements that had a pattern, that learners were constantly offering answers, and that one concept was being focused on intensively (Table 2.3, points 1, 2, 8, and 9). Without having picked out what the Direct Instruction Model actually posited, however, Roger still might not have made the connection. For us, the key question is: How can a teacher be guided by others or become self-guided to interpret theory? Perhaps at some point Roger will ask some focused questions about communicative functions (actional competence; Table 2.2, 4.3), which could be an interesting way to understand more about CC. This may point the way to the consideration of a possible *should* for Roger and perhaps also an *is* as his teaching evolves.

Reflective Projects

1. What middle-level or public teaching theories do you know about? Name them and list at least one teaching activity associated with each. Recall that many terms might be used for theory in the sense

we mean it in this chapter: Approach, image, method, philosophy, tradition, and so on.

2.   For number 1 above, did you list Communicative Language Teaching? What is Communicative Language Teaching? In contrast, what is Communicative Competence?

3.   A colleague asks you about the Direct Instruction Model. What do you tell him or her?

4.   We listed only some of Roger's low-level theories in Table 2.4. Can you find others in the case study? Do they directly relate to teaching, or do they perhaps relate to theories of language or theories of learning? Can you find additional theories about assignments, syllabuses, and classroom management? Are they Roger's theories, or theories of administrators, textbook authors, learners, or the marketing statements of the school?

5.   Roger would like to do a classroom research project on teaching and asks you for advice. Based on what you know about Roger and his situation, give him one or two issues that he could investigate.

6.   How might Roger's teaching be explored? Would it be worth it for Roger to audio-record himself? What might he learn from what he says or does in class?

7.   We have suggested that teachers should learn to interpret theories. A few suggestions were offered in this chapter. What were they? What steps would *you* suggest to interpret a theory for the purposes of teaching or at the very least, thinking *about* teaching?

CHAPTER THREE

Theories of Learning and Teachers

Why This Chapter?

This chapter focuses on the interaction of theories of learning and second language teachers. By theories of learning we mean any middle-level theory that specifies how learners develop awareness, knowledge, and competence. Like Chapter 2 on theories of teaching and teachers, Chapter 3 is foundational. Partly because persons learning a second language comprises the reason teachers and learners are together, whether in a classroom, in an office, in a living room, or in a virtual space. Learning is the overarching goal of the language education enterprise (see Chapter 8 on institutions for language education goals related to society). And partly because this is the first chapter in this book that examines learning as a topic. And finally because some of our most widespread and accepted conceptions of learning hide behind names that include the word "teaching" in them but not "learning," for example, Communicative Language Teaching (CLT) and Task-Based Language Teaching (TBLT). When teachers first encounter the category of learning, it is often through courses featuring teaching methods or teaching approaches (Chapter 2), with the idea that good teaching is essential to improved student learning. It would be rare to find CLT, TBLT, or other teaching methods described as conceptions of learning (see, however, Larsen-Freeman and Anderson 2011: 122, 149, 159). We think teaching methods courses aim at helping teachers to become classroom managers who can design linear, time-bound experiences for learners. Messages about how humans form knowledge, awareness, and competence may be only implied. As teaching education specialists Hattie and Donoghue note, "The teaching of 'learning' has diminished to near extinction in many teacher-education programs" (2018: 98). Further, as with teaching theories, learning theories may be manifest as high-, middle-, or low-level theories and yet may not be labeled clearly as theories (see the High Middle Low Theory Model, Chapter 1). Thus, in this chapter, we continue our work to help readers recognize theories when they appear in the course of their everyday work lives.

In this chapter, we first examine theories of learning very broadly, from the field of psychology. While second language learning theories are certainly germane to the work of second language teachers, many second language learning theories that are identified explicitly as such have their bases in psychology. As we outline the middle-level theories, many of them will seem familiar to those readers who have studied or are studying second language learning theories, as many of our theories have been usefully adapted from other fields. We also note that most of us work in second language education, with the emphasis on "education." We have many types of problems to solve, and for that reason, within education and schools there are many intellectual traditions and theories present. It is what makes working in a school so interesting but also confusing. We presented one probable source of confusion above, that of widely accepted, albeit implied, conceptions of learning that have the term "teaching" but not the term "learning" in them.

Second, we focus on a significant middle-level theory area, that of CLT. We define CLT as a theory area because numerous commentators, scholars, methodologists, and theorists have contributed to it, each with different interests and priorities. We describe CLT in terms of its 1970–2000 formulation as First Generation (CLT 1st Gen), but then also in terms of its later form (2000–present) as Second Generation (CLT 2nd Gen). We have suggested by its inclusion in this chapter that CLT has to do with learning, despite its being popularly thought of as having to do with teaching.

Third, we examine the strangely intriguing history of Presentation, Practice, and Production (PPP), a widely known and used lesson planning pattern. PPP is fascinating because of its ability to survive the repeated attempts of our field to ignore, if not kill, it. We argue that its hardiness may be attributed to its near-status as a middle-level theory. PPP in its traditional form does not have a theoretical basis in learning. It is nonetheless a force to reckon with due to its prevalence and possibly due to its resemblance to a named middle-level learning theory. Veronika, our case study teacher, wrestles with PPP, particularly the Practice and Production parts, as will be seen. A Ukrainian, she teaches adult learners in a half-day English language program. To examine her low-level theories of learning, we focus on the following artifacts: how Veronika prioritizes classroom activity, and how she eventually decides to use games. As with all chapters in this book, we follow each description of middle- or low-level theory or theory area with a table that suggests what the theory posits, or proposes, about teachers and theories of learning. We end with reflective projects to probe significant issues raised in the chapter.

How the High Middle Low Theory Model Applies to Theories of Learning and Teachers

As we argue in Chapters 6 and 9, theories of learning play an important role in teachers' professional lives, even if their formal preparation in them has been perhaps broad yet thin, or indirect and somewhat hidden within courses on teaching methods. We hope to plant at least one seed in this chapter—that focusing on a middle-level learning theory is rewarding for teachers for self-study. Learning theories are fascinating, sometimes offering unexpected insights and answers for the often practical questions teachers ask. Veronika, our teacher in this chapter, has to clear up her own confusion about what it means for learners to practice the second language but then also to communicate with and use the second language. In doing so, on the one hand, she relies on PPP, in reality a nontheory, to increase learner practice time. But on the other hand, she returns to half-remembered learning theories from her MA days and the simmering intellectual conflict that began in those days of combined study and teaching. Namely, how might learners engage in CLT activities in ways where together they use their recall to review and remember important language knowledge? In other words, how do learners use their social selves to engage their cognition?

Teachers' low-level theories on learning are also well worth self-study. This is harder to do in that their own theories are seldom stated and thus hard to pin down. Nonetheless, teachers do have theories about learning, based on their own experiences as language learners (see Bae, Chapter 6: "Learners are cognitive beings. They can be guided to think about what works well for them, and class time is a good time for that"; Felicia, Chapter 8 "Reading authentic posters and sales pamphlets from the community in bits and pieces adds up and helps reading over time"), and cumulative professional experience (see Aisha, Chapter 9: "For learners to succeed in an English-medium campus, they should be guided to figure out what they mean to say first, then think about language forms they could use").

Middle-Level Learning Theories

Theories of learning come from many fields such as psychology and education. Some theories have descriptive names as found in Dunn (2002), some are best known by the name of their originator as found in Licensure Examination for Teachers Reviewer (2020), and some are named with a suffix (-ism) as if they were a philosophical way of life as found in Harris (2014; see also Barrs 2022). These sources reflect the commonly known terms, or in the case of Harris, common functional groupings, for the theories. We also chose these sources because they are easily accessed, but also heavily accessed, suggesting utility to a wide variety of users. We note that the list in

Table 3.1 Learning Theories

Descriptive Names	Famous Originator Names	Suffixed Names
1. Sensory Stimulation Theory	1. Jean Piaget (Cognitive Development)	1. Cognitivism
2. Reinforcement Theory	2. Lev Vygotsky (Social Development)	2. Behaviorism
3. Cognitive-Gestalt Approaches	3. Jerome Bruner (Spiral Curriculum)	3. Constructivism
4. Holistic Learning Theory	4. Sigmund Freud (Psychoanalytic Theory)	4. Connectivism
5. Facilitation Theory	5. Benjamin Bloom (Mastery Learning)	
6. Experiential Learning	6. Howard Gardner (Multiple Intelligences)	
7. Learning Styles	7. Erik Erikson (Psychosocial Theory)	
8. Action Learning	8. Abraham Harold Maslow (Human Needs Model)	
9. Adult Learning		

Source: Authors.

Table 3.1 is not exhaustive. Theorizing learning has been historically a true priority for scholars and an area of intense interest. See Table 3.1.

Some of these theories are well known, and it is likely that most teachers are at least familiar with their names. It is not likely, however, that many teachers are familiar with all of these theories or that they have an in-depth understanding of even a few of them. As we argue in Chapter 1 and in other chapters, theory in general and even a truly representative and relevant sample of specific theories learned in-depth are not part of the academic training of most language teachers. Given this situation, how can we understand the collection of learning theories offered in Table 3.1? Second language learning theorists Sato and Loewen (2019) offer a suggestion, namely that learning theories may exist on a continuum from cognitively oriented, or occurring within the brain, to socially oriented, or occurring within social interactions. In other words, learning theories with a cognitive orientation view learning as best explained by the brain, the mind, and thinking procedures. For example, applied linguists Richards and Rodgers (2014: 23) note: "A cognitive view of language is based on the idea that language reflects properties of the mind." Richards and Rodgers do something curious here—in an enumerated list following this statement, they slip seamlessly and without announcement from describing *language* as cognitive representations (memories) to describing *learning* as cognitive, involving "abstract knowledge acquisition" (23). Theories of learning and language are perhaps not seen as separate.

Socially oriented learning theories on the other hand take the view that learning takes place between people, especially a person who knows less (and who wants to know more), often called a student or a learner, and a person who knows more, often called a teacher, lecturer, or instructor (and who is willing to teach or instruct). Applied linguists Gaspar and Berti (2019) working in a multiple literacies tradition (Chapter 9) note that they see learners as being mentored, and that social contact with more able peers and teachers forms the main processes of learning. We wonder if reducing learning theories to a single two-ended continuum risks oversimplifying the diversity of learning theories, but we admit even Table 3.1 does that. We have to start somewhere.

What follows are three thumbnail examples of cognitively oriented learning theories (Table 3.2) and three examples of socially oriented learning theories (Table 3.3). For each, we offer what we think teachers, at minimum, might want to know about a learning theory: (1) what the theory seeks to explain, (2) what the learning theory posits as the causes of learning, and (3) who uses the theory. Item 1 speaks to a problem a teacher might want to solve; item 2 speaks to a specific thing a teacher may ask a learner to do or have learners experience to bring about learning; and item 3 speaks to where a teacher might go (a discipline, a conference, or a journal) to learn more about the theory.

We note that while most, if not all, learning theories come from psychology, many psychologists such as Bruner (2009; see also Table 3.1) applied their work in other fields of their own interest such as curriculum (Chapter 9) and education. The same holds true for the socially oriented learning theories found in Table 3.3. Vygotsky (translated by Hanfmann, Vakar, and Minnick 1962), also a psychologist, applied his thought and energy to specific classroom practices in schools (pedagogy), and was in fact for a time a secondary school teacher (Barrs 2022). As will be seen later in the chapter, CLT as a learning theory area draws from both cognitively and socially oriented learning theories. Trying to provide a single answer to each of the three questions posed in Tables 3.2 and 3.3 (what it [a theory] explains; what causes learning; and who uses it [a theory]) becomes fairly complicated for CLT.

Communicative Language Teaching 1st Gen—1970s, 1980s, 1990s

Our past is relevant today. To understand learning theories suggested by CLT, one needs to know the theory of language underpinning CLT. This view of language sees a shift from understanding language as form to language as use

Table 3.2 Three Examples of Cognitively Oriented Learning Theories

Sensory Stimulation Theory

1. What it explains	The role sensory experiences have in learning
2. What causes learning	The causes of learning are primarily added visual stimulation (such as colors) but also sounds and sensations
3. Who uses it	Psychologists engaged in research with adult learners

Reinforcement Theory

1. What it explains	Why humans do certain actions but avoid others
2. What causes learning	The causes of learning are positive and negative reinforcement
3. Who uses it	Psychologists engaged in research; teachers, to promote or discourage certain learner actions

Cognitivism

1. What it explains	How information is processed in the individual mind
2. What causes learning	Learning occurs through mental processing, which could include learned strategies such as different kinds of memory games, review techniques, and summarizing information and mind-mapping
3. Who uses it	Teachers, to plan instruction in strategies and strategy use; applied linguists engaged in research

Table original to this book; information sourced from: Dunn (2002) and Harris (2014).

(Communicative Competence, Chapter 2; language as use, Chapters 4, 7, and 9). This shift (Figure 3.1) resulted in a set of understandings that learning itself needed to be accomplished by using language and not a static contemplation of a static system of linguistic forms (see Figure 3.1). In the sections that follow, we will first explore some fairly seismic, historic shifts in our theory of language and then follow up with CLT 1st Gen conceptions of learning.

Shifts in a Theory of Language—Austin and the Performative

Austin (1975), a philosopher, worked out his ideas on language in a series of lectures at Oxford during 1952–4, delivered them in guest lectures at

Table 3.3 Three Examples of Socially Oriented Learning Theories

Theory Name or Theory Family	
Action Learning	
1. What it explains	How learning may be linked with actions generated by small teams.
2. What causes learning	Learning is caused by instruction, insightful instructor questioning, and reflection sessions within small teams of four to eight people.
3. Who uses it	Human resource workers, to solve complex, real-life problems with teams of people.
Connectivism	
1. What it explains	The role of independent, interactive, and shared information collection and use in learning in digital environments.
2. What causes learning	Learning is caused by learners and teachers using informal digital networks in the form of e-mails, forums, blogs, and YouTube videos to access and use needed information in pursuit of valued outcomes, usually projects.
3. Who uses it	Teachers and learners both in and out of class.
Social Development Theory	
1. What it explains	To explain the role of culture and social relationships in learning both in and out of school.
2. What causes learning	Learning is caused by interaction between a more knowledgeable other and the zone of proximal development (ZPD) of a less knowledgeable other. ZPD defined as what a person can do by him- or herself and what he or she can do with the help of a more knowledgeable other. If the joint activity takes place within the ZPD, the learner can learn.
3. Who uses it	Psychologists engaged in research and designing learning interventions; Applied linguists engaged in research and planning learning interventions.

Table original to this book; information sourced from: Barrs (2022), Dunn (2002), Harris (2014), Licensure Examination for Teacher Reviewer (2020), Marquardt and Banks (2010), World Institute for Action Learning (2021).

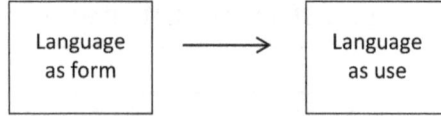

FIGURE 3.1 Shift in a view of language, shift in learning theory.
Source: Authors.

Harvard University in 1955, and then published them in 1962 and again in 1975. Immersed in the intellectual traditions in his own field of philosophy, Austin was working against assumption that statements or utterances (language) are limited to describing things or stating facts that are true or false (1). Austin offered examples of what he called Performatives such as "naming" and "betting": "I name this ship the Good Ship Lollypop" and "I bet you a dollar it will rain tomorrow." By simply saying "I name this ship" and "I bet you," the speaker performs something. These performative utterances have to be done in the right social situation by persons willing, able, and authorized to do them, and listeners willing and able to participate. In other words, these performative utterances require an appropriate social context. Austin called his insight a revolution in philosophy (3). Austin had just described a speech act and had laid the groundwork for the necessity of an appropriate social context and language use.

Shifts in a Theory of Language—Searle and the Speech Act

Searle, a student of Austin's, offered a view of language as utterances (what we say), characterizations (conventional linguistic descriptions), and explanations (conventional grammatical rules). An example of an utterance is "That's an apple." A linguistic description is "Apple is a noun." And a rule or explanation for the utterance and characterization just given is "The rule of the indefinite article preceding a noun beginning with a vowel requires an *n* as in an apple" (Searle 1969: 15).

Searle hypothesized that "speaking a language is performing speech acts, acts such as making statements, giving commands, asking questions, making promises, and so on" (Searle 1969: 16). "That's an apple" would be an example of making a statement, at least in most social contexts. His claim is that the basic unit of linguistic communication is the performance of the speech act. In so doing, Searle took the notion of speech act from Austin and expanded it from an edge concern to a central concern. One can, of course, study language without studying speech acts, but that would be like studying the rules of baseball without studying it as a game. Baseball, and also language, has rules, but the rules arise from the game. The game does not arise from the rules. Rules (grammatical structures) are necessary to understand the game, but they are not the game itself. Rather, the game is social contact, and making and interpreting meaning. Speech acts are the basic unit of communication and include what the speaker means, what their utterance means, what the speaker intends, what the hearer understands, and what the rules are (21). A sole focus on language as form (teaching only grammar) is attending to the rules while ignoring the game. Rules are necessary and important, but they are not the game, which is communicating and using language for the purpose of social contact with others. The game is the reason we watch the players.

Pedagogical Principles Emerging in Communicative Language Teaching 1st Gen

A pedagogical principle is a value that is objectified with implications for what teachers will lead learners to do in classrooms. These can involve activities, games, textbook exercises, puzzles, dictations, and so on. See Larsen-Freeman and Anderson (2011) for an account of a full-length CLT class meeting. For the purposes of this chapter, then, we describe CLT in terms of four principles: a need for authenticity; a key role for negotiation; the importance of group work for achieving negotiation; and a continued desire on the part of some pedagogists and scholars to continue the use of a structural, or grammatical, syllabus upon which to organize a course (see Chapter 9 on the high-level theory of curriculum). This last principle figures large in still continuing debates over a theory of language and a growing dissatisfaction with one still current form of CLT.

Authenticity

Authenticity is commonly referred to as the quality "realness" and can be understood in two senses. One sense is that teachers might ask learners to use authentic texts or materials also used by native speakers of the language being studied (Larsen-Freeman 1986). These might be menus or weather reports or train announcements. This type of authenticity was prized for social purposes in that learners could connect their efforts to the real world. A second sense of authenticity is when some event or some location is used for the purpose intended (Macnamara 1973). For instance, Breen (1985) notes that a classroom is intended to be used for learning. His example of authentic interaction taking place in a classroom, then, is learners having been asked to read the teacher's comments on homework from the previous year and then to assess the usefulness and appropriateness of the teacher's feedback. On the board is written: "What comments from the teacher would have been most helpful to the students whose homework it was?" and "What kind of homework and homework feedback would you recommend as the most helpful to you now?" While the learners' engagement with the homework, the feedback from the previous year, the text on the blackboard, and their assessment of the feedback are not "real world" as in outside the school, it is nonetheless true, or authentic, to the immediate learning setting.

Negotiation
This refers to negotiation between learners and between learners and teachers using the second language. Canale (1983) considers negotiation a crucial feature of communication because the information we have is never complete. As social beings, we are always needing, seeking, and getting additional information. Further, the social context changes and what we need changes. Thus, our purpose may change (Candlin 1980) with concomitant changes in communicative functions we need to use. What we need to *mean* changes, even mid-utterance, and thus we must adjust the language forms we use. This suggests that negotiation is extemporaneous (unplanned and unscripted) language use. Finally, what we mean to say may be incomplete or misunderstood by another. He or she may signal misunderstanding, and we must notice this and adjust accordingly and try again.

Group Work
Christopher Brumfit (1984), an early and influential CLT scholar, argued that group and pair work promotes a more authentic, social use of language. Working in pairs or groups increases talking time for learners and the chances for more creative and personalized talk, which is more similar to real-world communication outside the classroom and more likely to result in negotiation.

Continued Use of a Structural Syllabus
Despite the emphasis on free, extemporaneous, authentic communication in CLT, some pedagogists in CLT 1st Gen wanted to preserve the role of grammatical syllabuses in organizing CLT courses. For example, Morrow (1981) argued that part of communication involves correct grammatical forms and if learners do not have them, they cannot communicate. This is a sentiment offered today by many teachers working with beginner-level learners. Roger, our teacher of ESL in Chapter 2, and Rick, our teacher of French in Chapter 4, also grapple with this issue without too much awareness of it. Stern (1981) argued for a "layered" (variable) syllabus that moved between grammatical structures and communicative functions, linking forms and meanings (see seminars on communicative functions given by our teacher Roger's teaching director and regional manager; Chapter 2).

What CLT 1st Gen Posits about Learning
CLT is, in its broadest conception, a zeitgeist, or a spirit of our time (Chapter 1). CLT as zeitgeist has lasted as long as it has because its directly observable teaching techniques have become so varied (Larsen-Freeman and

Anderson 2011) and could be attributed, to the untrained or unsympathetic eye, to almost any teaching principle, such as "letting students play because they need to let off steam." This does a serious disservice to CLT and the significant theories of language and of learning that have emerged from of our lengthy and productive engagement with CLT. For this and other reasons, we are less likely in the present day to see CLT purely as an identifiable teaching method with conceptions of learning underpinning it.

In contrast, CLT 1st Gen in the 1970s, 1980s, and 1990s was seen as a teaching method similar to other commonly acknowledged teaching methods such as the Audio-Lingual Method, Total Physical Response, or the Natural Approach. A teaching method has recognizable teaching techniques that teachers then use according to known principles and beliefs concerning language, learning, and the role of teachers and learners (Larsen-Freeman and Anderson 2011; see also Chapter 2). One basis for looking at CLT in this way is that earlier writers (pre-1990) explicitly refer to CLT as a method. Taylor (1987: 45) says that CLT is a teaching method that stresses the interaction of learners with the language they are studying "to acquire it by using it rather than learn it by studying it." In foundational, contemporaneous sources to Taylor, CLT is either named as a method or enumerated among other methods (Larsen-Freeman 1986; Richards and Rodgers 1986). We note both 1986 books are first editions by these authors. These first editions name emerging assumptions about learning in CLT. Richards and Rodgers (1986: 72) note that at that time little was written directly about learning theories and CLT, saying rather that "elements of an underlying learning theory can be discerned in some CLT practices." See Table 3.4 for what CLT 1st Gen posits about learning.

Communicative Language Teaching 2nd Gen—2000–present

We are using the turn of the past century as a convenient way to mark a shift in CLT from a period of time used for defining what it is (CLT 1st Gen) to a time multiple generations of language teachers responded to it (CLT 2nd Gen), and, as might be argued, some scholars reimagined it as TBLT. Despite powerful theoretical insights that merged language meaning and form (Figure 3.1) and concomitant shifts in learning proposals, most language teachers continue to have only a fuzzy conception of what CLT is (Klapper 2003: 33). Klapper suggested that CLT has been a failure at "linking attention to linguistic form with the communication of meaning" (34). In other words, despite a new theory of language described above, there has been an inadequate translation of the theory into something teachers or learners think they can use. As illustration, consider one possible interpretation in which we purposefully oversimplify CLT: on one hand, CLT may be seen as a wonderful movement in which language learners can develop their own identities in exploration

Table 3.4 What Communicative Language Teaching (1st Gen) Posits about Learning

1. Communicative Competence, including discourse levels of language, cohesion and coherence, socially appropriate uses of utterances, and suprasegmental aspects of pronunciation, is a worthy aim of learning.
2. Learners need to learn about the social contexts of utterances.
3. Strategies for interpreting language by native speakers are worthy aims of learning.
4. Learners should aim at comprehensibility in pronunciation.
5. Real communication between a listener and a speaker is interaction.
6. Interaction causes negotiation of meaning in which a listener and speaker must work together to make meaning clear.
7. Negotiation of meaning may cause a listener to give a speaker feedback on non-understanding.
8. Negotiation may cause a speaker to revise or repeat what they said, and this may cause learning.
9. Interacting, negotiating, and communicating cause learning; it is direct and immediate practice.
10. Struggling in the act of communicating causes learning.
11. Direct and immediate practice in communicating (doing real communication) allows for internalization and automization of plans for language system use.
12. Learners working in small groups increases communication practice.
13. Doing tasks increases opportunities for communication.

Paraphrases and interpretations original to this book have been sourced from:
Larsen-Freeman (1986), Richards and Rodgers (1986), Taylor (1987).

of other cultures and means of expression. Learners are social beings who use language and learn to accomplish social acts of their own choosing. On the other hand, CLT does not have an adequate theoretical or pedagogical basis for linking language meaning and form. What is "meaning" exactly? We are thus left with linguistic forms, which we know a lot about. In other words, teachers such as Roger (Chapter 4) or Anna (Chapter 7) could, within reason, say: "Yes, we ought to wish to help learners learn to communicate, and yes we sort of care about their social lives and futures (but really, their own language use is their own business and whatever meanings they might wish to say we cannot predict anyway), and how is this to be done if they have no language (forms) to begin with?" "We know what language forms look like, and language forms are learnable and teachable." "Language is content." "This content can and should be mastered." But then also consult Felicia (Chapter 8) and Aisha (Chapter 9) for powerful counterarguments to Roger's and Anna's lines of thought. Note here how, like Richards and Rodgers (2014) above, we have slipped into seeing a theory of language and a theory of learning as perhaps similar.

Swaffar and Arens (2005: 13) show how the persistence of the separation of language form and meaning plays out in second language departments in US colleges: "Language courses are divided from content courses which appears in the difference between lower-level courses and upper-level courses." In the lower-level courses (first- and second-year courses), learners focus on grammatical forms and vocabulary. In upper-level courses (third- and fourth-year courses), learners finally "get" to the real thing—meaning and depth—namely, literature and culture. This traditional separation implies an assumption that learners can only handle meaning after mastering some requisite number of language forms.

Strong and Weak Versions of CLT

Embedded even in CLT 1st Gen and continuing into 2nd Gen was a discussion of different versions of CLT that focus on, once again, the uneasy and shifting theoretical, practical, and educational conceptions of language form and language meaning. Two versions emerged and became known as "strong" CLT and "weak" CLT. The terms were introduced by Howatt (1984) and then elaborated by Ellis (2003). In strong CLT, tasks (having learners use language) are primary and grammar (teaching learners grammatical points) is secondary. In weak CLT, grammar is primary and tasks are secondary. For the purposes of this discussion, we rely on Candlin's (1987: 10) definition of "task" as a problem-posing activity that involves second language learners and teachers working together toward a social goal.

Howatt (1984) says the claim of the strong version of CLT is that language is acquired through communication. One of our classroom artifacts in this chapter is how a teacher prioritizes time to different classroom activities. This simply refers to how much time a teacher asks learners to engage in a particular activity, such as listening to an audio file and completing a table, or talking to classmates to get their opinions, or reading a passage and underlining specified verb endings. This also includes how much time a teacher ends up just lecturing. In general, the more time spent doing something, the better learners get at whatever the activity focuses on. Then, in terms of Howatt's perspective on strong CLT, learning takes place when teachers prioritize learners' engagement in tasks in which they are using the second language to communicate and award most class time to that. Here, however, the concern is that learners will learn to communicate using ungrammatical utterances. The implication of communicative tasks is that they are meaning-focused and that learners will use language in whatever ways they need to accomplish a task (Nunan 1989; Skehan 1998). This is an enduring concern of teachers but also an enduring point of interest to second language acquisition researchers as was demonstrated in the emerging literature on TBLT (Larsen-Freeman 2015; Bygate, Skehan, and Swain 2001; Newton and Kennedy 1996; Samuda and Bygate 2008; see also Chapter 6). Second language learners apparently process meaning in many cases and demonstrate this by comprehending utterances just fine. But why can they not so easily or accurately produce second language forms?

In the weak version of CLT, the teacher explains selected grammar points and the class practices them. Although he never uses the word "task," Howatt (1984: 279) says that the weak version of CLT, like the strong version, "provide[s] learners with opportunities to use their [second language] for communicative purposes." But Ellis (2003: 28) then stipulates that in the weak version, tasks (listening to an audio file and completing a table, talking to classmates to get their opinions, working with a classmate to draw the floor plan of a house using a written description, etc.) are a way of practicing structures previously introduced by the teacher. The primary concern is that learners must first understand the grammatical points taught before practicing them. A teacher working within a weak CLT version would then prioritize more class time to grammatical instruction. We wonder if there are not quite a few teachers like Roger in Chapter 2 and Veronika in this chapter, who, if they are aware of it, would choose a weak version of CLT. For them, it is hard to be passive observers who assign less teacher-controlled activities such as tasks and then step aside as their students practice, make mistakes, and use language in unexpected, and in perhaps mystifying and dissatisfying, ways. Would such teachers also find socially oriented theories such as Connectivism and Social Development Theory in Table 3.3 equally irrelevant to their educational purposes or at odds with their low-level theories? Needless to say, while CLT is still in wide use in second language education, many of the doubts and questions raised from its inception continue today.

Presentation Practice Production

Presentation Practice Production is a teacher-initiated way of presenting and handling language teaching materials. It is so established that it approaches being an unquestioned "default" or automatic way of asking learners to experience new language content (Larsen-Freeman 2015). In essence, it is a time-honored but theoretically flawed way for a teacher to organize learners' learning experiences, at least as it is traditionally construed (for compelling alternatives, see DeKeyser 2007). The teacher (with the textbook) identifies something to be studied (the Presentation part); that something is practiced in some controlled way, usually at the sentence level (the Practice part); and finally, learners produce that something in some longer form such as a conversation, dialog, or some connected sentences (the Production part) (Samuda and Bygate 2008). The past of PPP is fairly clear: it came to be associated with language learning when learning grammar was more firmly considered equivalent to learning a language (Chapter 4). The progression of conscious study → controlled practice → free practice became persistent in second language education because it was, among other things, thought to promote learning according to learning theories and a view of language extant in the mid-twentieth century and still persisting today (see "Reinforcement Theory" in Table 3.2; and Chapter 4, "Persistence of Language Seen as a System of Forms"; see also Samuda and Bygate [2008] and Willis and Willis [2007]). For instance, controlled practice ensured learners would avoid making mistakes and thus avoid bad habit formation, a hallmark of Reinforcement Theory (Table 3.2; see also Samuda and Bygate 2008). Even recent language education scholars argue that learners engaging in output practice (Production) is necessary for L2 learning, although for reasons based on a quite different theory (Larsen-Freeman 2015; Muranoi 2007).

Nonetheless, PPP has been repeatedly attacked as a failure on both theoretical and methodological grounds (Ur 2011). In terms of learning theory, one emerging finding from TBLT has been that learners cannot incorporate new grammar points (forms) into their productive repertoire (meaning). It is nearly impossible to pay attention to form and meaning at the same time (Ahmadian and Tavakoli 2010; Willis and Willis 2007; see Chapter 6, sections on "noticing" and "attention"). Further, PPP assumes a grammatical syllabus (Chapter 9) that sets a particular order in which language forms are introduced (Presentation). Second language acquisition theorists have argued that if learners are not ready to learn a grammatical form, they will not learn it, no matter how well it is presented or how thoroughly it is practiced (Ur 2011; see however Swan 2005). In terms of methodology, many teachers have experienced learners seeming to use the given grammatical forms without error in the Practice stage, and even do well on quizzes and tests they think approximate Production but then are stymied by learners being unable to then use the grammatical forms extemporaneously in speaking or writing. Practice does not make perfect. This seems to be the case to Rick, our French teacher in Chapter 4. Muranoi (2007) raises the question: Is it because output-type practice itself is poorly understood? Ahmadian and Tavakoli (2011) seem to agree when they simply proceed to offer empirical and practical arguments and examples that teachers must provide learners planning time and support to use language forms that teachers want students to learn and use in language production. In other words, they need to prioritize classroom time to planning and offer more support before and during the Production phase.

But now we come to the intriguing thing about PPP: It will not die, and it will not go away. It is a convenient means for teachers, and textbook authors and publishers, to program the beginning, middle, and end of a given lesson. The three stages of conscious study → controlled practice → free practice give an easily remembered structure to any lesson plan. Learners may come to depend on this structure as part of a "normal" classroom experience, leading to expectations of what they think proper teaching ought to be (Chapter 5) and how they think a second language ought to be treated—in other words, as a series of consciously learned forms (Chapter 7). Most intriguing is that PPP has the appearance of being theoretically adaptable and not necessarily wed to the behavioristic model of learning that birthed it ("Reinforcement Theory," Table 3.2). Ranta and Lyster (2007) point out an eerie similarity of PPP to Anderson's cognitively oriented three-phase learning model, Adaptive Control of Thought (ACT; Anderson 1983, 2005), which is widely accepted in second language education and actively pursued in second language research agendas (see, for example, Ahmadian and Tavakoli 2011).

The ACT learning theory posits three stages of learning that could be seen to correspond to the three stages of PPP. Stage 1 of ACT is posited as a cognitive phase that is dominated by learning rules and facts from a teacher, with learners watching or trying on their own (like Production in PPP). Typically, this phase is seen as slow and full of errors. It results in declarative knowledge, which learners can consciously state, yet not easily used in extemporaneous language use. Stage 2 of ACT is posited to be an associative phase in which learners' declarative knowledge becomes procedural knowledge through practice (like Practice in PPP). Stage 3 of ACT is posited as an autonomous stage that is characterized by increasing levels of performance, which is automatic, error free, and with little demand on working memory or consciousness (like Production in PPP) (Ranta and Lyster 2007). But the surface resemblance ends here. At the very least, Anderson's ACT Model posits much more time at each stage than a single PPP lesson would offer, or even an entire unit made up of many and multiple PPP lessons. The ACT model predicts, among other things, that learners may persist in using a single form for a single meaning to meet communicative needs when pushed to do so in productive activities (Larsen-Freeman 2015). Any use of new forms may take place only gradually, and in a very irregular way, correctly sometimes and incorrectly at others.

As we will see, PPP is used by Veronika in a quite different and unexpected way: as a means of self-reflection of how she prioritizes time to classroom activities.

Low- and Middle-Level Theories Concerning Learning and Teachers: A Teacher of English

Veronika is Ukrainian. She is married with a young child. Due to enduring geopolitical tensions in Ukraine and its eastern border, she and her daughter are in Poland, while her American husband stays in Ukraine for work. Veronika is now teaching English in Poland, and even though she has professional qualifications to teach English, French, Russian, and Ukrainian, given the current job market and political situation, she will likely teach English for some time to come. Veronika began studying English in early grade school but did not think the school lessons were interesting or that her teacher was good. She asked her mother and had a private tutor who came to her house, and sometimes her friends would join. Together they studied grammar and played vocabulary games; so it was not boring. It did not occur to her that her tutor was doing much the same thing as her schoolteacher but simply adapted the Practice part of what they did to a kind of speed "game" format where Veronika had to give missing words to sentences or unscramble sentences quickly and in competition with her friends. Veronika was proud to be gain admission to university, where she studied English, French, and Russian linguistics and where her courses were lecture driven. She studied the syntax, morphology, phonology, and also the rhetoric of those languages. She especially enjoyed making comparisons between the languages. As an added bonus, she took pedagogical certificates in the three foreign languages and also in Ukrainian so that, if she wished to, she could teach.

After graduation, she married an American man she met in Ukraine and moved to the United States where she enrolled in an MA in applied linguistics program. She was prized as a French and a Russian speaker and supported herself as an instructor teaching those languages. When people meet Veronika now, most believe they are talking to a friendly, outgoing American English native speaker. She and her husband moved back to Ukraine for his business, and there they had a daughter. Now Veronika, her daughter, and Veronika's mother live in Poland temporarily. With her language skills and qualifications, Veronika quickly found a job with a refugee and relocation organization. One of their programs provides foreign language education. Thus, Veronika teaches in a half-day English as a foreign language program.

Veronika and Learning

When Veronika theorizes about how her students learn, she relies on her experiences as a student at the university in Ukraine, despite a course she took in second language acquisition in her MA program. She does not really differentiate between a theory of language, a theory of learning, and a theory of teaching. Partly, her theory of language is that language is a system of forms: vocabulary, morphology, grammar, and perhaps rhetoric. She was taught language as a system, step by step, and she consciously studied it and practiced it, step by step. For her, conscious study and practice was learning. She spoke sentences aloud, she practiced dialogs with her classmates, and she wrote out sentences on her own. She thought that the second language acquisition course she took in her MA program made some interesting points, but she saw no use in trying to figure out if her students were "ready" to learn a grammatical structure if she was responsible for a class of twenty-five students and if she was assigned to teach a set number of grammatical structures in a given semester; twenty-five students could all be at different stages of readiness to learn. And if the textbook had those structures in the assigned units, what was she supposed to do about it? The second language acquisition course did not seem to touch on the one aspect of learning she was interested in—the idea of review and memory. She begins to ask a question she would ask again and again in her professional life—do not review, memory, and practice go hand in hand?

At the same time, Veronika has a healthy respect for games and songs, and creating a change of pace for learners. But there is a limit to that—songs and games are for children, and her students are not children. She herself was a serious student of language, and she expects that her students now, in Poland, will be serious even though she has trouble motivating them. Just by chance, she took a course on materials design in her MA program and almost by accident learned about something called Communicative Competence (Chapter 2). The teacher in that course suggested that learners could tackle longer texts such as stories or full song lyrics if they did so in stages using communicative tasks, and by focusing on something different each time and building up comprehension. Perhaps learners could reconstruct multiple lines this time or notice the endings of certain words another time. Meeting the texts multiple times would help learners. Some of the tasks the teacher demonstrated were high energy and had Veronika and her classmates working together. They almost seemed like games. They were very social, with laughter and self-generated suggestions and many revisions on whatever product a task called for; for example, a completed table or a constructed summary. Other tasks the teacher demonstrated were quiet, such as matching images created within a song to phrases or lines from the song that could be either provided in written form or not. Veronika became very interested in the different tasks, particularly because of the repeated use of the texts, perhaps spread out into multiple lessons. It felt like the repetition of text use could be practice, but then also like games because of the group work, and yet also like review because of the quiet work. But what the teacher was suggesting, especially with the game-like tasks, was disturbing to Veronika. It was messy.

Veronika objected to her teacher: "If my students have poor language skills, how can they talk to each other and correctly use the sentences I want them to use?" The teacher answered,

> That might not be the point of the task they are working on at right that moment. One thing at a time, right? We're getting them to notice a single feature here, in this case the way those conjunctions are used. Perhaps learners will even notice more than we expect. They may make mistakes

when they then come together to talk, and they may self-correct. They may certainly use grammatical constructions we never taught them to work on a task. And what if they begin using phrases and utterances we don't expect, and in novel ways, while they work together? I'm not sure I want to regulate them so tightly at this moment. Yes it's messy, and maybe uncomfortable for me. But I have to remind myself, perhaps at that moment, it is not strictly a speaking skills task, or an accuracy skills task, is really what I mean to say. I may wish to have learners communicate and exchange meaning at the moment, if I am satisfied they have noticed the features I want them to.

Veronika was *not* satisfied. She felt pretty sure that leaving learners to say whatever they wanted while practicing was not the right way to go. Should not students be guided and strictly controlled during practice? That the teacher was using the term "task" slipped by Veronika owing to her mingled interest and confusion. The teacher then said to the class,

I don't know. I think if I wanted at some point to bring to reinforce learners' attention to specific sentences, or reinforce their use, I might do it toward the *end* of a unit. Perhaps I might ask them to recall what utterances, or even better short exchanges, they did use to complete a task and then ask them to compare the utterances I provide. An end task might then be focused on the comparisons.

Veronika was quite confused by this point. This was not what she thought practice was at all.

Veronika and Her Classroom Teaching

Like any language teacher, Veronika has her troubles. One is motivating her students. Even though they want to be in school, and they are grateful to be finding a way to move on to the next chapter in their professional lives, they seem to forget Veronika's lessons almost as fast as she teaches them. They seem sluggish in class and do not seem to remember anything that happened a little while ago, much less in a previous lesson. Sometimes Veronika spends the whole class period patiently and clearly explaining a grammar point, using mostly English and board diagrams. Learners nod and take notes in their textbooks, which are provided by the school.

When the learners come back from break or the next day, Veronika is eager to move on to practicing the points. But when Veronika moves to review and elicits the vocabulary or grammar to get ready to practice, she finds that the students do not seem to remember the content. Even worse, they cannot talk about the grammar points or use the vocabulary or words in sentences to demonstrate they understand a word meaning or a grammatical rule that Veronika takes to be review, and thus the first stage of successful practice. This not only frustrates Veronika but leads her to think her students are not serious.

What with her living situation, Veronika has not had time or money to attend conferences, online or not. She feels lucky, however, that the organization that sponsors the English language school sends an academic director to her school branch twice a month to hold workshops. The constant theme is CLT and, in particular, how to get the teachers to talk less and the learners to talk more. The aim of classes is to get learners to communicate. The best way to learn how to communicate is by communicating. Veronika listens and participates and tries to connect everything with her coursework in her MA program. Much seems familiar. But she feels a bit stuck the same way she was back then, too. The MA courses then seemed to encourage her to have learners communicate and use language, yet the French and Russian textbooks the university gave her then seemed to just go from grammatical point to grammatical point and from vocabulary list to vocabulary list. Each chapter began anew. Veronika feels she is faced with much the same thing now in Poland. There is pressure to prioritize classroom time to learners communicating through activities and games and talking, but then there is different pressure from a textbook to prioritize classroom time to focused mental operations using a lot of written language. How can learners build up knowledge the way the book implies they should without a lot of disciplined practice and review? She feels there is not enough time to master the grammar and vocabulary and get enough practice in increasing the communicative ability of her students to function as English speaking workers or guests in English speaking countries.

Games, PPP, Some Old Teacher Resource Books, and Some Changes in Prioritizing Classroom Time

Veronika keeps coming up with the idea of games. She still thinks of playing games as childish. What she then realized with some clarity, and a little pain, is that she knew very little about how to adapt grammar points, vocabulary, and practice exercises from textbooks she had to use so they could offer more practice *and* be more communicative. Was the answer games? Her learners were still sluggish. They needed to be motivated. So, step one was decided; she was going to try games and to teach using them.

This took her to step two—how to get learners to talk more? The answer was for Veronika to talk less. Veronika vaguely remembered something called PPP from her university pedagogical training in Ukraine. She asked a Chilean EFL teacher friend at her school about it, and Kevin replied that it was actually "Presentation Practice Production." He said that the idea was a little old but that it might offer her a way to prioritize more classroom time to learner activity and maybe communication. Simply spend less time on Presentation and more time on Practice and Production. It was not clear to Veronika what the difference between Practice and Production was, because if you practiced something, were you not also producing it, and if you produced something, were you not also practicing it?

Veronika found an old book of games in the teachers' room (*Games for Language Learning* [1979] by Wright, Betteridge, and Buckby). One called "The Odd Man Out" (59–60) interested her. The current chapter in the textbook had an awful lot of new and unrelated vocabulary, and Veronika was searching for a way to help learners organize the vocabulary into learnable categories that might also help learners relate the new vocabulary to vocabulary previously appearing in the textbook as a means of review. In the game, five words are put on the board, one of which is odd or does not fit with the others. The point of the game is to identify which word is odd and to say why. The next class, Veronika wrote five words on the board (the first set of five words from the game book—if the game was good, she could start using old and new vocabulary from the textbook). The words were horse, cow, mouse, knife, and goose. Veronika assumed the obvious answer was "knife," but one student argued for "cow" because it had only three letters and that made it different from the others. That both interested and amused Veronika because it showed that the apparent simplicity of the game rested upon the complexity of various ways of classifying things. The game worked, and Veronika was impressed with the amount of discussion, most of it in English, the game generated. She was startled by one further point. In looking more closely at the book, she realized each game was categorized by the authors as "controlled," "guided," or "free." "The Odd Man Out" was listed as teacher "guided," she supposed, because learners only had to say which word was odd and why, yet her students took off with it as though it were a "free" communicative task. Veronika had said not a word.

A few weeks later, Veronika wanted to find another way to get learners to practice and produce sentences the textbook chapter focused on. What was another way she could do that with a game? Veronika's students were interested in vocabulary; the success with "The Odd Man Out" suggested that. She found *New Ways in Teaching Vocabulary* (Nation 1994) and a simple exercise named "Vocabulary Match-Up and Sentence Writing" (Mannon, in Nation 1994: 105). It had only three steps, which Veronika simplified into three steps in her lesson plan:

Step 1: Select some vocabulary you want to review. Make two cards: one for the word and one for the definition with enough cards so each student has one, but only one. So if you have ten students, make five vocabulary cards and five definition cards.

Step 2: Form students into pairs by randomly handing one card to each student and asking them to find the person with the corresponding card.

Step 3:   When all the students with the word cards find their partner with the definition cards, sit down and write a sentence using the word. Write the sentences on the board. Read the sentences aloud and correct if necessary. Teacher can collect the papers for later use as quizzes or reviews.

Veronika was intrigued by the game because she thought it might allow learners to practice writing sentences, and that was something she wanted them to pay attention to and get some accuracy over (step 3). The learners did fine. For step 3, they wrote sentences they already knew how to write, and Veronika had to nudge them a little to write the new sentences from the textbook, such as what a student wrote: "1982 was a great year for my family. I was born in Kiev," changing it to "My family lived in Kiev *when I was born*. It was 1982." The learners went on break and Veronika had a thought. She erased the board. When the learners came back, she had them come to the board and put everything back from memory, including the textbook sentences. "Can you remember any other sentences from this part of the textbook? You can change them a little if you like," she said. The learners together filled the blackboard with reasonably accurate sentences, a few of them original. Veronika spoke only if a learner group asked for assistance.

Veronika wondered: Was this practice? She thought so. Learners had to use their memory. They reviewed. They used their minds. Yet, at the same time, they worked together. She heard them proposing different answers to each other. Some of the time they stayed in English. Well, then, what they did, was it communicative? In a strange way, she thought perhaps it was. There was still a lot of structure to learners' practice. Their production was not completely free. See Table 3.5 for what Veronika posits about learning.

Veronika has an applied linguistics MA degree, and she speaks and uses multiple second languages, particularly English, with better-than-average Communicative Competence. Yet despite her professional coursework and her own learning, which has likely involved processes beyond practicing a specified set of linguistic forms (linguistic competence), Veronika operates as though learning is conscious study and practice. In essence, she bases her decisions about teaching, at least in the beginning of this case study, on her own remembered experiences of second language learning. At the same time, Veronika is greatly advantaged by her MA in combination with in-house teacher workshops in that they have reawakened a genuine intellectual conundrum she is now poised to pursue. The MA program offered her concepts, and her teaching experiences then, as now, seem to conflict with those concepts. Learning is supposed to take place as a result of communication, which is messy. How can that be practice? And how can a textbook be adapted to accommodate more practice, and perhaps more communication? And another question then follows: If learning involves memory and thinking, would not second language learning also involve

Table 3.5 What Veronika Posits about Learning and Teachers

1. Language is vocabulary and grammatical structures. Language forms are the proper objects of learning.

2. Learning is a cognitive activity.

3. Learning is comprised of conscious study and practice of language forms.

4. Proper practice is scripted and controlled.

5. The purpose of practice is to gain linguistic accuracy on specified linguistic forms.

6. Review, memory, and practice are mutually supportive.

7. Practice is pointless if learners do not understand the language point.

8. Learners need to learn linguistic forms before they can communicate.

9. Communicative tasks are messy and may not provide true practice.

10. Games promote learning because they increase the amount of time prioritized to learner practice; they *may* promote learning because they may cause learners to communicate.

11. Communicative tasks *may* cause one kind of learning while textbooks cause another kind of learning.

Source: Authors.

that? Just because her second language acquisition instructor did not cover content quite like this does not mean that other scholars in second language education do not pursue these topics (see Chapter 6, for example). As a well-trained teacher and experienced instructor confronted with a novel teaching situation, Veronika is in a good position to benefit from self-study of not only her own low-level theories but also middle-level theories about learning.

Reflective Projects

1. Consider a second language you have learned. It does not matter how good you think you are at it. How did you learn it? Think of at least five specific memories of how you learned it. Were there some things you did that you liked more than others? Were there some things that you thought were more effective than others? If you are teaching a second language now, can you make a connection between your early language study practices and your teaching practice?

2. If you had formal professional training, what middle-level learning theories did they actually teach? Were you encouraged to consider your own low-level learning theories? Looking back or looking at your program now, can you say what your program posits about learning, or posited about learning?

3. Review the middle-level learning theories in Table 3.1 or Tables 3.2 and 3.3. If you were to further study one learning theory, which one would it be and why?

4. We offered three aspects as a tool to evaluate learning theories: (1) What the theory seeks to explain; (2) what the learning theory posits as the causes of learning; and (3) who uses the theory. To review: Item 1 speaks to a problem a teacher might want to solve. Item 2 speaks to a specific thing a teacher may ask a learner to do to bring about learning. Item 3 speaks to where a teacher might go (a discipline, a conference, or a journal) to learn more about the theory. Apply the three questions to any of the learning theories that appear elsewhere in this chapter and in this book, including Task-Based Language Teaching, the Noticing Hypothesis, Metacognition, Multiple Literacies, Adaptive Control of Thought, Communicative Language Teaching 2nd Gen, and so on.

5. When describing CLT 1st Gen, we named four principles: a need for authenticity; a key role for negotiation; the importance of group work for achieving negotiation; and a sustained desire on the part of some pedagogists and scholars to continue the use of a structural, or grammatical, syllabus upon which to organize a course. If we were to treat the principles as theories of learning, we begin to see how CLT is truly a theory area with many contributors. This is especially true when posing our three questions: What does the theory seek to explain? What does the learning theory posit as the causes of learning? Who uses the theory? Going back to the part of the chapter where the principles are described, try to answer the questions with particular attention to the third question. What is the background and interest of the person who posits the principle?

6. Have you ever had a conscious change in your low-level theory about language learning? What caused the change? What did your belief change from and what did it change to?

CHAPTER FOUR

Theories of Language and Teachers

Why This Chapter?

This chapter focuses on the interaction of theories of language and second language teachers. The practices or artifacts we use as discussion points are books on the teacher's desk, content and skills a teacher emphasizes, and tests and quizzes a teacher makes and uses. By theories of language we mean how language is characterized, studied, and commented and acted upon by scholars, administrators, teachers, and learners in the second language education field.

Theories of language have an important role in second language teachers' working lives (Kelly 1976). As one novice teacher in a Japanese foreign language program said,

> I want students to communicate more and to exchange ideas. Some students have done homestays in Japan and other students want to know what that was like, maybe get some tips on what to say and how to act. Some others want to be able to read menus in restaurants and use Japanese language websites. But the textbook my boss chose does not help me with that. Instead, 80% of the textbook is on grammar explanations with single sentences and drills. When we get to the next lesson, we start all over again with a new set of grammar rules. I wish at least the grammar rules were recycled more.

These comments may seem to relate more to teaching methods. But underlying these comments are contrasting views of language. This teacher's commentary illustrates how these contrasting theories of language are expressed by different stakeholders in second language education, including teachers, administrators (the teacher's supervisor), and textbook publishers. It is also apparent that the teacher feels the contrast between wanting learners to exchange meaning and read texts (language as use) and the demands of the supervisor and the textbook to focus learners' attention on words, sentences, and grammar (language as form). See Chapter 8 for more information on stakeholders, a concept from Evaluation, a high-level theory area.

What teachers know and believe about a second or foreign language comprises a significant impetus to nearly every aspect of their professional lives. It is the language itself, however it is characterized, treated, and acted upon, that makes up the content of the course (Strevens 1987). A teacher cannot easily be a teacher if he or she does not know the course content. It is the language that is taught and learned. It is the language that learners ask questions about, that teachers can provide answers and guidance for. Thus, it is likely that teachers spend a significant amount of time working to understand more about the language by consulting books, websites, and other resources. Teachers' ever-developing theories of language offer a conceptual or knowledge source that they rely upon to plan their lessons, prioritize content and skills, choose materials, and write quizzes and tests.

In this chapter, we outline how the High Middle Low Theory Model (Figure 1.3) applies to theories of language. We offer specific high, middle, and low-level theories which account for and explain commonly observed aspects of daily classroom life. We do this in two ways. First, we offer a table after each major section which states what a particular theory posits. By posit we mean stating the assumptions or principles that a theory suggests. Second, to illustrate the theories of language, we offer the case study of Rick, a French teacher in the United States. We describe how he teaches his lessons, and how high, middle, and low-level theories may account for that. We also describe his online and conference-based interactions with a German language teacher whom he has befriended and who lives in another state. Their interactions offer contrasting working theories of language. We finish with reflective project ideas for readers.

How the High Middle Low Theory Model Applies to Theories of Language

For the purposes of this book, we outline two ways in which language is characterized. This brings context to the high-, middle-, and low-level theories we describe in this chapter. These are: language seen as form and language seen as use. A third view, language theorized as a means of identity formation (Multiple Literacies), is also relevant but is dealt with in Chapter 9.

Language Seen as Form

First, language can be characterized as a formal system in terms of sounds, vocabulary, word formation, phrases, and sentences (Dupuy and Willis Allen 2012; Fox 1993; Johnson 2009; Kelly 1976; Kumaravadivelu 2006; Mitchell, Brumfit, and Hooper 1994; Robins 1997). Linguistics as a field of inquiry has a long history of its own (Robins 1997), with a long but uneven interaction with second language teaching (Kelly 1976). At the risk of oversimplifying either field, the language as form view described here reflects a view of language dating from the mid-1950s. A teacher or scholar working within this characterization may simply refer to language as "grammar." There are multiple historical sources for this characterization of language. In her history of the field of second language acquisition, Thomas (2013) describes early known traditions to teach learners not only the foreign language but also a metalanguage for language, in other words, a specialized language for talking about language. This grew out of a practical need felt by foreign language teachers of seventh-century Europe to describe learners' first language and then use the metalanguage to explain the foreign language being learned, Latin in this case (Thomas 2013: 26).

This view of language might be seen as the subject matter that language teachers must know in order to teach (Alamarza 1996; Andrews and McNeill 2005; Borg 2003, 2006; Johnson 2009). We argue that this theory of language is common in second language education and may be a kind of default way for teachers to think about language. The French teacher in our case study has two reference books on his desk. One is on French grammar and the other is a book on grammar simply as a topic of its own.

Language Seen as Use

Second, language can be characterized as language use. To study and discuss language in the context of human use and communication is not new (Kelly 1976; see also Kumaravadivelu [2006] for a review). However, in its contour most recognizable to second language teachers today, language is seen in terms of language learners using it to accomplish general types of social acts such as making and accepting invitations; asking and answering personal questions; or asking for and following directions to a place. This would be a view of language that focuses on language users making and interpreting meaning. Each of the three examples given above are called communicative functions in scholarly literature, textbooks, teacher resources, and course syllabuses in second language education. See Austin (1962), Searle (1969), and Wilkins (1976) for classic sources on communicative functions (see Chapter 3). See the *Common European Framework of Reference (CEFR)* for many examples of what the authors call micro- and macro-functions (Council of Europe 2001: 30, 42).

Here is an illustration: There might be any number of ways language users together may accomplish the social act of making and declining an invitation. They might say for inviting: "Could you join me?" or "Please come to dinner" or "Are you free tomorrow night?" Note that three different linguistic forms (in this case, questions or sentences) can accomplish the act of inviting. The person wishing to decline may respond with silence (Wong and Zhang Waring 2020) or he or she may say "I don't know" or "No, thank you" or "How about a rain check?" These illustrate yet more conversational actions (silence) or linguistic forms (sentences) being used to accomplish the act of declining an invitation. Inviting and declining an invitation may take five or more turns by users in a conversation or while texting (Wong and Zhang Waring 2020). The social function of making and declining an invitation would be considered or taught as a unit, or a communicative event. At the advice of his German teaching friend, the French teacher in our case study has printed out materials from a professional teaching organization and turned them into a notebook. The materials, in part, offer descriptions of communicative functions as suggestions for planning classroom activities.

Texts

It is argued here that a perspective of language as use implies a necessary focus on *texts*. Halliday and Hasan (1976: 1–2) offer this definition: text is a term "used in linguistics to refer to any passage—spoken or written, of whatever length, that does form a unified whole." Further, "a text is a unit of language in use. It is not a grammatical unit, like a clause or a sentence; and it is not defined by its size" (1–2). Halliday and Hasan further note that a text is defined by its meaning as a "semantic unit" and not necessarily by its form. Thus, a text can be a short conversational exchange, or it can be a poem, a short story, a blog post, a discussion following a post on social media, a newspaper or radio advertisement, a conversation during office hours, or a small group discussion in a language classroom. The point is that these different texts, whether spoken or written, or produced or interpreted, are communicative acts. Each requires language users/learners to use different aspects of their communicative competence (see discussion below) to interpret and produce them. The relevance of the concept of texts will become more apparent in the case study of our French teacher. As will be seen, the French teacher and the German teacher portrayed in the case study think of texts, using quite different theories of language.

Persistence of Language Seen as a System of Forms

The two characterizations of language described here do not operate in isolation from one another in second language education. Teachers and other stakeholders adhering to one or both of the high-level theories described below (Proficiency and Communicative Competence) would likely say that their overall aim is for learners to use and communicate with the second language—in other words, successfully expressing, interpreting, and exchanging meanings. Nonetheless, teachers operationalizing language as form seem to think and act as though language forms comprise the content of second language courses. Alamarza (1996), working with pre-service teachers, reported that her research participants were led to view language "with an emphasis on structures and forms and no real difference between the written and spoken means of expression" (61). Some commentators argue for teaching language as a formal system to teachers but also focus on helping teachers transform this declarative knowledge into procedural knowledge (Andrews 1994; Andrews and McNeill 2005). This would help teachers to present and explain grammatical rules, to draw learners' attention to regularities in word formation, and so on.

The idea that teachers treat language as a system of forms is persistent in the literature. For instance, Gorsuch (2012) found that some ESL teachers working with high intermediate learners compartmentalized the Communicative Competence model, focusing on linguistic competence (language as form) (see also Fox 1993; Johnson 2009). Dupuy and Willis Allen (2012) worked with novice Spanish language teachers to explore language as a means of building learners' social identities through guided interaction with authentic texts. Nonetheless, the novice teachers persisted in teaching discrete grammar points and vocabulary even with materials and texts not particularly suited to that purpose (293, 295). See also Johnson (2009) on the prevalence of linguistics courses in teacher preparation programs.

High-Level Theories of Language

Two high-level theories relevant to the French language teacher and the German language teacher described in this chapter are Proficiency and Communicative Competence. Both are termed high-level theories because they are public theories and widely written about, commented on, and debated. Communicative Competence models have been decades in the making (for accounts, see Celce-Murcia, Dornyei, and Thurrell 1995; and Fulcher and Davidson 2007). Even today, there is no one unitary, agreed-upon model of Communicative Competence, although there are common elements to the various extant models. This shows the sustained, continued salience of the model to second language scholars and educators. It is still the object of commentary and interpretation. Further, both Proficiency and Communicative Competence have had profound and lasting effects, "sometimes unintended, on many levels of the educational enterprise, including textbook design, classroom instruction, and teacher education" (Gorsuch 2019a: 414). The theories comprise teachers' and administrators' working universes. It is essential to note that the two terms are often used interchangeably, despite significant differences between them not only in terms of what they try to explain but also in terms of how they have been adapted to practice.

Proficiency

Proficiency is the ability of learners to use the second language for "some future activity" (Davies 1990: 20). One way to understand Proficiency is to consider how it is tested. A proficiency test captures general language ability "on the basis of typical syllabuses" (20) of second/foreign language courses. Proficiency tests are intended to capture "what has been learnt but in a much more vague way . . . it exhibits no control over previous learning" (20). The Center for Open Educational Resources and Language Learning (2010) states that learner proficiency levels are not indications of learner achievement but rather what "individuals can and cannot do regardless of the curriculum." Achievement tests, in contrast, are designed to capture previous learning in a course. Achievement tests are the common tests and quizzes made by teachers and used to assign course grades and to offer feedback to learners. Teachers use many concrete strategies in designing their achievement tests to capture previous learning in the courses they teach (Gorsuch 2019a). In general, teachers do not write proficiency tests (Gorsuch and Griffee 2018).

Examples of proficiency tests are the OPI (Oral Proficiency Interview) administered by ACTFL (American Council for the Teaching of Foreign Languages 2012a), the TOEFL (Test of English as a Foreign Language; Educational Testing Service 2019), the IELTS (International English Language Testing System; IELTS 2018), and the TOCFL (Test of Chinese as a Foreign Language; Taipei Economic and Cultural Office 2011). Like these tests, which contain unpredictable content by design, Proficiency as a theory does not necessarily take into account specific language use contexts or tasks, and the effects of these contexts or tasks on learners' second language use (Gorsuch 2019a). Authors of *Performance Descriptors for Language Learners* (ACTFL 2012b) state that learners can engage in interactive activities in classrooms and be graded by teachers on their performances. However, they also state that learner performance and proficiency "are not the same" (4). In other words, teachers cannot assume that learners' performances in an interactive speaking task in classrooms have any clear relationship to their "proficiency level" on the ACTFL *Guidelines* (4). Rather, learners must do multiple interactive spoken performances and then collectively the performances might "generally" be related to a "proficiency level" (4). This underscores an important feature that differentiates Proficiency from

Communicative Competence. In a Communicative Competence framework, a learner's performance on a communicative task would be taken as direct evidence of their ability on that task, in that particular setting.

It is argued here that the various ACTFL materials such as the *Guidelines* and *Performance Descriptors* are middle-level theory expressions of the high-level theory of Proficiency (see commentary by Fulcher 1996; Gorsuch 2019a; Kissling and O'Donnell 2015). The *Guidelines* and *Performance Descriptors* will be described in more detail later in the chapter. See Table 4.1 for what Proficiency posits (what it theorizes).

Communicative Competence

Communicative Competence "seeks to explain language use as cognitive and social events" (Gorsuch 2019a: 416). It is, like Proficiency, second language ability, but is seen as an interaction between: (1) learners' second language knowledge, (2) learners' ability to plan and monitor, and (3) the characteristics or demands of the language use situation (Bachman and Palmer 2010; Fulcher and Davidson 2007). See Table 4.2 for a model of language knowledge, the first of the three components (Bachman and Palmer 2010: 44–5).

In order to use these various components of language knowledge (Table 4.2), learners must make sense of what is required (the characteristics or demands of the language use situation) and then use Metacognition (the ability to plan and monitor) to do communication (language use). See Chapter 6 on Metacognition. Note how grammatical knowledge in Table 4.2 may comprise the sole content of many second language courses, yet grammatical knowledge as theorized by Communicative Competence is but one component of language knowledge, which itself is only one component of Bachman and Palmer's (2010) whole model.

A Communicative Competence perspective on language use focuses on making and interpreting meanings but is conceived of in terms of learners accomplishing more specifically stated social or cognitive goals. Examples

Table 4.1 What Proficiency Posits

1. Language is characterized as language use.
2. Proficiency is the ability to use language.
3. Proficiency is the ability to use language across multiple, unpredictable language use situations.
4. Proficiency is most properly tested using scientifically developed tests with unpredictable content (norm-referenced tests or performance tests).

Source: Authors.

Table 4.2 Communicative Competence Model of Language Knowledge

Organizational knowledge: "How utterances or sentences and texts are organized"	
Components (2)	*Definition and Examples*
Grammatical knowledge	"How individual utterances or sentences are organized," including vocabulary, word order, word formation, pronunciation, graphology
Textual knowledge	"How utterances or sentences are organized to form texts," including cohesion and "conversational organization"

Pragmatic knowledge: "How utterances or sentences and texts are related to the communicative goals of the language user and the language use setting"	
Components (2)	*Definition and Examples*
Functional knowledge	"How utterances or sentences and texts are related to the communicative goals of language users," including the ability to get other people to do things (manipulative functions) or teach things (heuristic functions)
Sociolinguistic knowledge	"How utterances or sentences and texts are related to features of the language use setting," including genres, language varieties, levels of politeness, and cultural references

Source: Table original to this book; Information sourced from Bachman and Palmer (2010: 44–5).

are: (1) following directions to install computer software; (2) composing an important email to a client from work describing a proposed change in a contract; or (3) reading a simple short story to identify the main characters, and (4) offering and receiving opinions in a classroom discussion on story characters' problems and their solutions to their problems. There are general communicative functions underlying the examples here, such as "following directions" and "describing changes" and "offering and receiving opinions." However, the purposes or end goals of the communicative acts are specific and go beyond single, general communicative functions. The function of "offering and receiving opinions" by itself could not adequately describe what learners must do for example 3 given above (read a story, select information relevant to the task, prepare for a verbal discussion, etc.). See a proposed "chain" of communicative functions needed for "purchase of goods and services" found in the *Common European Framework of Reference (CEFR)*: "Finding the way to the shop," "exchanging greetings,"

Table 4.3 What Communicative Competence Posits

1. Language is characterized as language use.
2. Language use is a social and cognitive event.
3. Communicative Competence is an interaction between learners' second language knowledge, their ability to plan and monitor, and the characteristics or demands of the language use situation.
4. The characteristics and demands of different language use situations will change how learners use language.
5. Language use situations are complex with multiple underlying communicative functions. We must be prepared to describe them to understand what aspects of Communicative Competence are being demanded of learners.

Source: Authors.

"seeking information," "agreeing to prices of items," "agreeing addition of total" (Council of Europe 2001: 127).

These elaborated purposes or goals may require more extended attention by language learners. Learners would be seen as systematically using different aspects of their Communicative Competence (language knowledge, cognition, understanding of what is required by the situation) to address a specific language use goal in ways of their choosing. For instance, reading and following instructions to install computer software would be a different operation than reading for pleasure. For reading instructions, learners might direct themselves to read very carefully and slowly for brief periods, and to return to specific words, phrases, and passages multiple times to enhance comprehension or resolve misunderstandings. When learners read for pleasure, we might see them read long passages at length, depending on their comfort with the text. They may choose to read a section of prose or dialog aloud. Their reading speed may be faster than it would be for reading directions on software installation. See Table 4.3 for what Communicative Competence posits (theorizes).

Middle-Level Theories Concerning Language

As discussed in Chapter 1, middle-level theories deal with specific domains of interest, such as how learners plan doing tasks based on experience (Self-Efficacy Theory; e.g., Bandura 1997; Siegle 2000) or how learners learn a second language (second language acquisition theories; e.g., Shehadeh 2002; Van den Branden 1997). Middle-level theories are often public and discussed or debated. They are general, and thus it would take careful thought to apply them to specific learning settings. In terms of language, the middle-level theories focused on in this chapter are: language use description frameworks and the Proficiency Movement.

Language Use Description Frameworks

A language use description framework is defined as a collection of publicly available documents, publications, guides, or resource materials that apply the high-level theories of Proficiency or Communicative Competence to program and classroom planning and practice, and to materials and textbook selection, writing, and use. In essence, language use description frameworks attempt to create a common understanding of second language ability "by having prose descriptions of learners' abilities using the language set on an intuited, continuous, linear scale" (Gorsuch 2019a: 423). The two most visible examples in our field are the ACTFL *Guidelines* (American Council for the Teaching of Foreign Languages 2012a) and the *Common European Framework of Reference (CEFR)* (Council of Europe 2001, 2018) (for reviews of each framework, see Gorsuch 2019a). The ACTFL *Guidelines* have an overall scale with eleven points ranging from "distinguished" to "novice low," while *CEFR* has a seven-point scale from Pre-A1 "basic user" to C2 "proficient user." ACTFL added the "distinguished" level at the top end of their proposed scale in 2012, and *CEFR* added the "Pre-A1" level at the bottom end of their proposed scale in 2018. Here are examples of prose descriptions (called "descriptors") for low-level learners, common to first- and second-year US college foreign language classes. According to the ACTFL (2012a: 9) *Guidelines*, L2 speakers at the "novice-mid" level can

> communicate minimally by using a number of isolated words and memorized phrases limited by the particular context in which the language has been learned. When responding to direct questions, they may say only two or three words at a time or give an occasional stock answer. They pause frequently as they search for simple vocabulary or attempt to recycle their own and their interlocutor's words.

According to *CEFR*, L2 speakers at the "A1" level engaged in "overall spoken interaction" can

> interact in a simple way but communication is totally dependent on repetition at a slower rate of speech, rephrasing and repair. Can ask and answer simple questions, initiate and respond to simple statements in areas of immediate need or on very familiar topics. (Council of Europe 2018: 83)

CEFR has a separate set of descriptors for "understanding an interlocutor" at the A1 level. "Understanding an interlocuter" is considered a permutation of "spoken interaction."

Can understand everyday expressions aimed at the satisfaction of simple needs of a concrete type, delivered directly to him/her in clear, slow and repeated speech by a sympathetic speaker. Can understand questions and instructions addressed carefully and slowly to him/her and follow short, simple directions. (84)

Note that both ACTFL and *CEFR* characterize language as language use. Gorsuch (2019a) has argued that the ACTFL *Guidelines* as a language use description framework is an expression of the high-level theory of Proficiency, and that *CEFR* is an expression of the high-level theory of Communicative Competence (see also commentary by Center for Open Educational Resources on Language Learning 2010; and Council of Europe 2018).

The ACTFL *Guidelines*

The language use description framework focused on here is widely known in the United States—the ACTFL *Guidelines* (American Council for the Teaching of Foreign Languages 2012a). The ACTFL *Guidelines* have had a lifespan of more than thirty-six years (Liskin-Gasparro 2003) and have evolved over time, with panels of consultants and authors adding one level to its scale and details to its descriptors. The teacher depicted in the chapter's case study teaches French in Utah at a college. His colleague/friend teaches college-level German in Colorado. They met while attending the annual ACTFL conference, which focused on the ACTFL *Guidelines* and applying them to teaching and programs.

Theorizing Language Use

One way the *Guidelines* get applied to instructional planning and classroom teaching is by theorizing three general contexts in which language use takes place: "interpersonal," "interpretive," and "presentational" (ACTFL 2012a: 7). For instance, according to the ACTFL *Can-Do Statements*, written for learners (ACTFL and National Council of State Supervisors for Languages 2018), a learner at the novice-mid level who is *interacting* using the L2 "can express basic needs related to familiar and everyday activities, using a mixture of practiced or memorized words, phrases, and questions" (7). A novice-mid learner who is *interpreting* written texts (either "informational" or "fictional") can "identify some basic facts from memorized words and phrases when they are supported by gestures or visuals" (3). A novice-mid learner who is *presenting* information in the L2 ("presentational" language use) can "present information about myself, my interests and my activities using a mixture of practiced or memorized words, phrases and simple sentences" (4). Having learners interact in the L2, interpret L2 materials, and do presentations in the L2 are all familiar classroom activities to teachers, particularly those who ascribe to the Proficiency Movement (see description below).

The ACTFL *Performance Descriptors* (2012b) further theorizes these three basic language use situations to suggest ways teachers may plan instruction and emphasize content and skills. Thus, the corporate authors of ACTFL theorize how to encourage language use in classrooms. For language use in interpersonal "mode," learners engage in "active negotiation of meaning" and "observe and monitor one another to see how their meanings and intentions are being communicated" (7). For interpretive language use, learners engage in "reading (websites, stories, articles), listening (speeches, messages, songs), or viewing (video clips) of authentic materials" (7). Finally, for language use in presentational mode, learners engage in "writing (messages, articles, reports), speaking (telling a story, giving a speech, describing a poster), or visually representing (video or PowerPoint)" (7). None of these statements suggest specific techniques or lesson procedures. They do offer images of language use processes and skills to focus on, including "negotiation of meaning," and observation and monitoring, reading a variety of texts, listening to a variety of texts, telling stories, and describing things.

The authors of *the Performance Descriptors* (2012b) also offer seven "parameters" or "language domains" that theorize learners' classroom language use. These "language domains" offer images on: teachers' classroom task or activity selection, skills/processes selection, and text selection (8); and criteria by which teachers can judge learners' performances on those tasks or activities. See Table 4.4 for "language domains" on planning classroom tasks and activities, and selecting texts for novice learners.

For instance, a second/foreign language teacher may select content from the required textbook such as an authentic short poem with pictures. Perhaps the poem is about a child looking in a shop window. The teacher may ask learners to narrate and describe the pictures in pairs (functions–interpersonal) or listen to a speaker narrate and describe the poem and pictures and then have learners indicate recognition of elements of the text (functions–interpretive). The same teacher may then search for and then record additional authentic texts for more listening practice (text type–interpretive). To aid his search for listening texts, he would poll learners on their topic familiarity with specific shopping websites, folk tales, children's stories, and any other narratives that touch on the themes of wanting, admiring, standing on the outside looking in. He would then choose authentic texts based on topics with which learners are most familiar. The teacher may ask learners to give a short presentation where they recount the poem or poems or note their personal reactions to the poems using sentences they have practiced (text type–presentational).

The four remaining "language domains" suggested by the ACTFL corporate authors are in essence very general theories for scoring criteria teachers can use for judging learners' performances on the class activities and tasks learners do with specific texts. In the language testing field, scoring criteria are theoretical categories (Gorsuch and Griffee 2018), or ways of specifying language use, upon which teachers can judge aspects of learners' language use ability, as in "Adele used very good pronunciation but she still needs to work on her vocabulary." "Pronunciation" is one criterion, and "vocabulary" is a second scoring criterion. Scoring criteria are in essence scoring scales, much like the ACTFL *Guidelines* themselves, but focusing on something more specific. See Table 4.5 for theorized criteria from the *Performance Descriptors* (2012b) by which teachers can judge learners' performances on those tasks or activities suggested in Table 4.4.

Given the tasks and activities described in the paragraphs above, the teacher may then judge learners' language use on one or more of the four "language domains" in Table 4.5. We offer these examples as reasonable extrapolations of the "language domains" and classroom activities proposed by the ACTFL *Guidelines* (2012a) and ACTFL *Performance Descriptors* (2012b). See Table 4.6.

The examples we devised and offer here describe a general scoring criterion for, or a means of judging, learner language use while engaged in specific classroom tasks. The examples also include a standard by which a teacher might judge success on a given task. For instance, where learners give a presentation, a teacher may specify 80 percent accuracy on spoken and written words, phrases, and sentences (language control), and also that learners speak more or less continuously for at least one minute (also an element of language control called "fluency"; see Chapter 5).

Some readers may note what seem like missing scoring criteria, such as grammatical accuracy, appropriateness of pronunciation, accuracy with spelling or logographic character writing, and correct word formation. These traditional, form-focused criteria are used in many teacher-made achievement tests even if the criteria are not consciously applied or even defined (Gorsuch 2019a). They are simply used. We think many teachers looking at the ACTFL *Performance Descriptors* (2012b) would likely theorize these traditional, form-focused criteria as being part of the "language control" category in Table 4.6 above. Yet, it is interesting to note that there is no mention of criteria such as "grammatical accuracy" or "spelling" in the *Performance Descriptors* (2012b). Such traditional scoring criteria will be discussed later in the chapter in the section on low-level theory. Our two case study teachers have a disagreement on just this topic.

A Contradiction between Proficiency and What Learners Do in Classes

For better or worse, it appears there is an intractable contradiction between the high-level theory of Proficiency and the ACTFL *Guidelines*, a middle-level theory-based application of Proficiency. As one of the main, publicly accessible documents interpreting ACTFL's mission, the *Performance*

Table 4.4 "Language Domains" on Planning Language Use Classroom Tasks, Activities, Texts for Novice Learners

"Parameters" or "Language Domains"	Definition	Examples	Interpersonal, Interpretive, or Presentational "Mode"
Functions	Global tasks the learners can perform	Ask formulaic questions; initiate, maintain, and end a conversation; create with language; narrate and describe; make inferences	Novice *interpersonal*: Listing, naming, identifying Novice *interpretive*: Word and formulaic phrase recognition Novice *presentational*: Presents simple basic information through words, lists, notes
Contexts and content	Situations in which the learner can function Topics which the learner can understand and discuss	Oneself; one's immediate environment General interest; work-related	Novice *interpersonal*: Personally relevant contexts that relate to basic biographical information Novice *interpretive*: Texts with highly predictable, familiar contexts Novice *presentational*: Personally relevant contexts that relate to basic biographical information
Text type	Texts that the learner is able to understand and produce in order to perform the functions of the level	Words, phrases, sentences, questions, strings of sentences, connected sentences, paragraphs	Novice *interpersonal*: Highly practiced words and phrases and an occasional sentence Novice *interpretive*: Authentic texts supported by visuals or when topic is very familiar; lists, phrases, sentences Novice *presentational*: Highly practiced sentences and formulaic questions

Table original to this book, information and categories sourced from: The Performance Descriptors (2012b: 8, 14, 16, 18; used with permission), and Gorsuch (2019a: 432–3; used with permission).

Table 4.5 "Language Domains" on Criteria for Judging Learners' Performances on Classroom Tasks and Activities for Novice Learners

"Parameters" or "Language Domains"	Definition	Examples in Interpersonal, Interpretive, or Presentational "Mode"
Language control	The level of control the learner has over certain language features or strategies to produce or understand the language; "How accurate is the language learner's language?" (The *Performance Descriptors* (2012b: 9)	Novice *interpersonal*: Can comprehend highly practiced and basic messages; can control memorized language sufficiently to be appropriate to context Novice *interpretive*: Primarily relies on vocabulary to derive meaning from texts; may derive meaning by recognizing structural patterns that have been used in familiar or some new contexts Novice *presentational*: Produces memorized language that is appropriate to the context
Vocabulary	Vocabulary used to produce or understand language; "How extensive and applicable is the language learner's vocabulary?" (9)	Novice *interpersonal*: Able to understand and produce a number of high frequency words, highly practiced expressions, and formulaic questions Novice *interpretive*: Comprehends some . . . highly predictable vocabulary Novice *presentational*: Produces a number of high frequency words and formulaic expressions; able to use a limited variety of vocabulary on familiar topics

(continued)

Table 4.5 (continued)

"Parameters" or "Language Domains"	Definition	Examples in Interpersonal, Interpretive, or Presentational "Mode"
Communication strategies	Strategies used to negotiate meaning to understand text and messages and to express oneself; "How does the language learner maintain communication and make meaning?" (9)	Novice *interpersonal*: Able to imitate modeled words, use facial expressions and gestures, repeat words, resort to first language, ask for repetition, indicate lack of understanding Novice *interpretive*: Able to skim and scan, rely on visual support and background knowledge . . . rely on recognition of cognates, may recognize word family roots Novice *presentational*: Able to rely on a practiced format, use facial expressions and gestures, repeat words, resort to first language, use graphic organizers to present information, rely on multiple drafts and practice sessions with feedback; support presentational speaking with visuals and notes
Cultural awareness	Cultural products, practices, or perspectives the language learner may employ to communicate more successfully in the cultural setting; "How is the language learners' cultural knowledge reflected in language use?" (9)	Novice *interpersonal*: May use culturally appropriate gestures and formulaic expressions in highly practiced applications; may show awareness of the most obvious cultural differences or prohibitions Novice *interpretive*: Use own culture to derive meaning from texts that are heard, read, or viewed Novice *presentational*: May use some memorized culturally appropriate gestures, formulaic expressions, and basic writing conventions

Table original to this book, information sourced from: The Performance Descriptors (2012b: 8–9, 14–19; used with permission).
Note: *For examples of scoring criteria, descriptors for "Novice" level are given.*

Table 4.6 How "Language Control," "Vocabulary," "Communication Strategies," and "Cultural Awareness" Might Be Judged on Tasks and Activities at the Novice Level

Task or Activity	How "Language Domains in Table 4.5 Can be Used to Judge Learners' Language Use
Learners narrate and describe a poem and pictures in pairs (interpersonal)	*Language control*: Learner/speaker speaks somewhat continuously for a least one minute. Learner/speaker uses appropriate phrases and sentences 70 percent of the time. Listeners' notes reflect at least 70 percent of the phrases and sentences of what the learner/speaker said. *Communication strategies*: Learner/speaker and listener use three out of the following strategies: imitating words, using facial expressions, using gestures, repeating words, using first language (briefly), asking for repetition, indicating lack of understanding; other strategies used (asking for clarification, using rising intonation, etc.) are noted and accepted.
Learners hear a poem and check concepts, phrases, and words they hear (interpretive)	*Language control*: Learner writes a check on 70 percent of all words, phrases, and grammatical structures on the worksheet that also appeared on the audio file, but less than 5 percent of the words, phrases, and grammatical structures on the worksheet that were not on the audio file. *Vocabulary*: Learner is able to define most of the words they checked on their worksheets by writing notes or definitions in either the first or second language and/or by finding definitions appropriate to the context of use in a dictionary.
Learners hear a new poem or story on the same theme and check concepts, phrases, and words they hear on a worksheet. They find concepts, phrases, and words that are in common with the first poem they studied in an earlier class (interpretive)	*Vocabulary*: Learner is able to define most of the words they checked on their worksheets by writing notes or definitions in either the first or second language, and/or by finding definitions appropriate to the context of use in a dictionary. *Vocabulary*: Learner is able to identify at least five words in common between the new poem or story, and the first poem, and to successfully compare the use of the words between the two texts by identifying differences or similarities in meaning between the two contexts of use.

(continued)

Table 4.6 (continued)

Task or Activity	How "Language Domains in Table 4.5 Can be Used to Judge Learners' Language Use
Learners give a presentation where they recount the poems they read and give their personal reactions (presentational)	*Language control*: Learner is able to write and say words, phrases, and sentences on their poster (or power point, etc.) at an 80 percent accuracy level. They are able to speak with some pauses for at least one minute. *Cultural awareness*: Learner uses at least two culturally appropriate phrases or gestures that may be used to emphasize information or a personal reaction.

Source: Authors.

Descriptors (2012b) characterize language use in classrooms and programs. The descriptors are: "designed to describe language performance that is the result of explicit instruction in an instructional setting" (3). Thus, the corporate authors theorize that second language use that is learned and done in a classroom ("performance") is different than "proficiency" language use. The authors define Proficiency as "the ability to use language in real world situations in a spontaneous interaction and non-rehearsed contexts and in a manner acceptable and appropriate to native speakers of the language" (4).

What does this contradiction mean? One implication is that language use in classrooms is seen as limited in scope in terms of different language use situations teachers can reasonably set for learners. A second implication is that classroom language use and learning is theorized as bound by learners' efforts and experiences, namely those of memorization and rehearsal (ACTFL 2012b: 4). Nonetheless, teachers are urged to design instruction to "focus on real world-like tasks with the anticipation that learners will be prepared to do the same outside the instructional setting" (4). The two positions are contradictory, suggesting intractable problems with the application of a high-level theory (Proficiency), which stipulates that language use has little relationship to classroom achievement. Indeed, the *Performance Descriptors* are designed to offer "more detailed and more granular information about language learners" (3) and as a "companion" to the ACTFL *Guidelines*— "a document that describes broad, general language proficiency regardless of when, where or how language is acquired" (3). In developing and publishing the *Performance Descriptors*, the authors may themselves see the contradiction. See Table 4.7 for what the ACTFL *Guidelines* seem to propose theoretically.

Table 4.7 What the ACTFL *Guidelines* Posit

1. Language use takes place in classrooms. It is termed "performance."
2. Classroom language use is posited as interactional, interpretive, and presentational.
3. These three basic contexts of use in item 2 can inspire teachers' selection of tasks, activities, skills, and texts.
4. Two processes that contribute to language use and learning in classrooms at the novice level are memorization and practice.
5. Classroom language use can be described from the point of view of both learners and teachers.
6. Classroom language use can be characterized and encouraged by teachers selecting "functions" (global tasks learners can do), situations, topics, and texts.
7. Classroom language use can be characterized and judged as language control, vocabulary use, use of communication strategies, and evidence of cultural awareness.
8. Proficiency (language use in the real world) is not the same as performance (language use in classrooms).

Source: Authors.

The Proficiency Movement

We identify the Proficiency Movement as a middle-level theory concerning language that has to do with the skills and content teachers emphasize in second language classes. The skills and content emphasized suggest a view of language use, what it is for, and what it is used to learn. In a nutshell, it is argued here that the productive skills of speaking and writing are emphasized in Proficiency Movement classrooms and that the use of productive skills is seen as a means of using, practicing, and learning grammar. As such, grammar (language as form) comprises a substantial chunk of course content, even if it is treated inductively or indirectly in a course, usually as homework or "self-study" modules.

The Proficiency Movement in second language education dates from the early 1980s (Lantolf and Frawley 1988; Liskin-Gasparro 2003). It has conceptual links to the ACTFL *Guidelines* (American Council on the Teaching of Foreign Languages 2012a; see Ringvald 2006 as an example). The Proficiency Movement carries with it a sense of progressivism and professionalism (Liskin-Gasparro 2003; see also Center for Open Educational Resources and Language Learning [COERLL] 2010). It has been convincingly argued that the ACTFL *Guidelines* and its mainstay of assessment and accountability, the OPI, through the Proficiency Movement, have had a profound influence on high school and college foreign language education in the United States (Lantolf and Frawley 1988; Liskin-Gasparro 2003; Manley 1995). The movement has reached into teacher preparation programs, curricula, course syllabuses, testing, and textbook design. Liskin-Gasparro (2003) mentions "a new generation of pedagogical materials" coming out of the movement with "student-to-student interviews, set-ups for role plays and skits . . . free writing" (486), which before the time of writing might have appeared hidden away in an obscure corner of a teacher's manual.

Productive Skills Valued

On one hand, course syllabuses inspired by the Proficiency Movement may mention the four skills of speaking, listening, reading, and writing. See example syllabuses for a Spanish course in Texas: "Spanish 1501 is a four-skills course" (available at https://www.ttu.edu/courseinfo/); and a "World Languages First Level Proficiency" German course in Iowa: "Understanding and speaking 'everyday German'; reading and writing skills" (available at https://myui.uiowa.edu/my-ui/courses/details.page?id=877359&ci=147038).

Nonetheless, the productive skills of speaking and writing, particularly speaking, are primary in this tradition. Learner-to-learner oral communication is a kind of default activity in class. Partly this is because of the early basis of the ACTFL *Guidelines* in the Oral Proficiency Test (Lantolf and Frawley 1988) but also because of the lasting frustration on the part of teachers that learners seem to learn about language but remain unable to use it (Adair-Hauck and Donato 2002). Ringvald (2006) suggests that having learners talk and write allows them to negotiate meaning and thus "acquire" language, rather than learn about it. Grammar, instead of being a centerpiece of instruction, becomes "a support skill" for learners to practice while talking or otherwise producing language (Liskin-Gasparro 2003: 484; see also commentary by Andrews and McNeill 2005; Breen 1991; Burns 1996).

Low-Level Theories Concerning Language and Teachers: A French Teacher

The best way to approach identifying and describing low-level theories of language is through a case study description of Rick, a French teacher at a college in Utah. First is a description of Rick's language learning experiences. Teachers learn the language they are teaching both formally and informally, and both kinds of experiences shape their conceptions of the language they teach (Alamarza 1996). The books on his desk will be named, and the content and skills he emphasizes and the tests and quizzes he writes will be described. Finally, Rick's low-level teacher theories will be identified and matched to his practices.

Rick as a Language Learner

Rick is in his forties. He learned French in high school and college. It was an eight-month-long study abroad program in Reims, France, that made him want to continue studying French. He loved that he experienced how French was used. His study abroad brought life to the classroom French he had been studying, with its emphasis on grammatical rules presented in sentences and lists of words. In Reims, he had to learn how to keep conversations going, something his classroom learning back home had never touched on. Upon graduation, he went to another state in the United States for his MA in French literature, where he was supported as a teaching assistant. He was mentored to teach much as he had been taught in high school and college with the same textbooks. After getting his MA, he went to yet another state and got a PhD in French translation. He was then hired for a college job in Utah. Because he was the youngest hire, and because he had to take French linguistics classes for his doctorate, he was told to administer the undergraduate French program. His department chair told him, "If you understand Linguistics, then you know about language. You can teach it, the rules, vocabulary, what the students need."

Rick enjoys his job. He still works actively on his own French language ability. He drills himself on grammatical forms and vocabulary and pronunciation. For instance, he has never been comfortable with the subjunctive form in French. He learned how to avoid using it and compensated by using different verb phrase forms that he could say fluently. Still, he wants to conquer the subjunctive. His friend, Felicia, who teaches German in Colorado, has suggested he learn the subjunctive with the form presented in longer texts such as authentic conversations or multiple paragraph-length written texts, where speakers' intentions and meanings are clearer. Thus, Rick has found and bought a book called *Contextualized French Grammar* (Bourns 2013). He has it now on his desk, and he is reading through the section called "The Subjunctive: What About When I'm Not Sure, or I Don't Believe, or Something Isn't All That Probable?" (116). He also works on his own pronunciation by imitating speakers on podcasts from a web-based radio program he likes called "Nostalgie" (https://www.nostalgie.fr/podcasts). He is working on imitating and saying longer and longer chunks of spoken language. Rick also has a general book on grammar on his desk, *Brehe's Grammar Anatomy* (Brehe 2018). He is reading a section on adjectives, as he is interested in how they behave in languages in general.

Rick's Teaching

Rick teaches three sections of second-year students. The learners are supposed to be "novice high" according to the college course catalog. Rick wonders where the term "novice high" came from. Some nameless previous teacher or administrator put it in the catalog and no one ever changed it. Rick looked around on the internet and found a website for the ACTFL *Guidelines* (2012a) that used the term. In reading through the *Guidelines*, he learned from the "speaking" section that appeared first that "speakers are able to express personal meaning by relying heavily on learned phrases or recombinations of these and what they hear from their interlocuter" (9). Two things attracted Rick: first that learners at that level ought to be able to use learned content (what he thinks of as grammar and vocabulary) and recombine them, piece them together. This accords with his own experience learning classroom French. Second, learners could recycle phrases they heard from an "interlocutor," which denotes a person you were talking to, of course. But in the context of language teaching, did it not also mean that learners needed an interlocuter? That would be learners talking together, right? That they could learn from each other? For the first point, he tries to get students to recombine sentences and also use a variety of different vocabulary in substitution drills. Learners have a list of words that they are supposed to use correctly in sentences from the textbook chapter. He is still working on the second point, but he is not sure how to get students to talk to each other, except to read aloud sentences from the textbook. Mainly, Rick is talking to students.

Rick went to his department chair and got the department to help pay for him to go to a regional second language teaching conference so he could learn more about the term "novice high." He went to a presentation with an interesting title: "Teaching Grammar Implicitly through Language Use." This topic touched exactly on some teaching issues that have been bothering him. Given what Rick had read from the ACTFL *Guidelines* (2012a), his novice high students really sounded like one level lower and more like "novice mid." Learners are getting lots of exposure to grammar, and they spent a lot of time with vocabulary lists that Rick teaches them to use in sentences. Learners ought to be able to say and write more. Rick is getting very puzzled and frustrated over this. At the presentation, Rick met Felicia, who is a German teacher at a college in Colorado, a nearby state. He talks to her many times at the conference, and afterwards by email. They agree that the "implicit grammar" presenter at the conference had some interesting ideas. The presenter suggested the following:

1. Learners can learn grammar by using it in reading, writing, listening, and speaking activities.
2. They can be encouraged to talk to each other about what they think the rules are.

3. Teachers can help learners figure out the rules by asking questions or giving hints.

4. Teachers can also ask learners to compare the new grammar rules to the those of their first language.

At Felicia's suggestion, Rick prints out the *Guidelines* (2012a) and the *Performance Descriptors* (2012b) from the ACTFL website and puts them in a notebook on his desk.

Back home, he wants to try some of the things he learned at the conference. First, he changes his grammar drills. Instead of learners working alone on a drill from the textbook, he has them work in pairs to complete the sentences. Then learners say the sentences to each other to check each other's answers. He encourages the pairs of students to do this several times, eventually not looking at the book as they say the completed sentences to each other. He feels he cannot give up spending time on teaching on grammar, as grammar is the true content of the course. After all, learners cannot say anything if they do not have the "building blocks" of language. But having students work in pairs and confer about their answers is a nice compromise with the new things he has learned at the conference. Here is one of the textbook drills he uses.

1. Pour réussir un entretien professionnel, il est important de
_____ (s'habiller) bien.

2. Il est possible de/d' _____
_____ (être) chef d'entreprise si on veut travailler beaucoup.

(Eight items, from *Français Interactif*, Department of French and Italian, 2019: 287)

In line with his desire for students to talk more, he focuses more on pronunciation. To help students with this, he picks out the sections in the book called "phonétique." These sections have learners practice hearing and saying vocabulary that has been learned in a previous chapter. Learners turn on their own computers or cell phones and access the textbook's website. Using earbuds, they access the audio files of words. Learners seem to enjoy this. Rick also has learners study the words without audio and sometimes does dictation exercises where students spell out words that he says. In Rick's mind, these activities help learners with listening and writing.

Since the conference, Rick also requires students to visit him during office hours. When students visit his office hours, they often ask about grammar rules, in English. Grammar is featured on the course quizzes and tests, and students want to get good grades. He answers their questions. But Rick also has a new list of questions ready every week that come from the textbook. No matter what, Rick finishes off his individual meetings by asking students questions from his list at random. He wants them to answer in French, if they can. For instance, this week the textbook chapter is on work and the professional world. One of his questions is: *Qu'est-ce qu'il faut étudier pour devenir biologiste?* (What does it take to study to become a biologist?). He is hoping that learners will respond with some intelligible version of *Il faut étudier la biologie et les maths* (You have to study biology and mathematics) (Department of French and Italian 2019: 283). A few students can answer, but most of them have poor pronunciation at the sentence level, and they cannot scrape up the vocabulary they need to answer. It does not seem to matter that they had already studied vocabulary they could have used to answer. Often Rick is left to ask learners basic personal questions in French. He does not want students to feel they have lost face. And when it gets right down to it, learners can only really answer very simple personal questions about themselves. Just the other day, one young man spent five minutes telling Rick about his summer vacation using the present tense, as though it had happened today, instead of four months ago. The young man's description was a bit painful to listen to, but Rick did not want to stop him. The young learner was using extended speech, which Rick thought was rare and a good thing.

Twice, students really shock Rick by answering his textbook-based questions this way:

> Rick: *Qu'est-ce qu'il faut étudier pour devenir biologiste?* (What does it take to study to become a biologist?)
>
> Student 1: *Oh Euu . . . Ohh c'est intéressant . . . la biologie c'est . . .?* (Oh . . . um . . . that's interesting . . . and "biology" is what?")
>
> Rick: *Qu'est-ce qu'il faut étudier pour devenir biologiste?* (What does it take to study to become a biologist?)
>
> Student 2: *Quoi? . . . Eu . . . Vo- Vous avez dit biologie . . . c'est ca?* (What? Uh . . . Did you ask about "biology"?)

In both cases, Rick laughed and then responded by repeating his original question, *Qu'est-ce qu'il faut étudier pour devenir biologiste?* The students laughed too, but the conversations came to an end. Later, Rick looked at his printouts of the ACTFL materials and realized the students had been using "communication strategies" appropriate to their level (Table 4.6). He wonders if he could have responded differently and engaged students in a more ordinary way by responding in French with *Oui, tu sais, la biologie, l'étude de la vie? Un biologiste est quelqu'un qui étudie les sciences de la vie?* (Yes, you know, biology, the study of life? A biologist is someone who studies life science?). Would that have helped learners to answer his first question after they asked him to clarify it? But would they have understood his response explaining what "biologie" meant? He was not sure.

Content and Skills

Rick was pleased to find a digital textbook on the open access list of his college. Students had been complaining for months about the high cost of their textbooks. The book was *Français Interactif* (Department of French and Italian 2019). He was intrigued that the authors included many videos of their own students who were doing study abroad in France. He thought the videos would motivate his own students, ten of whom were going to France for further studies in a few months. Rick also saw sections of the book familiar to him, such as vocabulary lists and activities organized by grammatical forms. They looked very teachable. The book had an interesting treatment of vocabulary. Students did a lot of listening to sentences and deciding the grammatical form they were listening to. Rick thought students could do those at home, but once, with an extra ten minutes before the end of class, he had students log onto the website and do a listening exercise in class. The students listened intently and seemed engaged. He started asking them to give their answers to the listening exercises, which they could do in French, with the support of the textbook prompts. Rick also noticed an exercise called a dictogloss, where students watched a video of a student and then in groups completed some blanks in a paragraph. Perhaps this was the "larger contexts" or "texts" of language his friend Felicia wanted him to use in his own learning of French? He tried one of them in class. He saw the students were using more French, and using mostly English but some French to discuss which answers were best. They could not really discuss anything in French, but they could say the sentences from the paragraph to each other with the correct and incorrect answers. To his surprise, students asked Rick to play the audio file four or five times. Since they had the extra time, he did so.

Tests and Quizzes

Under pressure from his department chair, Rick has been giving a final oral test to his students. He agrees to do this, with the understanding that the students will get a regular paper-and-ink final exam, as well as an oral test. The paper-and-ink quizzes and the final tests are not hard to put together. The content of Rick's quizzes and tests are grammar and vocabulary, which he takes directly from the textbook. They are fill in the blank and matching exercises. Sometimes, Rick will adapt content from the textbook and have learners recombine phrases into new sentences. He wants them to be prepared for their quizzes and the test, so he has consciously matched them to the kind of experiences learners have in class. Because his teaching has changed recently, he wonders whether he should include some listening test items in the final exam. He decides to do so, and the learners listen to ten uncompleted sentences and choose the correct missing word from a list. Rick grades students on whether the word they choose is appropriate and also whether the word is spelled correctly and in the correct form for the grammar used.

When it comes to the oral exam, Rick does not want to repeat the embarrassing and uncomfortable experiences of his office hours, where, really, none of the students could respond correctly to his interview questions taken directly from the book. He has learned that his school has a freely available software where students can make a slide show and then narrate it with an audio file. They can then upload their "show" where Rick can see and grade it. He tells the students they must make two slides for their show. One slide should have at least seven sentences in French about their daily routines. The second slide should have at least seven sentences about their plans with their families for the following year. Both topics, the grammatical structures, and necessary vocabulary come from the textbook. Learners have a week to complete their slides (idea adapted from Glick 2019).

Rick grades students' slides on how many sentences they have used on each slide, and how well they used grammar and spelling. He also gives students a grade on how "comprehensible" their recorded sentences are. This meant he listened to specific words the students said and focused on the clarity and accuracy of their pronunciation. He called his friend, Felicia, in Colorado and talked to her about his oral test. They had a disagreement. Felicia told him that having students compose and record sentences might not actually be using language. It was not really an oral test where learners responded to questions, or were recorded talking to each other while they solved a puzzle or did a textbook exercise together. They argued over whether Rick's oral test was "interactive" or "presentational." Rick thought it was interactive, simply because learners were speaking. Felicia thought the test was presentational because learners were simply presenting information (Tables 4.4 and 4.5).

Felicia has questions about Rick's oral test. She asked, "What if the sentences have no relationship to each other and students just give you a list?" Rick was a little surprised. He told her, "Well it's just talk about their routines and their plans. There will be a natural order to their sentences." Felicia said she was not sure about that. "Just to get a grade, could they just not keep repeated the same general ideas with just one different piece of vocabulary?" Then, she made a suggestion about Rick's grading.

> Why focus on grammar and pronunciation? Students will never be very good at that, at the novice level. Those linguistic accuracy sort of details masks their ability to orally communicate something they mean to say. What about grading on whether their routines or plans hang together and create a normal sounding narrative text? What about grading on whether their reports would attract a further comment from an interlocuter? Think about whether someone talking to the student could respond to what students say, if they wanted to? I mean, are you not interested in whether learners can use communication strategies?

Table 4.8 What Rick Posits about Language

1. Language is a system of forms.
2. The basic units of language are words and sentences.
3. Language forms comprise the content of a foreign language course.
4. Learners should only be asked to say or write language forms they have learned in class (the course content).
5. Language forms should be tested on quizzes, tests, and oral tests.
6. Spoken language is based on written language.
7. Textbooks and learning materials are chosen that offer practice materials organized by language forms.
8. Pronunciation is best judged at the word level.

Source: Authors.

Rick and Felicia ended up not agreeing on his test plans. Rick told Felicia he thinks her ideas are interesting, but even with the ACTFL printouts, he had no idea how he could grade on the things she mentioned. See Table 4.8 for what Rick's low-level teacher theory seems to say about language.

Rick's teaching is undergoing change, and there may be resulting changes, however small, in how he sees language. These might be attributed to middle-level theories described in this chapter, the ACTFL *Guidelines* (a language description use framework), and the Proficiency Movement. For instance, Rick appears to believe that learners' levels can be described through a language use description framework such as the ACTFL *Guidelines* (2012a). He notes that his learners seem more like novice-mid than novice-high. He also notes that learners only seem to be able to talk about themselves, and that a few of them may be trying to use communication strategies at the novice-mid level. He is, in his own way, trying to get learners to talk more, which is a skill valued by the Proficiency Movement. Overall, it is not apparent he sees language as use. When he asks learners to talk, he views it as an opportunity for learners to focus on forms, including pronunciation. He does not see learners' talk as a social event or as communicative functions.

Reflective Projects

1. Do a self-inventory of books or websites that you consult as a language learner and/or a language teacher. What are the books' or websites' names? What are the books or websites about? What view

of language do you think informs the books or websites: language as a system of forms? Language as use? Use concepts from this chapter to formulate your reasons, including:

- communicative functions
- texts
- Communicative Competence
- Proficiency
- Do books in your self-inventory use these terms or concepts? Do they talk about the concepts, but perhaps without using the actual terms? Find examples in your books.

2. How did you learn the language you are teaching? Did you learn the language formally, in a classroom? Or did you learn the language naturalistically, without textbooks? Tell a classmate or a colleague about your language learning experiences.

   Further reflect on your own experience by completing the table. If you can, imagine how someone learning a foreign language in a way different than you, might see language differently.

Someone learning a language in a classroom	Someone learning a language naturalistically
Things such a person might be good at:	Things such a person might be good at:
Things such a person might not be good at:	Things such a person might not be good at:
Methods such a person might use to improve. What materials or resources might they use?	Methods such a person might use to improve. What materials or resources might they use?
How such a person might describe language. What terms might they use? What units of language?	How such a person might describe language. What terms might they use? What units of language?

3. Either do a self-inventory or interview another teacher. Find answers to the following questions.

   - What is the main content of the course you teach?
   - In terms of the four traditional skills (listening, reading, speaking, writing), what skills do you emphasize in your course? How do you know? What does a review of the lesson plan for a typical

lesson tell you about time spent on one or more of the four skills?

- What additional skills do you emphasize in your course?
- In terms of the textbook you use in class, what is the main content?
- What skills do you choose from the textbook to emphasize?
- Please describe a typical activity you might do from the textbook.

After the self-inventory or the interview, analyze the responses to the questions. Were the terms communicative functions, texts, Communicative Competence, or Proficiency used? Were there other terms used that have to do with language, such as grammar, vocabulary, or other terms? What were they? Together, what do the responses tell you—does the responder (either yourself or another person) see language as a system of forms or language as use?

4. In this chapter, a number of skills are mentioned. Aside from listening, reading, speaking, and writing, what were they? Could you find activities in a textbook or another source that would help learners with them? Thinking back to Rick, the teacher in this chapter, what would you tell him about these "other" skills? How could he work with learners on those skills?

5. The teacher in this chapter, Rick, believes that learners should be tested on similar things to what they experience in class. Do you think he accomplished that with his paper-and-ink final test and his final oral exam? Thinking back about the description of his teaching, how could Rick make his tests match learners' experiences more closely?

6. Evaluate the interpretation of low-level teacher theories in Table 4.8. Can they be matched with specific examples of Rick's actions and thoughts? Are there other explanations (theories) you can pose, based on his actions and thoughts?

PART TWO

Learners

CHAPTER FIVE

Theories of Teaching and Learners

Why This Chapter?

This chapter focuses on the interaction of theories of teaching and learners. As we stated in Chapter 2, a theory of teaching is a middle- or low-level theory that explains how teachers instill knowledge or skills in learners. Generally, teachers do not wander about their classrooms in an aimless way. The actions of teachers are goal and direction oriented. We think that what gives direction and purpose can be called a theory of teaching, whether or not the teacher can identify it by name or even describe it.

The purpose of this chapter is to further illustrate our thesis that teachers operate out of theories; that these theories may be unknown or invisible to the teacher; but that with care they can be identified, investigated, and used for actions in the classroom. We do this by introducing the middle-level theories of Fluency from linguistics and Expectancy from the field of sociology. We think these middle-level theories are far more prevalent in ordinary classrooms than one might think. We introduce Fluency Theory and note that most of us, most of the time, operate out of a naïve or layperson's perspective as to what we mean when we say that a person is "fluent in a language." We introduce five constructs (components) of Fluency. We refer readers to Chapter 1 for a discussion of constructs and their relationship to theory. We believe these five constructs should be included in Fluency Theory. We conclude our discussion of Fluency by discussing the implications of our model. We also introduce our second mid-level theory area, namely Expectancy Theory, which we believe has given rise to much scholarship in our field more recognizable to us in the form of "expectations." See Chapter 7 for additional comment on learner expectations. This chapter, Chapter 5, offers the philosophical and scholarly roots of this field of inquiry.

In order to instantiate Fluency Theory and Expectancy Theory, we introduce two classroom artifacts. One is listening fluency (derived from Fluency Theory) and the other is learner resistance (derived from Expectancy Theory). Both of these artifacts, presented as low-level teacher theories, appear in the case study of a junior high school English in Japan. Her name is Noriko, and she is a licensed teacher who is interested in getting her young learners to listen to longer dialogs spoken at a natural rate by native speakers, instead of very short dialogs spoken at an artificially slow rate. As with all chapters in this book, we follow each description of middle- or low-level theory with a table that suggests what the theory posits, or proposes, about learners and theories of teaching. We end with reflective projects to probe significant issues raised in the chapter.

Fluency

Fluency is one of those words that have meaning for most persons. We surmise this because the phrase "X is fluent in language Y" is a common utterance. Because of that, most everybody has a working definition of the term "fluency." This kind of knowledge, the kind held by an average citizen, is known as folk or lay knowledge. For a discussion of Folk Linguistics, see Chapter 7. Given that there are many areas of knowledge in applied linguistics and second language teaching, we can assume that unless we have acquired specialist level knowledge in a certain area, we ourselves are probably operating at the folk or lay level. Nowhere is this truer than when it comes to an understanding of Fluency Theory.

At this point, we remind the reader of our discussion of theory in Chapter 1. There we maintain that one way to think of theories is that they are or are composed of constructs that can be divided into concepts. We demonstrate this here. After a review of the literature, we conceive of the construct "Fluency" as having five conceptual areas: smoothness, linguistic accuracy, communicative goal achievement, vocabulary, and creativity. See Figure 5.1.

1. Smoothness

First is smoothness. The word "fluent" comes from the Latin *fluere* meaning flow (of a river) and by metaphorical extension the flow or way of moving of other phenomenon such as physical actions but also words (Brown 1993). For example, Samuel Johnson in his dictionary of the English language (Johnson and Chalmers [1843] 1994) acknowledges the Latin origin of fluent meaning liquid and its smooth flow. Thus, for our purposes, the historic meaning of fluent is smooth flow of speaking.

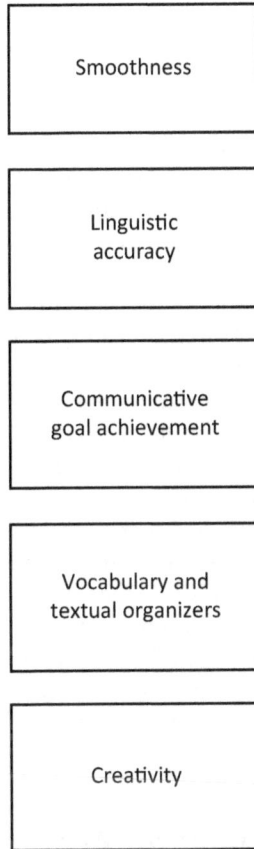

FIGURE 5.1 A model of Fluency Theory.

Source: Authors.

An early-twentieth-century example of the promotion of fluency as a smooth flow of speech can be found in Palmer ([1917] 1968, 1921) who worked in Japan from 1922 to 1936 as an advisor to the Japanese Department of Education. He served as director of their Institute for Research in English Teaching. Palmer ([1917] 1968: 118) argued for fluency not only of expression (speaking) but for fluency of understanding (listening). In fact, Palmer (1921: 87) stressed that comprehension was primary:

In the first place we must set out to sharpen our powers of receiving and retaining knowledge communicated to us orally. This may be difficult; we have become so accustomed to acquiring information from the written word *via* the eyes that we feel very bewildered and incapable when deprived of this medium. We hear a foreign word or sentence, and this auditory impression is such a rapid and transitory one that we feel that we cannot possibly retain it in our memory; we feel that we require at least one good look at the word so that we may hereafter reproduce in our imagination the written form. But we must resist this tendency.

One pedagogical approach that Palmer (1921: 88) called "ear-training exercises" was having the teacher read words and phrases and later sentences and even paragraphs of text multiple times. We will see in later works on fluency the central theme of smooth and rapid online cognitive processing (see also section on attentional resources in Chapter 6).

The understanding of fluency as smooth flow remains remarkably persistent. One example is Fillmore (1979) who in describing his first of four characteristics of a fluent speaker mentions the ability to continually talk. Actually, he is more emphasizing the flow of speech rather than the smoothness of speech. An example of this aspect of fluency is a host of a TV news and commentary show. Another example comes from Hedge (1993: 275) when she states that one current definition of fluency "is the ability to link units of speech together with facility and without strain or inappropriate slowness or undue hesitation." As to the mechanics of how smoothness and flow of speech is achieved, Gorsuch (2011, 2013) describes five speech characteristics that promote the smooth flow of speech and which, if violated, demote smooth flow: intact thought groups; self-repairs also known as false starts; one- or two-word fillers without semantic meaning also known as fillers; rate of speech; and a variety (not monotone) of appropriate rising, flat, and falling tone choices.

2. Linguistic Accuracy

This is the ability to keep going in a coherent way. Fillmore (1979: 73) says, "The main ingredient in this kind of ability appears to be a mastery of the semantic and syntactic resources of the language." An example would be a speaker who can express his/herself in a concise yet logical way. For example, a TV political commentator who can answer complex questions in a short period of time. In the United States, former president Barack Obama also comes to mind. When this ability is lacking, if the topic is complex, we find the speaker confusing and hard to follow.

3. Communicative Goal Achievement

This is the ability to use linguistic accuracy to achieve one's goal in multiple situations and genres, or as Fillmore (1979: 73) says, "the ability to have appropriate things to say in a wide range of contexts." Achieving a goal in this sense is a linguistic or communicative success rather than a real-world success. For example, you are in a situation where your second language is spoken.

Perhaps you are on holiday. You go into a shop and ask for an item. Goal achievement does not mean they have the item; perhaps they do not have it. Rather, it means they understood what you were asking for. Multiple situations and genres means that not only can you negotiate at the shop just mentioned but also later attend a lecture and even participate in a panel discussion on a topic within your area of expertise. Thus, task complexity, familiarity, and the role you play are appropriate variables to consider in goal achievement.

4. Vocabulary and Textual Organizers

Vocabulary is what we, as language teachers, normally mean by "vocabulary," namely words that we can understand and use to express ourselves and accomplish our communicative goals. In addition to vocabulary, Pawley and Syder (1983) posit an understanding of fluency through the use of textual organizers, which can be divided into memorized chunks and lexicalized sentence stems. A memorized chunk or sequence is a string of words that native speakers use as whole utterances. Pawley and Syder claim that the experienced speaker of a language knows thousands of these sequences (179). Some examples include "need any help," "is everything OK," "if you believe that you'll believe anything," and "that's easier said than done."

Although similar to memorized chunks in that they are group of words that are often used together, a lexical sentence stem seems to be a unit of cultural thought around which multiple spoken expressions can be made. We say "seems to be" because Pawley and Syder admit they cannot define exactly what a lexicalized sentence stem is. We think of them as a lexical form of a cultural concept or metaphor. For example, English speakers use the term "headache" as a lexical sentence stem, but not the term foot ache or finger ache even though feet and fingers may experience pain. Thus, we might say "I have a pain in my foot" or "my foot hurts," but not "I have a pain in my head." Of course, it is possible to say, "I have a pain in my head," but it would sound unnative-like as opposed to the more native-like "I have a headache." From the stem, many expressions can follow: "I have a headache" (an acceptable excuse for not doing something), "It's a real headache" (a difficulty), "This assignment is a real headache," "the city's biggest headache is traffic control." Pawley and Syder (1983: 195) claim that the key to native-like fluency "is this store of memorized constructions and expressions," and fluent speech is built from prefabricated pieces of connected speech chunks and stems.

5. Creativity

The final aspect of fluency is the creative use of language such as the ability to write novels and poetry and in speech to make puns and jokes.

For example, the present authors were once visiting the United Kingdom and Scotland. During a stay in Edinburgh, we needed to have some clothes washed and visited a neighborhood laundry. We asked for a special service and the middle-aged attendant quickly assented saying, "Not just another pretty face." That was years ago, and we still remember her quick and creative retort to our request.

* * *

Implications and Questions for Our Theoretical Model of Fluency

Given our theoretical model of fluency (Figure 5.1), we suggest four questions become apparent. The first question has to do with something called dimensionality, which is a way of thinking about complexity in a way that is attuned to how we might measure or judge something like fluency. Put in a simpler way, a dimension is a part or component. Our first question is whether fluency is unidimensional or multidimensional. In other words, is fluency one thing or would it be more accurate to think of fluency as composed of more than one thing? If, for whatever reason, we decide fluency is unidimensional, then smoothness and flow would probably be the most popular description. And this, in fact, is the answer for persons at the folk level. When an untrained person is asked what they mean when they say that John or Joan, who is an English born and bred native speaker, is fluent in, say, German, they mean speaks German in a smooth way. This unidimensional understanding is, however, insufficient for exploring and understanding fluency for research or pedagogical purposes. A multidimensional view of fluency is needed that will explains how a speaker can be judged more fluent in one aspect of language and not as fluent in another aspect.

A second question that is raised by the model of Theory of Fluency in Figure 5.1 is: Does a theory of fluency apply equally to a native speaker speaking their L1 and a non-native speaker speaking their L2? Historically, fluency was a category applied only to language learners speaking their L2. When speaking their L1, they might be called articulate or even well-spoken. We can see no difference in how our model would apply to one of these categories in Figure 5.1. This might result in some persons being judged fluent in their L1 and others being judged not fluent in their L1, for example, some foreign language teachers judged more fluent in the L2 they teach than some native speakers of that L2.

The third question is: Is each fluency dimension a yes or no decision or should each fluency dimension be considered on a continuum? Take, for example, the first dimension in Figure 5.1—smoothness. The third question is: Should smoothness be judged as present or absent, or should smoothness be judged along a continuum, say from one to five on a Likert scale. We would argue that fluency is a point on a continuum. If hesitancy or pausing is a sign of dysfluency, how much is allowed as normal before it is noticed and judged dysfluent? Using a five-point Likert scale to answer this question, each of our five conceptual areas would require its own Likert scale and each Likert scale would require five criteria.

The fourth question is: Can the term "fluency" be applied to more than speech? For most persons, including second language teachers, fluency refers to speech. This is true for at least two reasons. First, most teachers define fluency as a smooth flow of speech (Koponen and Riggenbach 2000: 6). This definition necessarily limits the application of fluency to speech. Second, for many teachers, increasing speech fluency is a primary concern. While this is true, Palmer ([1917] 1968; 1921: 90) emphasized listening fluency as a prerequisite to speaking. And Lennon (2000: 26), operating from a more inclusive definition of fluency, applies fluency beyond speaking. We, too, raise this question because we wonder, as Noriko our English teacher in Japan does, whether fluency might be applied to listening, or writing, for example. We explore this more below.

Contemporary Definitions of Fluency

Tavakoli and Hunter (2018) accept the characterization of fluency as "flow, continuity, automaticity, or smoothness of speech" (Koponen and Riggenbach 2000: 6) as a useful and practical definition. The definition we prefer, however, comes from Lennon (2000: 26) who defines fluency as "the rapid, smooth, accurate, lucid, and efficient translation of thought or communicative intention into language under the temporal constraints of on-line processing." We find this definition helpful because fluency is not restricted to speaking. See Table 5.1 for what the middle-level theory of Fluency posits.

Listening Fluency

We think "listening fluency" may be an unfamiliar term to many of our readers, and as a result we wish to explore it as low-level teaching theory in our teacher case study with Noriko, our junior high school English teacher. We think listening fluency has a basis in middle-level theory (see section above on Fluency and Figure 5.1), but for reasons we touch on below, we wonder whether we have developed as a field a solid theoretical basis upon which teachers can build lessons and adapt materials to develop learners' listening fluency, or as our teacher in our case study calls it, their "stamina" for listening in English. If fluency is the translation of thought or intention into language under time constraints as Lennon (2000) defined it, then we posit that the door is open to applying the term "fluency" to other language areas, including listening, reading, and writing. Listening fluency is the receptive translation of other person's speech into meaning, commonly known as understanding.

Table 5.1 What Fluency Theory Posits

1. Fluency primarily means a smooth flow in whatever area of language is under consideration. The opposite of fluency in this regard is hesitancy or choppiness.
2. Fluency requires the use of the grammatical and semantic system to express thoughts and ideas logically, coherently, and concisely.
3. Fluency assumes the achievement of communicative goals using a readily accessible repertoire of linguistic resources.
4. Fluency is built upon a readily accessible repertoire of culturally appropriate vocabulary, lexical sentence stems, and textual organizers.
5. Fluency assumes creative combining of a language user's cultural and linguistic resources.

Source: Authors.

Listening Is Ignored in Language Education

Listening is basic, primary, and as Palmer noted as early as 1921, a low level but necessary skill. However, even today, listening is still largely ignored and not considered important because it is difficult to understand and to teach. There are several reasons for this being the case. First, as Rost (2005) explains, listening is a complex process. Listening is a bottom-up process in which the second language learner must sort out multiple forms of data such as grammatical forms and vocabulary. Many factors make listening difficult: rate of speech, prosody, accent, phonology, hesitation, lack of background knowledge, vocabulary (Cross 2011; Graham 2006). Of special note is rate of speech, which many learners experience as a rapid flow of undifferentiated sound making it almost impossible to identify individual words. At the same time, listening is a top-down process in which learners must bring to bear their prior knowledge and linguistic goals. And all this must be done in real time. A second reason listening may be difficult is that to be successful, listening needs to be intensively and systematically taught, and most teachers are not prepared for either of these requirements (Renandya and Farrell 2011). For example, teachers would have to know the theory of what they are doing, how to select the practical teaching strategies, and how to integrate these strategies into their classroom curriculum. A third reason comes from Çakır (2018) who concludes from a study of fifty-one EFL teachers in Turkey that listening is not considered important because it is beyond the capacity of most teachers. This may be because less than half (48 percent) of the teachers studied English language training as opposed to English literature or linguistics. Fourth, learners cannot rehearse or plan listening, or as

Brown (2011: 3) put it, "listeners can't skim. The language comes rushing at them." Fifth is that listening creates anxiety in learners (Arnold 2000). Listening can be a threat to learner identity because of the disparity between the competent self the learner believes himself to be in the L1 and the L2 incompetent self he experiences in himself in the L2. The inherent complexity of teaching L2 listening and the other reasons listening is ignored in language education given above paint a bleak picture. They point to a lack of practical orientation with the end result that teachers will not know how to make listening materials, nor where to turn for guidance to adequately adapt materials.

We now transition to Expectancy Theory. We think teachers are going to care about this mid-level theory because any change in the status quo means that learners will be involved. Our case study teacher Noriko knows that modifications in high school entrance exams are coming, and as a result she plans changes to her traditional curriculum. She also knows that while students are interested in the exams, they view changes as threatening so that the more she knows about how to manage learner expectancy and resistance to change, the better.

Expectancy

Many readers of this chapter may be familiar with the term "expectations" in both their personal and professional lives. We explore the theoretical bases for the interest in expectations in general education that we think helps inform current inquiry in second language education. First, we outline a salient theoretical discussion and development of Expectancy Theory. Then, we pose Expectancy Theory in its original context, in terms of Teacher Expectancy, which is how teachers affect how much and what learners learn (see Table 5.2). Finally, we relate Expectancy Theory and Teacher Expectancy more transparently to learner expectations and resistance. In an article titled "Teacher Expectations and the Self-Fulfilling Prophecy," first published in 1983 and then later online in 2006, Derek Blease of Loughborough University of Technology outlined the structure of the theory of Expectancy in classroom settings. Our methodology will be to use Blease (1983) as our guide while at the same time consulting the original literature. Blease begins with the basic definition of Merton (1968), a sociologist, who himself sources Thomas (1928), Rosenthal and Jacobson ([1968] 1992), Leith (1977), Dusek (1975), and Finn (1972).

Merton's Definition of "Expectancy"

This formulation (Merton 1968: 475) is described by Blease (1983) as the initiation of the concept of Expectancy as it is understood today. Merton

(1968) begins with what he calls the Thomas Theorem: "If men [sic] define situations as real, they are real in their consequences" (Thomas 1928: 527). Merton discusses the Thomas Theorem as having two parts: the first part— "If men [sic] define situations as real"; and the second part—"they are real in their consequences." For Merton (1968), the first part is a belief about a situation rather than the truth about a situation, and the second part is the expectation based on the belief. He offers three examples that illustrate what he is talking about:

1a. A bank doesn't have enough money in reserve to cover depositors' demands

2a. Certain groups of people have certain characteristics (positive or negative)

3a. A student believes he/she will fail a course

Merton argues that the first part of the theorem includes what he calls the "objective features" of a situation but also the meaning that the situation has for them. In the case of the 1a example, the belief that a bank does not have enough money to cover depositors' demand gives rise to the meaningful belief that financial ruin is possible; in the case of 2a, an individual from that group has the characteristics attributed to the group; and in the case of 3a, the student will indeed fail the course. In essence, these beliefs build expectancy or expectations.

Merton argues that the second part of the Thomas Theorem implies that the meaning of a situation as described above determines action. He puts it this way:

Once they have assigned meaning to the situation, their consequent behavior and some of the consequences of that behavior are determined by the ascribed meaning. (Merton 1968: 476)

For example, as a result of 1a—the belief that a bank does not have enough money in reserve to cover depositors' demands—the action is panic and multiple withdrawal requests that cause the bank to fail. In other words, 1a (a belief that something is the case) causes 1b (the case to happen). "Teacher Expectation," the term coined by Merton, is defined as a pan-classroom, self-fulfilling prophecy that is basically false but nonetheless evokes a behavior among classroom stakeholders (the teacher and the learners) that makes the original false conception to come true. If stakeholders think X is true, they will take action Y, and action Y will cause X to become true. We think it is important to show how Expectancy Theory evolved over time, if simply to show how fruitful and significant this middle-level theory is, but also to show how theories are refined and changed by different stakeholders who work with theories.

Rosenthal and Jacobson's Refinement of Expectancy Theory

Blease (1983) next describes a refinement from Rosenthal and Jacobson ([1968] 1992), writing in the field of educational psychology, who argue that we can accurately predict a person's behavior in large part because we know his/her past behavior and also because our expectations form a screen through which we view the behavior. In other words, interpersonal self-fulfilling prophecies can be defined as "how one person's expectation for another person's behavior can quite unwittingly become a more accurate prediction simply for its having been made" (vii). The example given is that if we are introduced to person X and have been told that person X has characteristic Y (is a very cheerful person), we will tend to interpret what X says and does as cheerful. This assumes, says Blease (1983: 124), a "framework of interaction": a person has an expectation of another person's behavior, and these expectations are interpreted as fulfilled.

A Modification to Apply Expectancy Theory to Classrooms

Leith (1977) accepts the idea of a framework of expectations. He wants, however, to move the conversation from psychology (individual cases) to sociology (groups such as classrooms); he wants—as the title of his article suggests—to apply the framework of expectations in a school setting and place it in the context of education.

A Distinction between Expectation and Bias

After an extensive review of the research literature, Dusek (1975: 679) distinguishes between results from research using experimental design in which an external researcher manipulates variables based on natural teacher expectations of student achievement. The results from experimental studies show that the teacher changes her expectations regarding the performance of learners who were, in fact, equivalent on some objective measure. The results from these and other experiments similar to those of Rosenthal and Jacobson ([1968] 1992), Dusek refers to as "teacher bias." On the other hand, the results from the effects of teachers reaching their own conclusions he calls "teacher expectancy." Note we use the term "bias" here (see Chapter 1). The term "bias" will become important in our discussion below when we turn to learner resistance.

An Expansion from Teachers to Learners

Finn's (1972) hypothesis is that expectation is real, exerts a strong influence, and is a complex or multidimensional construct. It is to the nature of this multidimensional construct we now turn. Finn notes the general lack of empirical support for Teacher Expectancy and concludes that the problem is a narrow focus on only the teacher. The whole of the educational environment needs to be taken into consideration. He calls this the "Expectation Network" and includes all the possible influences in a learner's educational experience, including but not limited to the teacher, the physical setting, the curriculum, the learner him/herself, and the peer group. Teacher Expectancy as defined by Finn (1972: 390) can be stated as a conscious or unconscious evaluation that one person forms of another (or of him/herself), which leads the evaluator to treat the person evaluated in such a manner as though the assessment were correct. To this definition we need to add certain conditions for expectancy to be operative in classrooms (Blease 1983):

1. Observation must occur over an extended period of time.
2. There must be contact with members of "the expectation set" e.g., teachers, parents, classmates.
3. In the case of learners, they are personally concerned with their situation.
4. There is constant monitoring and feedback.

Figure 5.2 summarizes our thinking in this section about Teacher Expectancy and is formatted in terms of Expectancy and bias and applies to teachers, learners, parents, administrators, and other stakeholders.

Our main point is that Expectancy, as we understand it, is not unwitting or unconscious bias formed by external sources but rather a set of conclusions formed by our own experience and the entire Expectancy Network. "Expectancy" can be defined then as open-ended, conscious evaluations persons have of themselves and other persons that are arrived at by utilizing

Expectancy	Bias
Is witting or conscious	Is unwitting or unconscious
Has an internal source	Has an external source
Can be positive or negative	Can be positive or negative
Expectancy network	

FIGURE 5.2 Expectancy Theory: Self-fulfilling prophecy (the Pygmalion Effect).
Source: Authors.

Table 5.2 What Expectancy Posits

1. Expectancy assumes an individual recognizes a situation of interest or concern.
2. Expectancy requires an individual to form a conclusion or a belief about the situation of interest.
3. Expectancy requires a context: that is, a considering of all relevant factors. This is called a Framework of Expectancy.
4. Expectancy is not an unconscious or unwitting bias of an individual but rather a conscious and witting awareness.
5. Expectancy assumes an openness to monitoring and feedback by an individual and a willingness to change an expectation if there is evidence supporting a change.

Source: Authors.

all known information available over a period of time that is open to change or alteration by monitoring and feedback.

For learners, this could include being familiar with past classrooms, their arrangements, the curriculum, and administration given the expectation that current and future classrooms will and ought to be the same or similar. For learners in our case study, this includes an expectation that English lessons would be conducted mostly in Japanese and not noticing any contradiction about how this might negatively affect their learning of English. It also might include a group consensus that maintains a lack of self-confidence in speaking English. And finally, it might include the requirement to pass entrance exams to future educational institutions. Because of the lack of conscious thought processes being employed, these expectations fall in the bias camp.

For the teacher in our case study, her expectations include the same familiarity with junior high school classrooms and learner's lack of confidence with anything concerning the subject of English. However, she also believes that listening can be taught, and that if it can be taught, it should be taught. And finally, she knows that future entrance examinations for high school entrance will probably include a listening section.

Low- and Middle-Level Theories Concerning Teaching and Learners: A Teacher of English

In this section, we continue to deal with Expectancy under the conditions of change and learner resistance to change. See also Chapter 7 on learner expectations. In essence, we explore learner expectation and resistance when learners experience a violation of their expectations, something we believe is of intense interest to teachers and scholars alike. We begin by laying out a brief context, along with an actual report of learner resistance in Hong Kong in 2008 to an education innovation. Then we present our case study of Noriko, a Japanese teacher of English in a junior high school, and outline her problems and how she addresses them with her knowledge of materials design and show how to grapple with learner expectations.

Context—Learner Expectations

Learner expectations can be defined as near range anticipations—some explicit and some implicit—that learners have regarding their educational context (see also Chapter 7). These include classroom organization, teacher, time limitations, interactions with fellow learners, types of assignment, materials, tests, and evaluation outcomes (grades). Imagine a student new to a school and entering their assigned classroom for the first time. They will expect—among other things—to find a teacher, a place for them to sit, fellow students, textbooks that they will be given or are expected to buy, various evaluation protocols (tests), various time periods, including the number of minutes they are expected to be in the room per day, and a designated first and last day of class. All of these expectations form what we have referred to previously as the Expectancy Network (Finn 1972).

On the face of it, one can argue that teachers have the most power in classrooms and learners have the least. However, one might counter argue that learners do have some power (Griffee and Gorsuch 2016). For example, the category Learner Retention (keeping learners in school until graduation) assumes that retention is based to some degree on learner expectations and their acceptance of those expectations. This is because if learners believe that their expectations have been violated, they can and will drop out of their program. This shows that learner resistance to change can and does have consequences.

Types of Change in Classrooms and Expectancy

We think types of changes in classrooms may manifest differently in expectancy frameworks. Certainly, Bartunek and Moch (1987) discuss change in terms of three orders. To enable their discussion, they posit a concept they call schemata, a kind of organizing framework of thinking about the world, or alternative worldviews. These color our views of change itself. To illustrate, imagine an English as a second language class in the United States based on the literary works of Mark Twain. The instruction is teacher-fronted, and this is the norm for the upper-level classes, as the administration is preparing the learners for literature courses in an English department.

In this context, a first order change would be modifications that make sense within the usual framework. This might mean the lectures are supplemented by movie clips ranging from ten to fifteen minutes. The class is studying *The Adventures of Tom Sawyer* and the movie clips are from a movie based on the same novel and illustrate the scene or point the teacher is making, such as how narrative is developed using dialog. A second order change is a modification of the framework. For example, the teacher dresses as one of the historical figures in the novel and talks from a first-person point of view. A third order change is a change in the framework itself. For example, the class is taken to an historical site where actors dressed in period costume reenact scenes, talk directly to the learners, and invite the learners into the storyline, and perhaps change the novel's conclusions.

Here is an example then that illustrates resistance. This example will show the three levels of change (first, second, and third order) in terms of the resistance they might generate with the announcement to learners of changes in a curriculum, specifically in something unexpected, such as listening, an area we suggest learners already have little experience with. A first order change might be that new instructions are given with the listening section in each chapter in the textbook. Learners are simply asked to look at the sentences in the section while the teacher reads the sentences. The teacher promises that she will explain new vocabulary and any grammar questions learners might have. We can expect a mild student response but general acceptance of activities. A second order change might be that the teacher will read the sentences aloud from the existing listening section and the learners are then expected to answer some questions that also appear in the textbook. However, there is a catch: learners cannot look at their textbook while they are listening to the teacher reading aloud. This is more of a challenge and also a departure from past practice and might produce some objections. Nonetheless, the teacher promises to read slowly and to repeat if requested. A third order change might be the same assignment as the second order change, but the person reading the passage aloud may be an unfamiliar native speaker of the second language. In the case of Noriko, our case study teacher, it is a young Irish assistant language teacher assigned to the junior high school where Noriko teaches. The "guest reader" will read the sentences from the listening section only once and at normal speed. We can now expect a stronger and more resistant learner response, and perhaps even a general uprising as learners righteously express their resistance. Bartunek and Moch (1987) claim that if a teacher plans to make changes in her classroom style or content, it would be helpful to decide which order of change because it would help her plan the change, increase learner acceptance, and decrease learner resistance.

An Historical Example of Change and Resistance

Five BATESL (Bachelor's degree in teaching English as a second language) graduates from a university of Hong Kong bachelor's degree teacher training program were interviewed one year after graduation to ascertain their progress as English language teachers, their views on education, and on the BATESL course itself (Urmston and Pennington 2008: 92). These five graduates became the respondents for the study because they had first-hand experience teaching English classes composed of learners in school in which Chinese was the medium of instruction. During the time of the study, a curriculum change in the teachers' school was implemented, and these five newly minted teachers were witness to the change. Their learners were required to attend something called an "English Enhancement Scheme," a special government-initiated program that took place over three or four mornings during school holidays using—and this is the important part— only English. It was designed to improve learners' English. Government education planners in Hong Kong were keen to introduce an oral English component to the state English language curriculum and improving young learners' oral English ability was seen as one way to do that. One problem: The government education planners forgot to ask the learners. Needless to say, learners resisted this top-down change.

Why Was There Resistance?

According to the BATESL graduates who served as respondents, the prevailing education culture of Hong Kong, and most importantly, those of the learners within that culture, was that English was a content to be learned and tested. Hong Kong society values education as measured by test grades. Resistance by the learners in the classes taught by the BATESL graduates occurred because the change proposed by the government violated the tacit agreement between school and learners when it introduced an element (oral English) that could not be tested in the usual way. Urmston and Pennington (2008: 96) concluded:

> The domination of examinations was felt in terms of teaching approach, as the teachers [the respondents in the study] believed that it was difficult to adopt interactive or innovative approaches [emphasized in the BATESL course] with higher level students who would expect examination practice, while on the other hand lower-level students might not have the proficiency required to engage in communicative activities.

Noriko

Noriko is from a large city in central Japan famous for its mountains and snow. She attended her home prefectural university, which was hard to get admitted to and famous for its English teacher licensure program. While in university, she read and translated American and British literature, discussing them in Japanese, but also in English with both Japanese- and English-speaking faculty members. It was not easy working in English, but Noriko and her classmates made it work with support from faculty members. Noriko remembers with fondness reading and studying the novels of Jane Austen, especially the novel *Emma*. One of her teachers, a former radio announcer on Japanese radio, encouraged her to seek comparisons between reading a novel and hearing dialog in movie adaptations of novels. How was the experience different? Was the experience different aesthetically? If so, could learners be engaged in this way? Noriko also took teaching methodology courses, including a materials design course, and also a course in listening and how listening might contribute to second language learning. She felt lucky that the listening course followed the materials design course. Her course project for the listening course built upon her materials design course project. For her materials design course project, she took a typical junior high school textbook English lesson (see description below) and added some games to make the grammar-based lesson more fun and challenging. For her listening course project, Noriko took the stilted little grammar-based dialog at the beginning of the lesson and rewrote it to be longer, and she thought, more natural sounding, and turned it into a listening lesson where students had to listen to and then re-create the dialog.

Noriko graduated with an English teaching license for junior and senior high school levels and has been teaching junior high school English for eight years in her home prefecture. She has observed that teachers with less experience than her seem insecure and not inclined to do much beyond the basics of classroom teaching; they appear to be in survival mode. At the same time, Noriko has noticed that one or two of her colleagues with significantly more experience are looking forward to retirement and seem less motivated to make any big changes in their teaching. Nonetheless, for a variety of reasons, Noriko is in a large group of mid-career teachers who have enough seniority to feel secure but at the same time enough confidence to consider trying something new. Many of them graduated from the same prefectural university Noriko went to. They have stayed in touch with the faculty members from the university.

Although Noriko has good English, good enough to carry on a general conversation with other English speakers, she has never traveled abroad. She works in a prefectural educational structure that supports a nationally funded program that employs foreign assistant language teachers who are native speakers of various languages, predominantly English. The assistant language teachers are assigned to schools and are intended to be resources to the schools and to the Japanese second language teachers. These assistant language teachers tend to be young, new to Japan, and to have no professional training or credentials. They are nonetheless seen as enthusiastic and, as Noriko correctly guesses, perhaps an unexpected and valuable resource. See https://jetprogramme.org/en/history/ for a history and description of the Japan Exchange and Teaching Program (JET). See also Miyazato (2011) for unique stakeholder perspectives on the JET Program and the role of Minoru Wada, a Ministry of Education official, who was instrumental in jump-starting the program in 1987.

Noriko's Teaching Situation

The realities of Japanese secondary English education as described by Gorsuch (2001) and later Binns and Johnston (2021) are a teaching method called (1) Yakudoku, (2) form-focused high school and university entrance exams that drive teaching in junior and senior high schools, and (3) inadequate professional training for junior and senior high school teachers. Yakudoku, a traditional teaching method, might best be understood as a variant of the Grammar Translation Method. It was adopted by the Japanese education system after World War II because Japan suddenly needed a large number of second language teachers who could teach English and other second languages but who could not necessarily use those languages. Yakudoku allowed, and still allows, teachers to explain grammatical points in Japanese and fosters the assumptions that grammatical structures are unambiguous in terms of their meaning, that they are capable of being sequenced in a curriculum, that they are learnable in an immutable and permanent way, and, as a result, that they are testable.

A second characteristic of Japanese education is high stakes high school and university entrance exams (Bjork 2015; Saito 2006). One mechanism for upward social mobility and social standing in Japan is young learners' success on high school entrance and university entrance exams. English is commonly tested on such exams. High school entrance exams thus unofficially drive English language teaching in junior high schools, and university entrance exams thus unofficially drive English language teaching in high schools (see Ozaki [2010] for a thoughtful essay on effects on university entrance exam content on high school curricula). Finally, a third characteristic of Japanese second language education is inadequate professional training for teachers. Japan, like any nation, has a history in this respect. Immediately after World War II, or what the Japanese call the Pacific War, there was a serious shortage of teachers and a shortage of teacher preparation programs, and yet a high demand for second language classes. Many teachers were needed, and shortcuts were made in teacher preparation programs, where teaching about second languages was emphasized as opposed to using second languages. This general pattern persisted for many years. Suemori (2020) reviewed literature that still found teachers to be demotivated by a lack of training opportunities, although more currently, Suemori also offers a more nuanced explanation of the effects of specific school contexts of factors that demotivate second language teachers in this regard.

Binns and Johnston (2021) validate Gorsuch's overall 2001 analysis. They say that although there is some openness to Communicative Language

Teaching (see Chapter 3) in secondary language education in Japan, the principles and practices of Communicative Language Teaching are not widely practiced. Rather, there is continued use of Yakudoku as the main teaching method. They underscore that the focus of the working secondary school curriculum and the teaching that goes with it is the preparation of learners for high school and university entrance exams. There is a concomitant and limited utilization of assistant language teachers. This is the general context in which Noriko finds herself.

Textbooks and Teaching

Noriko teaches in a public junior high school. Like all junior high schools in Japan, officially approved textbooks take center stage in the curriculum and in teaching. A primary focus on a course textbook for curriculum purposes is not unusual for second language education courses in many contexts worldwide (see Chapter 9). In Noriko's context, we can surmise the following. A typical junior high school textbook must: (1) be approved by both the both national and prefectural education authorities; (2) employ a grammatical syllabus; and (3) employ a list of vocabulary to learned. Beyond this, there will be little if any recycling of content. Further, language use, if represented in any way, appears in the form of very short spoken dialogs between fictional characters. As a participant in a textbook development group, Hardy (2007) provides additional description of junior high school textbooks in the Japanese context. He noted that his group had to use specified grammatical structures, along with specified nonpolitical content. They were motivated to include Japanese culture and to encourage in learners an awareness of Japan's place in the world. Hardy proposed that "despite periodic window-dressing measures initiated by MEXT [Japan's education authority] in which learners' Communicative Competence was to be cultivated [see Chapter 4], grammar-translation and/or audio-lingual methods remain entrenched in Japanese junior high school EFL classes" (14). We note that such methods reflect a view of language as form, not language as use (see Chapters 4, 7, and 9). Of relevance to this chapter and to Noriko (see description of her undergraduate study above), there is no mention of listening in Hardy's discussion of textbook development. Nonetheless, listening does appear briefly in national official curriculum documents freely available online. For instance, learners are "to pick up necessary information from the context about everyday topics if spoken clearly" (Ministry of Education, Culture, Sport, Science and Technology 2022: 2). Noriko, perhaps consciously, believes that the textbooks are aimed more or less at preparing learners to pass entrance exams for senior high schools. We note that in Japan, compulsory education ends in junior high school but the majority of students go on to senior high school.

What Noriko Thinks About

Noriko (1) is aware of national official curriculum documents and their newest permutations; (2) notices the assistant language teachers assigned to her school—they hang out in a group in the teacher's lounge; (3) enjoys using her own education and training; (4) continues to be intrigued by listening and its role in second language learning; (5) continues to be intrigued by materials design; and (6) knows from her eight years of teaching experience that learners expect to be prepared for senior high school entrance exams. For point 6, Noriko is aware that learners and their parents expect her to use Yakudoku to teach test preparation content.

Through discussion with her colleagues, Noriko is aware that some of the senior high schools in the prefectures have started including listening sections in their entrance exams. She is motivated by the perception that her learners may be disadvantaged if they sit for exams at those schools because her junior high school curriculum, based on the textbooks as they are currently used, do not include enough listening. She thinks more high schools will include listening sections in their entrance exams, and perhaps universities, too.

From experience, Noriko understands that while she is comfortable teaching using Yakudoku, she knows Yakudoku has limitations. For instance, learners will never become fluent speakers of English because Yakudoku makes them focus on form and not on actually using English in fluid and flexible ways. She knows from her own experience as a language learner, and never having been abroad, that good spoken fluency may not be attainable, but she wonders if good listening ability might not be attainable. Might not the idea of fluency, good, smooth ability, be applied to listening? Her learners, shy, gawky teenagers, cannot or will not speak in English but they can listen and, to some extent, understand what they hear in English.

Noriko's Thoughts on Fluency

Noriko is not an applied linguist, nor does she read widely in the field of linguistics or language education pedagogy. She has limited time to attend professional conferences but goes when she can. Nonetheless, she begins to approach a middle-level theoretical understanding of Fluency (Table 5.1) when she thinks of Fluency as a metaphor of capacity (see Chapter 1 on the role of metaphor in theory). She wants her learners' capacity to increase. She actually uses the English word "stamina" in her mind when she thinks of capacity. "Stamina" is a loan word in Japanese that even her junior high school learners know. She thinks of this idea of "capacity" in fairly specific ways in terms of materials design and teaching—learners will be able to handle authentic sounding dialogs, longer dialogs, and dialogs spoken slightly faster and more fluidly with more reduced speech. She believes this is a realistic possibility and that this will help learners with the trends in new entrance test listening requirements. She thinks that if learners work at this, and if she can show learners they can still comprehend progressively longer and more authentic dialogs, they might see this work as useful. She is deeply worried they will strongly resist, because they may see this as taking away from high school exam preparation. In other words, this kind of listening practice will not be at all what they expect. This thought actually gives Noriko physical pain.

From her undergraduate coursework, she believes there are three factors that affect the difficulty of listening to dialogs: how long a dialog is, how authentic a dialog is, and how naturally a dialog is spoken. The first factor is clear in Noriko's thinking. The second factor, that of authenticity, is less clear to her but she thinks of authenticity as having to do with whether a dialog is between native English speakers or not. Needless to say, an authentic dialog between native speakers might be more difficult for learners to comprehend. The third factor, that of naturalness, has to do with whether a dialog is spoken with natural and reduced speech spoken at a normal speed. Such speech would be harder for learners to comprehend than clear and non-reduced speech, as in "What are you doing" as opposed to "Whachya doin'?" Noriko's plan is to use the dialogs from her existing textbook and to ask the assistant language teachers to rerecord some rewritten dialogs to increase the length, authenticity, and naturalness of the dialogs. Noriko wants to add these features gradually to increase learners' listening fluency but to somehow prevent learners' immediate strong resistance.

Noriko's Unlikely Solution—Audio-Assisted Repeated Reading

We do not know exactly where Noriko learned about audio-assisted repeated reading. We do know, however, that Palmer's ([1917] 1968, 1921) thinking on the primacy of listening and the necessity of practice—although currently ignored—was introduced into the Japanese education system early in the twentieth century. And we also know that some Japanese and Japan- and Taiwan-based researchers have published on repeated reading (e.g., see Chang 2010). Finally, we know that Noriko has attended prefectural weekend workshops some of which are conducted by professionally trained Japan-based second language educators. This teaching sequence is adapted from Gorsuch and Taguchi (2008: 260), a study conducted in Vietnam with Japanese and US-based funding:

1. Learners silently read a short segment of a story.

2. Learners read the same segment a second and then a third time while listening to it on an audio file.

3. Learners silently read the same segment a fourth and a fifth time.

Noriko uses this same audio-assisted procedure (step 2), but in place of the reading passages, she substitutes the rewritten and rerecorded dialogs from the textbook. She starts with the original dialog in the textbook, usually between two persons on the topic of the chapter and always illustrating the grammatical points of the chapter. She rewrites the dialogs according to the three factors given above: length, authenticity, and naturalness. She goes about things gradually. She starts with only slightly longer dialogs, for example, and then adds the other factors.

Noriko begins teaching using the new materials by handing out a new dialog. She has learners compare the new, slightly longer dialog and their textbook dialog. Then, Noriko asks learners in the class to close their books. There is a murmur of resistance, but they do as she asks, and Noriko goes through steps 1, 2, and 3 as listed above. This first time she merely reads the slightly longer dialog aloud for learners. After she finishes, students quickly go back to the written dialog Noriko has handed out and also open their textbooks to the grammar pages. Noriko has not added any new vocabulary or grammatical points to the new dialogs. Rather, she has recycled and repeated them. A few learners ask questions about vocabulary and grammatical structures. Noriko answers all their questions quickly in Japanese without the usual long explanations. This was not done without some discipline on Noriko's part because these explanations are usually the bulk of the lesson. Then her class answers a ten-item multiple-choice comprehension quiz at the end of the chapter in the textbook. Learners do fine on it.

Some Larger Changes and Some Greater Learner Resistance

Noriko wants to increase her learners' capacity (their fluency), so she plans to increase the length of the dialog even more and to increase the authenticity of the audio input the learners get. However, she is keenly aware her students are interested only in what multiple choice scores they get on the comprehension quiz at the end of the chapter in the textbook, because they think this will predict how well they will do on high school entrance exams. Noriko sighs. In the next week of lessons, Noriko brings in two of the assistant language teachers assigned to her school, and they read the dialog aloud in step 2 above. Noriko's learners gasp a little but also lean forward in concentration. Noriko also tries a little experiment. After only one silent reading (step 1) and one audio-assisted reading (the first part of step 2), she asks the learners to take the multiple-choice quiz in the textbook and record their scores. Then she asks the learners to close their books and the assistant language teachers to read aloud the rewritten dialog a third time (the second part of step 2). Learners then

Table 5.3 What Noriko Posits about Teaching and Learners in Her English Language Class

1. The purpose of a junior high school curriculum is to prepare students to pass the entrance exams of some senior high school of decent standing.
2. Learners will resist any change in a curriculum that they perceive does not support the goal of passing entrance exams.
3. Learners have fairly fixed ideas of what activities in class predict passing entrance exams.
4. Fluency with some aspect of language is a reasonable goal of language learning. While this may not be spoken, other types of fluency might be more amenable to teaching.
5. Listening fluency may be a requirement for future success in high school entrance exams.
6. While teaching a language largely means teaching its grammatical structures, such traditional teaching will not help with listening fluency or fluency of any kind.
7. The key to building fluency is to build capacity gradually through introducing slightly more challenges and different types of challenges.

Source: Authors.

get to take the multiple choice comprehension quiz one more time. Some of the students gasped audibly at the increase in their scores. So, where Noriko expected more resistance, there was less. In the following weeks, Noriko made even more significant changes in the listening lessons. She asked the assistant language teachers to read aloud her rewritten listening dialogs in a different way. She asked them to read it slightly faster and in a more natural way without saying each word quite so clearly. Instead of saying cannot, they had to say can't, and so on. She recorded these on her cell phone. Noriko did have more trouble with learner resistance with these recordings. She offered to play the recordings multiple times. It took learners two to three more weeks before their multiple-choice quiz scores began to increase again. See Table 5.3 for what Noriko's posits about teaching and learners.

While Noriko does not have an advanced degree in teaching, she had focused coursework in materials design and a specific area of language, that of listening. The two taken together have continued to inspire her professionally in a focused way. She has been able to balance her knowledge of context (learner resistance) with her interests and expertise (materials design and fluency building).

Reflective Projects

1. Noriko is wondering what to do next. What directions for the future can you give her?

2. Noriko has started with listening passages based on the dialogues in her textbook that take only a minute or two. Gradually, she expands the time of the passages. What would you suggest is the maximum time she should aim for?

3. To this point, the listening passages are closely related to the theme and grammatical points presented in each textbook chapter. How can Noriko and the assistant language teachers expand their repertoire?

4. As with many teachers, some of Noriko's middle-level theory beliefs are in contradiction to each other. What are some of the contradictions?

5. In Figure 5.1, we list five components or dimensions of fluency. Could other dimensions be included? If so, what are they, how would you define them, and how would you argue that they could not be subsumed in one of the other five categories?

6. Thinking about what folk theory posits about fluency, make a table listing what you think should be included.

7. In your opinion, are folk ideas (about fluency or another topic that interests you) and theoretical ideas about (the same topic) irreconcilable?

CHAPTER SIX

Theories of Learning and Learners

Why This Chapter?

This chapter focuses on the interaction of theories of learning and second language learners. The practices or artifacts we use as discussion points are learning journals kept by students and a teaching log kept by a teacher of Korean. By theories of learning, we mean any middle-level theory that accounts for how humans form knowledge, awareness, and competence (Ausubel 2000; Bruner 2009; Meyer 1977; Vygotsky, Cole, and John-Steiner 1978; Sutton and Barto 2018), including second language (Gee 1997; Lantolf and Poehner 2011; Larsen-Freeman 2012; Swan 2005). These theories may come from applied linguistics, education, psychology, or second language acquisition. In this chapter, we focus on two theory areas. One is second language learner noticing of and attention to language forms, from second language acquisition (Schmidt 1990). This theory area picks up from Chapter 3 ("Theories of Learning and Teachers"), which briefly introduces Task-Based Language Teaching (TBLT). Chapter 6 takes this discussion a step further by highlighting how task repetition (having learners do a task a second or even a third time) enhances learners' noticing of and attention to language features (Bygate 1999; Hawkes 2012). The second theory area is Metacognition, from psychology, which refers to how learners handle what knowledge they have and how they form working plans to learn and to do things in life and in school (Pintrich and DeGroot 1990; Veenman, Van Hout-Walters, and Afflerbach 2006), including second language classes (Sato and Loewen 2018; Vandergrift 2002; Vandergrift and Baker 2015; Vandergrift and Goh 2012; Wang 2008; Wenden 1998).

In this chapter, we outline how the High Middle Low Theory Model (Chapter 1) applies to learners and theories of learning. We do this in two ways. First, we offer a table after each middle-level theory area description suggesting what the theories posit, or propose, about learners and learning. Second, we highlight middle- and low-level teacher theories by portraying classroom artifacts through a teacher case study. We finish with reflective projects for readers to probe important concepts from the chapter.

How the High Middle Low Theory Model Applies to Theories of Learning

Theories of learning have a significant role in teachers' working lives in that teachers are responsible for planning and carrying out lessons. Learners participate in lessons, and interact with teachers, other learners, and themselves, depending on lesson and course design. Thus, lessons and courses comprise a platform for learners' experiences, which ideally promote second language learning (Gorsuch and Taguchi 2010). The High Middle Low Theory Model helps to make sense of an interplay of identifiable low- and middle-level theories in teachers' thinking and actions. In terms of low-level theory, teachers' working bases for shaping learners' classroom experiences likely come from observations and reckonings teachers have made about what brings about learning. Teachers also have their own second language learning experiences, which shape their low-level, action-oriented theories of learning (see, for instance, the case studies of Veronika in Chapter 3; Rick in Chapter 4; and Anna in Chapter 7).

At the same time, teachers draw conclusions from what they hear about in professional journals, conferences, and post-qualification course work, which are potential sources of middle-level theory. Teachers may use their understandings of these theories to shift learners' lesson-based experiences (Hawkes 2012; Sato and Loewen 2018). The teacher in our case study, Bae, has been attending virtual professional conferences during the pandemic. As a result, he has become interested in what learners do cognitively while in his Korean language lessons. For instance, do his learners notice words and grammatical structures in the fun little Korean language stories he writes for them to review at the end of the week? He is not sure that they do. How would he find out? What could he do to push them a little more to notice features in the stories without just telling them to "study harder"? He senses that would not work well with his students, who are Australian first- and second-year college students. They are intelligent young people, but he wonders whether they are studying as effectively as they could be, or as much as they should. Bae, for whom English is a foreign language, has been a success at that. He thinks learning a foreign language requires a lot of persistence, thought, and small acts. He wonders how he could help learners with his experiences. Bae's developing middle-level theories of learning offer him some simple but interesting ideas for planning and carrying out lessons.

Middle-Level Theory Areas for Learning and Learners

In this section, we describe two middle-level theory areas. One is learner noticing of and attention to second language forms. Another is Metacognition, which describes attention, memory, and self-regulation functions of the mind. Metacognition is how learners organize their knowledge, thoughts, and actions to learn and to do things using the second language (Vandergrift and Baker 2015). The two theory areas are complementary, particularly when viewed in the context of task repetition. By doing a task twice or more with some added teacher-designed features, learners may see and reflect on language features they had not noticed before (Gorsuch and Taguchi 2010; Sato and Loewen 2018). This noticing and attention takes place in real time and is ongoing during learning tasks. It is then Metacognition that may aid in "catching" the feature for future self-directed learning and language use (Wenden 1998).

Noticing

This theory area, from second language acquisition, suggests that in order to learn second language words, word forms, syntax, and pronunciation, learners must first notice them in comprehensible input (Schmidt 1990). In essence, the Noticing Hypothesis posits that "all second-language learning requires the conscious noticing of linguistic elements" (Swan 2005: 379). What is noticed might be held briefly in short-term memory, if learners have sufficient attentional resources to do so, meaning, if learners are not grappling with too many pieces of information at once or are relatively skilled to begin with (Schmidt 1990: 136). This issue of attention and attentional resources will be further explained below. To continue with Noticing: features that are noticed and held in short-term memory may be then committed to long-term memory (Wenden 1998). Items held in long-term memory might be retrieved for use as declarative knowledge (knowledge a learner can consciously state and use in controlled ways) (Borelli 2018; Pica, Kang, and Sauro 2006). Words, word forms (morphology), syntax, and pronunciation are referred to variously in second language acquisition research as "language structures," "syntactic information," "linguistic features," "a grammar structure," "L2 form," "language form," "formal aspects of language," "features," "linguistic elements," and "formal aspects of language." In essence, the middle-level theory area of Noticing concerns itself with aspects of language at the sentence level and below, reflecting a preoccupation primarily with the linguistic competence component of Communicative Competence, or what Gorsuch (2019) refers to as a "narrow conception" of Communicative Competence (see Chapters 4 and 9).

Second Language Acquisition Research on Noticing and Tasks

As noted in Chapter 3 on theories of learning and teachers, Communicative Language Teaching (CLT) suggests that learners best learn to communicate in the second language by using the second language (Brumfit 2001; Larsen-Freeman and Anderson 2011). One way was to have learners engage in meaning-focused tasks that would cause them to communicate. In such tasks, learners' primary focus was on accomplishing things using the second language (Nunan 1989; Bygate, Skehan, and Swain 2001). This might be putting everyday objects (pans and teapots) in the correct locations on a picture of a kitchen in response to spoken instructions from a teacher (a receptive, nonreciprocal task; Ellis 2001), or working with a classmate to draw the floor plan of a house given a written description (a productive and receptive interactional task; Nunan 1989, from Prabhu 1987).

Second language acquisition researchers were quick to see the potential for tasks to explore theoretical issues in their own domains of interest (Bygate, Skehan, and Swain 2001), such as why learners might comprehend second language utterances or texts (meaning they can catch meaning) but then not be able to produce second language forms accurately (meaning their minds might not be handling language forms in such a way as to make them available for productive use). If learners are not handling language forms, why might that be? In other words, what is the nature of learners' cognitive processes as they use the second language? Might those "default-meaning-but-not-form" processes be manipulated? Michael Long, for instance, proposed that tasks, by design, could have a "focus on form," which would engage "learners' attention to grammatical forms that arise while learners are communicating" (Larsen-Freeman 2015: 266; see also Bygate, Skehan, and Swain 2001; Mackey 1999; Newton and Kennedy 1996). In other words, tasks could be designed to have learners engage in meaning but also prod their minds to notice and handle words, word forms, and syntax. Learners engaged in communicative tasks provided, and still provide, a platform for considering these issues in both lab settings (Mackey 1999; Pica, Kang, and Sauro 2006) and in classrooms (Sato and Loewen 2018).

With Noticing and tasks, a central theoretical issue, then, has been whether learners notice language forms, and whether this notice can be sharpened through changes in task design (Bygate, Skehan, and Swain 2001). One major proposal was that learners would notice when there was a "gap" between what learners knew and the "target equivalent" being emphasized in the task (Swan 2005: 380). For instance, a teacher might purposefully point out the gap, as in this exchange (K. Michelson, personal communication, November 30, 2021):

Student: *Madame, j'ai une question grammatique.* (Madame, I have a grammatic question.)

Teacher: *Une question dramatique?* (A dramatic question?)

Student: *Non, GRammatique!* (No, GRamatic!)

Teacher: *Dramatique?* (Dramatic?)

Student: *Non, une question GRAMMATIQUE!* (Non, a GRAMATIC question.)

Teacher: *Ah! Une question grammatiCALE!* (Oh, a grammatical question!)

In this case, the correct form (*grammaticale*) was directly negotiated by the teacher and thus brought to the attention of the learner in the context of learner-initiated language use. As a second example, teachers might point out a gap in learners' responses with a correction and then an additional request and assistance for learners to work out and say the correct form, thus "pushing" them to focus on the forms they need to use (Bygate, Skehan, and Swain 2001; Pica, Kang, and Sauro 2006; Swain and Lapkin 1995). From Samuda (2001: 133):

Student 1:   She must she must has many, many, MANY boyfriends

Teacher: (*laughing*) She must has?

Student 1:   Must yes uh must have

[Student 2]: Have

Teacher: Yeah she must have LOTS of boyfriends—look at all these phone numbers.

In effect, this might potentially cause learners to mentally compare their original utterance with a new and more accurate utterance and thus notice the feature (Oliver et al. 2019). A third example is where teachers might emphasize desired language forms in learners' input (Sato and Loewens 2019), as in Ellis's (2001: 51) experiments with instructions that learners get to complete a task. "Can you find the scouring pad? A scouring pad— scour means to clean a dish. A scouring pad is a small thing you hold in your hand." "Scouring pad" is the form being emphasized here. There is a presumption that learners may not already know "scouring pad."

A fourth and final example portrays how task directions and design might bring about noticing "the gap" but then also shows problems inherent in language use tasks where learners interact as autonomous language users, who have their own priorities (Bygate, Skehan, and Swain 2001). In other words, learners may not notice, or use, the target grammatical structures. The grammatical structure being focused on in the example is third-person reported speech in English ("She said she likes . . ."; M. Zhang, personal communication, December 13, 2021). Learners' instructions, which one learner read aloud, were: "Find out what movies your partner likes. Then report to another group what your partner said. Be sure to use He said he likes . . . or She said she likes . . . for your report." Here is what might happen:

Student 1: What we do?

Student 2: We talk—we have to talk about movies.

Student 1: Oh.

Student 2: Um . . . movies . . .

Student 1: What movie do you like?

Student 2: *Spider Man.*

Student 1: OK [goes to another group to report what she learned] She likes *Spider Man.*

Student 1 might have noticed a "gap" between what she said, "What we do," and Student 2's self-correction, "We talk—we have to talk," but that is not certain (meaning Student 1 may or may not have realized she could have said "What do we have to do?"). And Student 2 might have noticed her own self-correction ("We talk—we have to talk about movies"). But it was also hoped that Student 1 would tell learners in another group "She said she likes *Spider Man*," but instead she said "She likes *Spider Man*." And, given the communicative task learners were set to do, "She likes *Spider Man*" is a perfectly normal thing to say. But did she notice the target form? It is not clear. As can be seen, learners can successfully complete tasks without ever using the language forms the teacher wishes them to use (Bygate, Skehan, and Swain 2001). This may be a missed opportunity for learners to handle the form in short-term memory, and then to commit it to long-term memory for future retrieval, further handling and practice, and extemporaneous use. It is precisely this kind of problem our Korean teacher Bae runs into. As a result, he looks at other ways to increase learners' noticing of language forms, as we will see in the case study. He has also decided to ask students to keep a diary. He wonders if learners' diaries will offer evidence of them noticing the language forms he intends.

Tasks, Noticing, and Attention

All humans have hard limits on how many mental processes they can handle at one time (Flavell 1987). Language use, whether in the first or second language, is a complex process requiring a lot of a person's attentional resources (Ahmadian and Tavakoli 2010; Schmidt 1990; Yuan and Ellis 2003). This is evident when, even using the first language, a speaker who is given an unrehearsed topic to talk about will have many long pauses between utterances, along with false starts, and shorter and less syntactically complex utterances. This "problem" disappears when the speaker gets to rehearse, with resulting talk that is more fluent and complex (Butterworth 1980). The limitations on attentional resources are more evident in second language use where learners at all levels take longer to access vocabulary, among other language features, whether in listening, reading, writing, or speaking (Ahmadian 2012; Ellis 2001). Thus, when we ask learners to do a communicative task, the requirements of the task may consume so many of learners' attentional resources that they cannot notice intended language forms (Schmidt 1990). This then subverts the learning processes posited by the Noticing Hypothesis. Second language acquisition researchers have experimented usefully with task conditions to allow learners more attentional "space" with which to notice and use language forms of interest (Bygate 1999, 2001). One of these is task repetition.

Repetition as a Means of Freeing Up Attentional Resources

Two theories, Automaticity Theory and Verbal Efficiency Theory, predict that when individuals engage in a complex cognitive task, they can, with training, commit fewer attentional resources to "lower level" processes (LaBerge and Samuels 1974; Perfetti 1985; Young, Bowers, and McKinnon 1996). In other words, learners' lower-level processes can become automatic and be used without much thought (Fukkink, Hulstijn, and Simis 2005; Larsen-Freeman 2012). This automaticity for learners "frees up" attentional resources so that their "higher-level" processes can engage (Dougherty and Johnston 1996; Samuels 2006). These higher-level processes then allow learners to take notice of additional details of a task. In first and second language education, these theories have been applied to reading fluency and comprehension (Gorsuch and Taguchi 2008, 2010; Pikulski and Chard 2005; Samuels and Flor 1997; Stanovich 1987; Taguchi, Gorsuch, and Mitani 2021; Walczyk 2000). In second language reading, word recognition and basic decoding of clauses are considered "lower-level" processes while comprehension (extracting main ideas and details, taking note of rhetorical structure and connecting it to intended messages, etc.) is considered a higher-level process (Gorsuch, Taguchi, and Umehara 2015). This helps explain why second language reading is effortful and a kind of torture for most learners (Anderson 1999; Shimono 2018). Poor automaticity with lower-level processes (retrieving and recognizing words) prevents them using higher-order comprehension processes (Chang 2010), locking them out from realizations such as "Oh, I think Stan is lying to Amelia. There is going to be trouble." For learning purposes, more important is that second language users who are pretty adept at lower-level reading processes can notice more language form features in the text, such as new words and new grammar, or known words and grammar in actual use, perhaps for the first time (Gorsuch and Taguchi 2010). While Bygate (2001) and others note that repeating a task helps learners notice language forms in speech production, they do not necessarily mention Automaticity Theory or Verbal Efficiency Theory, possibly because they are operating out of different theoretical models more relevant to their research (see the speech processing model in Bygate 2001: 24; and Larsen-Freeman's [2012] comments on working memory and repetition). Nonetheless, we think the theories are useful here for illustrating limits on learners' attention and how repetition, interspersed with teacher interventions, can help learners notice language forms and get experience handling them in short-term memory.

Second language acquisition studies have been done where simple task repetition is done, and where task repetition plus some intervention is done. Bygate (1999) experimented with task repetition where a learner did a narration task and then did the task once more a few days later without being warned of it. The author posited that the learner's attention might be drawn to different aspects of her language production by doing a repetition. The first time a task is done, he believed, learners would be focused on communicating meaning whereas "on subsequent occasions this familiarity [with intended meaning] gives us time and awareness to shift attention from message content [meaning] to the selection and monitoring of appropriate language" (41). During the task repetition, the author noted the learner "repeated rather to self-correct *after* producing words and phrases" (42; original emphasis). This suggested to the author that the learner was paying attention to language form. The first time the learner did the narration task, most of her pauses and repetitions came *before* saying words and phrases, suggesting the learner's attention was consumed by expressing meaning and doing so in the real-time conditions imposed by the task. In later commentary, Samuda and Bygate (2008) posited four factors that might be manipulated to get learners to pay more attention to language forms: task repetition, learner planning for tasks, learner task familiarity, and learners working with different interlocuters on different iterations of a task.

Other studies have focused on task repetitions and interventions as a means of increasing learners' attention to language forms. Hawkes (2012) worked with beginning English language learners at the junior high school level. One of his basic tasks was learners exchanging spoken opinions on fast food restaurants. The intended language forms were offering opinions and giving reasons ("I think that . . ." and "I feel that . . ."), language forms used to show agreement or disagreement, and comparative and superlative forms (336). His multistage lesson included: (1) a pre-task stage where learners brainstormed and listened to an audio recording of two advanced speakers doing the opinion exchange task; (2) the main task where learners

Table 6.1 What Noticing Posits

1. Learners must consciously notice language forms to learn them.
2. The object of study is language forms at the sentence level or below.
3. One means of noticing is to draw learners' attention to a "gap" between what language form they know or wish to use, and the correct or different form.
4. Language forms that are noticed will be handled in short-term memory and possibly committed to long-term memory.
5. Learners will handle language forms in short-term memory if they have the attentional resources to do so.
6. Communicative tasks, which emphasize language use and meaning, may consume learners' attentional resources, impeding them from noticing language forms.
7. Communicative tasks can be manipulated to draw learners' attention to language forms.

Source: Authors.

exchanged opinions; (3) a form-focused intervention where learners were shown a transcript of the audio recording they heard in the pre-task and attention drawn to the target language forms; (4) direct teacher instruction of the language forms along with "controlled repetition" of the forms (330); and finally (5) doing the opinion exchange task once again. There was evidence from recordings of learners that in the second task (step 5) they used more of the target language forms, most notably the language of agreement and disagreement and comparative and superlative forms. Learners also did more self-corrections of the forms. This suggested that learners noticed the forms, and that they had sufficient attentional resources to do so, likely because of task repetition and the various interventions done by the teacher. As will be seen, Bae works with task repetition but also with an intervention in between task repetitions in the form of direct instruction. See Table 6.1 for what the theory area of Noticing posits.

Metacognition

The second and final middle-level theory area for this chapter is Metacognition. These psychological theories suggest that we potentially have an awareness of and control over our own thought (cognitive) processes (Eva and Regehr 2005; Flavell 1979; Graham 2006; Nicol and MacFarlane-Dick 2006; Paris and Winograd 1990; Veenman, Van Hout-Wolters, and Afflerbach 2006). As we make plans, carry them out, and accomplish things, such as studying for a test and then taking the test, we engage in multiple, simultaneous, thought processes to do so (Flavell 1979; Oxford 1994). Flavell (1979, 1987) suggests a three-component Metacognition Knowledge Model: First, we have to be aware that we are cognitive actors, meaning that we know we can do things with our minds to prepare for a test, for example (what Flavell calls knowledge of "person"). Second, we need some realistic picture in our minds of the demands of what we need to accomplish (knowledge of "task"). For instance, we need to think through the test question types and content that might appear so that we can estimate what we are still not good at, or what we are already capable of doing. Third, we ought to develop an array of thinking-oriented (cognitive) strategies we may choose from to be successful with the test questions and content (the task) we have visualized (knowledge of "strategy"). Sato and Loewen (2018, 2019) offer lucid descriptions of Flavell's three-component "person, task, and strategy" (1979: 907; 1987) Metacognition Knowledge Model. Anita Wenden, an early proponent of applying Metacognition theories to language teaching, famously describes a learner preparing for a summary writing test (Wenden 1998: 523–4). Applying Flavell's model, the learner is aware he can use his knowledge and experiences to prepare (Flavell's "person" component). The learner also considers the task of writing a summary using his discourse knowledge, drawing on what he knows about writing summaries (Flavell's "task" component). As he reads the article to be summarized, he decides to write down unknown words on a separate list (Flavell's "strategy" component). For a detailed review of the many Metacognition models proposed in psychology, see Meijer, Veenman, and van Hout-Wolters (2006).

Commentators generally posit that Metacognition is not a given, and that it can and should be cultivated for learner success (Eva and Regerhr 2005; Flavell 1979; Veenman, Van Hout-Wolters, and Afflerbach 2006). The same commentators also note that our Metacognition can and should be improved, as faulty Metacognition can lead to self-defeating behaviors that may not be self-corrective (Flavell 1979; Veenman, Van Hout-Wolters, and Afflerbach 2006). Veenman, Van Hout-Wolters, and Afflerbach's (2006) example is of a college student who believes she has committed adequate time to preparing for math tests, but then does not do well on tests. She wrongly attributes her continuing poor performance on how "difficult" the teacher makes the test, not to her preparation activities (4), which might be comprised of faulty estimations of the test item types and content, faulty estimations of one's own level of preparation (Paris and Winograd 1990), misapplying preparation strategies, or simply not knowing effective strategies. Eva and Regehr (2005) further suggest that persons who persist in poor Metacognition may have not been led to focus on specific errors, and that failures, if properly focused on and learned from, can improve Metacognition (S49) through more accurate learner self-assessment.

Improving Learner Metacognition

There is some consensus on how learner Metacognition can be improved. In his early commentary, Flavell (1979: 908) focuses on learners having metacognitive "experiences," which may add to or change metacognitive "knowledge" that Flavell characterizes as "stored world knowledge" (906). The implication is that teachers can be agents of improvement by creating such experiences that are "situations that stimulate a lot of careful, highly conscious thinking . . . in novel roles or situations, where every major step you take requires planning beforehand and evaluation afterwards" (908). One early and recognizable stage of Metacognition development is a learner's awareness of what he or she does not understand (self-monitoring). The implication is that learners need to learn to pay attention to feelings of puzzlement and uncertainty "about what is intended or meant" (909) in the object of study. This is one step to defining what is not understood. Flavell (1987: 26) later comments that learners can be encouraged to reflect on past, present, and future behaviors to develop "planfulness" at approaching problems or tasks (see also O'Malley and Chamot 1990: 198). Of direct relevance to Bae, our teacher of Korean, Flavell (1987: 27) suggests that having learners engage in writing offers "practice and experience with metacognition" because it allows retrospection and critical introspection "of one's own thoughts" (see also Negretti and Kuteeva 2011; Paris and Winograd 1990). As it turns out, Bae decides to have his learners regularly write in learning diaries. He is not immediately interested in whether learners write in English (their L1) or in Korean (their L2) as will be described in the case study below. Perhaps as a result, he learns several things that surprise him.

Additional ways teachers can develop learners' Metacognition is by teaching individual cognitive strategies and offering practice with them, helping learners match strategies to specific situations and tasks, working with learners to manage negative feelings when doing self-assessments, helping learners see studying as a series of choices depending on self-defined goals, and having learners share their own metacognitive processes as part of doing joint projects with peers (Paris and Winograd 1990; Yang 1992). These teaching ideas that focus on learners doing and practicing Metacognition are supported by Brown's (1987) adaptation of Flavell's three-component Metacognitive Knowledge Model. Brown (1987: 67) posits that there is metacognitive knowledge ("person," "task," "strategies") but also Metacognition "regulation," which means the ability to use metacognitive knowledge.

Metacognition in Second Language Education

Research interest in second language learner Metacognition is long standing (Dickinson 1987; Graham 2006, 2011; Kobayashi 2011; Noro 2004;

Padron 1992; Rivera-Mills and Plonsky 2007; Thompson and Rubin 1996; Vandergrift 2002, 2005; Wenden 1998; see also O'Malley and Chamot [1990] and Oxford [1990] on metacognitive "learning strategies," and Rose [2012], Teng and Zhang [2016], Tseng, Dornyei, and Schmitt [2006], and Tsuchiya [2018] on "self-regulation"). As a middle-level theory area, Metacognition is studied, commented on, and applied using multiple orientations. We present two orientations here: approaching Metacognition by describing discrete language learning strategies, and applying Metacognition theories in the design of instructional treatments. We present the first orientation because the field comprising "learning strategies" and "learning styles" was salient from the 1980s on (Rose 2012; Thompson and Rubin 1996). We present the second orientation because we believe this more recent application of a well-established Metacognition model to a specific and common feature of teaching, and thus to learners' classroom experiences, has demonstrable relevance to our first theory area in this chapter, that of Noticing and Attention.

Because Metacognition is a middle-level theory area, multiple orientations are, of course, present (Rivera-Mills and Plonsky 2007). Middle-level theory is tapped into to guide multiple research agendas depending on researchers' aims (Chapter 1). O'Malley and Chamot (1990: x) wished to develop an instructional approach that incorporated learning strategies for primary and secondary school English-medium content classes. To accomplish this, second language learning strategies, not all of them metacognitive per se, needed to be identified and described in use. In the case of Sato and Loewen (2018), the object of interest was learning whether teacher corrective feedback on a few language forms could be made more salient (noticeable) to learners if they participated in a theory-based Metacognition training sequence that foregrounded the language forms. In this instance, a learning-productive and common classroom practice (a teacher giving corrective feedback) formed the basis for developing "learners' awareness of their own learning processes" (Sato and Loewen 2018: 508). No one orientation to Metacognition can be comprehensive, or all-answering. The second orientation presented here (applying Metacognition theories) informs valuable changes to learners' experiences, and we hope that inquiry in this direction continues (see also Cross 2014; Vandergrift and Goh 2012).

The First Orientation—Language Learning Strategies

In this orientation, commentators describe and categorize learners' language learning strategies. Oxford (1990) published an inventory of some eighty language learning strategies organized by "direct strategies" (57) and "indirect strategies" (135). Within those two categories, she posited "memory strategies," "cognitive strategies," and "compensation strategies" as being "direct strategies"; and "affective strategies," "social strategies," and "metacognitive strategies" as being "indirect strategies" (15) (see also Fan 2003). O'Malley and Chamot (1990) employed student interviews, teacher interviews, and classroom observations of English language learners to describe twenty-three strategies in use such as "selective attention" where learners would "decide in advance to attend to specific aspects of input, often by scanning for key words, concepts, and/or linguistic markers" (119). Their twenty-three strategies were grouped as "metacognitive strategies," "cognitive strategies," and "social mediation strategies" (119–20). The "selective attention" example given above was identified by the researchers as a metacognitive strategy.

For the purposes of this chapter, we wish to differentiate between learning strategies and Metacognition. One example of a learning strategy would be a specific cognitive process, such as the word and phrase translation that Anna, our Mandarin language teacher in Chapter 7, used to learn English vocabulary. Another cognitive strategy she used was to make and review a personalized flashcard set. According to Oxford (1994: 1), language learning strategies are "specific actions, behaviors, steps, or techniques students use . . . to improve their progress in apprehending, internalizing, and using the L2." In contrast, Metacognition as defined by Flavell (1979) would be a learner's command (knowledge) and coordinated use of multiple strategies (ability to use) in response to his or her understanding of a specific task or text or need. That a learner is even aware of himself or herself as having thought-oriented strategies and plans, and that others around him or her are also cognitive actors, is also part of Metacognition as defined by Flavell. Oxford (1990, 1994) refers to the existence of "clusters" of learning strategies used to address "particular language skills or tasks," which sounds like Metacognition. Nonetheless, she refers to the totality of her research as "learning strategies" of which metacognitive strategies are only one category of strategies among five others. This may have the unintended effect of blurring the distinction between Metacognition and learning strategies. In any literature a teacher might consult, or in any conference presentation they might attend, they will likely discern these different orientations (see, for instance, Fan 2003; Lavasani and Faryadres 2011; Lee 2010; Macaro, Graham, and Vanderplank 2007; Negretti and Kuteeva 2011; Noro 2004; Seo 2000; Vandergrift and Goh 2012).

The Second Orientation—Application of a Metacognition Theory

Sato and Loewen (2018) applied Flavell's Metacognition model of person-task strategy to a study on increasing learners' attention to corrective feedback on specific language forms. They crafted a multi-lesson plan for college-level English language learners in which metacognitive instruction was done in five stages. In the first stage, learners were given an introduction to corrective feedback

Table 6.2 What Metacognition Posits

1. Learners potentially have awareness of and control over their thought processes as they learn and undertake learning tasks.
2. These thought processes include learning strategies.
3. Such awareness and control are valuable for learning through improved learner planning, and learner ability to make good use of learning experiences while under way and after the fact.
4. Metacognition models generally construe metacognition as knowledge and as use.
5. Metacognition knowledge and use can be developed in learners.
6. Teachers can be agents of learners' Metacognition development.

Source: Authors.

and the purposes for it ("strategy"). In the second stage, learners were given an explanation of the theories behind corrective feedback, including Noticing ("person" and "strategy"). Learners were also given examples of corrective feedback, highlighting the forms the authors wanted to study (the third-person singular -s and possessive determiners; Sato and Loewen 2018: 515) ("task"). In the third stage, learners were invited to ask questions about the metacognition introduction and examples. In the fourth stage, learners were exhorted to be on the lookout for corrective feedback from instructors "so you can improve your speaking!" ("person") (523). The fifth stage took place at the beginning of three ordinary language lessons during which teacher corrective feedback was given on the language forms under study. The teacher simply reminded learners what corrective feedback was for and to be on the lookout for corrective feedback in the lessons ("person" and "strategy"). Learners who received metacognition instruction improved their accuracy with the forms in extemporaneous spoken picture description tasks after the instructional treatments. The authors speculated that the metacognitive instruction enabled learners to notice the "evidence" of the forms offered in the corrective feedback (530). In other words, the metacognition instruction helped learners prepare for and monitor for the language forms. See Table 6.2 for what the theory area of Metacognition posits.

Low- and Middle-Level Theories Concerning Learning and Learners: A Teacher of Korean

This chapter identifies and describes low- and middle-level theories about learning and learners held by an experienced Korean language teacher named Bae. First is a description of Bae's background, including his own second language learning experiences with English and a description of his undergraduate degree and graduate certificate in teaching and Korean language. Second, Bae's beginning-level Korean class will be described. We will learn about his students and about his current interests and concerns, namely, what learners do inside their heads to learn Korean. Learners do not seem to "hang on" to language forms, and he wonders if this is because they cannot read the Korean alphabet very well. Or perhaps there are other reasons he has not thought of? Third, Bae's recent attendance at online conferences will be described. He uses and interprets ideas from the conferences to help him develop his interests and think through his concerns. The effects of Bae's responses are revealed in two artifacts. One is a learning journal kept online by students, and the second is weekly logs kept by Bae, in which he writes his concerns and plans on how to shift learners' experiences. Finally, Bae's low- and middle-level theories about learning and learners will be identified.

Bae's Background and Education

Bae is from South Korea and is in his mid-thirties. He has been teaching Korean as a foreign language for ten years in Australia. Bae became interested in teaching language during high school when he studied English as a foreign language. One of his teachers liked to explain English grammar by making direct comparisons between Korean and English and using the "comparison" lessons to educate the students about grammatical terminology such as "object" and "subject," with the terminology rendered in English. The article system of English (a, an, and the) just about drove Bae crazy because there is no such system in Korean. But he kept up with it with two-minute self-quizzes once a day. Bae's father would write out random English sentences, deliberately leaving articles, and other words, out. He would ask Bae to identify where the articles (if needed) ought to appear (before a noun). Bae's English teacher compared the English article system to the Korean particle system, which Bae realized was complicated. Particles would attach to Korean nouns and verbs, and one change would alter sentence meanings entirely, such as what was a subject or an object of a verb, or where something was located, or how certain a speaker was (Korean National Standards Task Force 2022; Lee and Ramsey 2000; N. Choi and J. Kong, personal communication, January 12, 2022).

Another of Bae's English teachers was big on reading using English language texts about Korean culture, history, language, and current news. While Bae and his classmates read silently, his teacher read the story aloud. Bae found this really helped him figure out how the strange English letters sounded. It made him slow down a bit and read more carefully, too. He was able to pick out and separate clauses, for instance. Reading helped him with English articles. The reading also helped Bae with his vocabulary. He found he would rather read a story to review vocabulary than just look at lists of words. But it was a Korean language arts (*gugeo*) teacher who got Bae really interested in language as a possible field of work. Bae's high school friends were bored with Korean language arts class, but Bae found that the teacher, an older woman, was very approachable. She would answer any question Bae might have about Korean folk tales and poetic traditions, and how Korean's writing system had changed over time. "Both spoken and written Korean is changing even now," she once told him. It was because of her that Bae enrolled in a Korean university that had a combined teaching and Korean language program. The campus had an official policy of being a bilingual Korean/English institution, and so Bae took courses using both languages. It was such a struggle with English! But he found if he read passages in required books at least twice, he understood more the second time. He took both an undergraduate degree and then a graduate certificate at the school. Then, he found a job teaching Korean at a college in Australia.

Bae's Work and His Students

Bae teaches Korean language courses at the beginning levels (basic, mid, and high). The college where he works is small, and he is the only full-time Korean teacher. Bae has changed textbooks a few times over the years and now he wants to change once more. Most textbooks and websites for Korean state over and over that the Korean alphabet (*hangul*) is "easy" and should take only a few weeks to learn. After a few perfunctory chapters on the Korean alphabet, all dialogs and exercises on grammar, vocabulary, and reading are in Korean using the Korean alphabet. Bae is not so sure that the alphabet is that easy for his English-speaking students. Yes, they can sound out most *hangul* symbols if they go slowly, and if Bae does dictation exercises with single words, learners do okay. But the problem comes when learners go above the word level, and beyond the immediate example sentences the textbook uses in a given week. Learners can more or less read the example sentences used in the textbook for grammar lessons *for that week*. But when they read sentences or little dialogs from previous lessons (where Bae has changed the words and rearranged sentence structure a little), it is very slow going, and it seems very easy for them to miss a key particle. He can see this on learners' performances on tasks and quizzes. This issue persists from the beginning level into the mid-beginning level.

On tasks, learners verbally exchange information from different pages in the book or do interviews with each other about daily routines. Bae also tries a task where one learner describes the position of an object in a room and the other learner draws where that object should go. This is really confusing because sometimes an object must be described as a possession of something else, requiring one particle and word order. But that does not hold true in many other cases. On all tasks, however, even though learners muddle through and complete the tasks, they do not use the grammatical forms and words that Bae hopes they will. It is frustrating that learners seem unable to use all their linguistic resources. In response, Bae starts writing little stories for learners to read that use the grammatical points and words from a lesson, which will be further described below.

On quizzes, given every two or three weeks, some learners do okay but others do poorly. Some quiz items are just as described above—rewritings of sentences and dialogs from previous weeks. Other quiz items are modeled on what Bae's father used to do for him. Within a little three- or four-sentence authentic dialog, Bae blanks out certain parts of words and then asks students to add particles, for example. Then, he asks learners to explain in English what the little text means because he wishes to get learners to connect changes in forms to changes in meaning. Learners who do well get at least half of the items right and can explain some sentences by saying, "Jinsol talked to her friends" when the *-na* particle is used to show past tense. But then the same students who do okay one week do not do well on the same structures some weeks later. And students who do poorly to begin with do not seem to improve. One student tells Bae, "I'm just no good at languages!" She has gotten poor quiz grades three times in a row. The sentences with blanked out characters are really getting to her.

As a way to get learners to practice particles more and "hang on" to their knowledge longer, Bae writes little fun stories for them based on "scary ghost tales" and childhood adventures his grandmother told him. But they seem to fall short somehow. Many readers do not read them, he thinks, because they sound taken by surprise when he mentions them after they should have read them outside of class. Or he might review some grammatical points by saying, "Can you remember what the story said earlier this week? Can you remember the example for . . ." and it is not clear they know what he is talking about. Perhaps he needs to think about what he wants the stories to accomplish for learners. Are students getting frustrated because their Korean alphabet knowledge is not that good, and they stop reading because the sentences in his stories just do not come together? Or do they not understand he is recycling what they already studied? This points out another problem with the current textbook: Each week there are new grammar points and vocabulary to learn. There is little recycling, except for a two-page review that appears every three lessons.

Two Conferences

The pandemic has forced the school to have classes online a few times, which neither the learners nor Bae enjoyed. He meets each class of twenty students five days a week for an hour each time. Bae is relieved to be teaching face-to-face at the moment. But the pandemic has had one positive effect. Bae has been able to attend more international conferences because so many of them are now online. He wants a few things: (1) to network with other attendees to find a new textbook series, (2) to attend presentations on how he can use tasks in class where learners use the grammatical forms more, and (3) to get perspectives on whether learners need more work on reading and decoding the Korean alphabet, and how he might help them with that. While his first purpose is related to teaching, the second two are related to learners' learning. He wonders whether the issues with tasks and grammar, and second language reading represent impediments to learning.

One of the conferences he attends is based in the United States. He finds a few instructors of Korean through an online group meeting on "less commonly taught languages," and he learns that teachers of languages such as Russian or Arabic or Swahili are in the same boat as him. There are few textbooks to choose from, and they are all more or less the same with new grammar points and vocabulary piled on each week with insufficient recycling. Still, he has learned about one textbook series he might look at, and he has made a new long-distance colleague who works for a Korean language school in Los Angeles.

At the same conference, he attends a workshop on communicative tasks. The presenter offers some startling but simple ideas for altering and extending learners' experiences. First, why not have learners do the same task twice, or even a third time? One attendee asks in the videoconference chat bar: "Won't students just get bored?" and the two presenters respond with a second simple idea: that each time the learners do a pair or group work task, there is some teacher-led intervention in between. This intervention could be corrective feedback, based on what the teacher is hearing learners say or seeing what they write. Learners could be asked to say or write the correct forms (whatever forms they used to accomplish a task). Teachers could also base corrective feedback on whatever forms they are looking for from, say, a textbook chapter being studied. They could lead learners through new restatements using the forms. Learners could work through basic reformulations of what they could remember of what they said or wrote the first time they did the task. Then, the learners do the task a second time.

One of the presenters offers a second intervention, one that would precede the first task and then also come in between the first and second time a task is done. The "pre-intervention" would have learners hearing an authentic audio recording of two speakers doing an oral task. The recording would include false starts and clarification requests between speakers, as would occur in ordinary conversation, but would also include the grammatical forms the teacher wants learners to focus on. At one point in the recording, one of the speakers actually says, "Did you say *walked*"? (the past tense was being focused on), and the other speaker says, "Yes, I said *walked*." Then, learners would do the task. The in-between task intervention would be a straightforward lesson on the past tense given by the teacher lasting no more than five minutes. Thereafter, the learners would do the task a second time. The presenter had tried this and found in audio recordings of the learners that they used the target grammatical forms more the second time.

Bae asks the presenters, "Are you thinking that learners will notice the grammatical forms more if you do these task repetitions and interventions? Is that what you're getting at? Noticing?" One presenter answers,

> Yes, we thought about the Noticing Hypothesis, for sure. We wanted to intensify learners' engagement with the forms. We thought that if learners could repeat the task, they might free up more of their attention so they could do the noticing we thought they needed. But we're still not sure what kinds of interventions work best. We think interventions between tasks are necessary, but we're still working out which ones work and which ones teachers could do routinely.

Another attendee asks, "Maybe learners are noticing more but perhaps they are using the forms more the second time because they are simply getting a better idea of what the task demands and what the teacher wants?" Bae thinks this is a good question, but he thinks that through either learning route, there is a chance that students would better remember the grammatical forms intended for that chapter. And he is intrigued with the idea that learners might simply understand a task better or can better address a task through an intervention and a second chance to try it. This still does not completely answer Bae's concern about whether learners could retain the grammatical forms and vocabulary over time.

Because Bae's time zone is different from where the conference originates, he can see some "early morning" presentations that are late at night for him. He clicks on one presentation on "learner self-regulation and Metacognition" because the "self-regulation" in the title intrigues him. He is not expecting any direct benefit on his main concerns, but in fact he gets an idea. The presenter talks about how language learners may need ideas on how to better learn language. "We need learners to explore things like reading strategies," says the presenter. "Learners need to know they *have* strategies, and that different classroom tasks or quizzes or reading sessions might need different strategies." There was that idea again, thought Bae, the idea that learners can learn to know how to do a task, or whatever. He thinks back to his days as an English language learner. He used lots of strategies to do well on any variety of tests and assignments. Would it help to talk to learners about strategies and how they helped him learn?

Bae goes to a second conference a few weeks later, this one on reading. There are teachers of languages such as Chinese or Japanese or Thai where the writing systems are different than that of the learners' first languages. Two presenters, one Japanese and another American, argue that American college students learning Japanese do in fact need help with reading fluency.

If the second language writing system is going to be used for learning grammar and vocabulary, then learners need to have fast and accurate decoding ability with the different characters used in Japanese writing. They suggest having learners read short passages two to four times in a row. For one or two of those times, they can listen to the text spoken aloud as they read along silently. This will increase their comprehension by the third or fourth time, because they will not be spending all their attentional resources on decoding characters. Bae is surprised on several counts: (1) he is hearing about attentional resources again; (2) he is hearing more support for learners doing something twice or more, whether it be reading a text, doing a task, or whatever; and (3) he remembers doing something similar while reading English texts in college.

Bae Makes Two Alterations for Learners

Bae chooses his mid-beginning course for a few changes to learners' experiences. He teaches four courses in total but wants to start small with just the one course. First, he sets aside one class meeting per week for a learner self-study class. He tells students that they will attend class as usual but that the one self-study class will be for them to ask questions, work on preparing for quizzes and tests, and otherwise study as they like. He requires them to log into the online course platform during the self-study session and write down anything that comes to their minds about themselves as they take the class. Learners have their own folders, which only the individual learners and Bae can access. It is in effect a learning diary. While students log in to write, so does he. He tells learners he is also writing in a log so he can better organize his thoughts about the learning he wants in the class, and to his surprise, students keep typing as long as he keeps typing.

During the rest of the self-study session, some learners sit to study together with a textbook, quietly going through the exercises. While they seem to use English, Bae can also hear Korean words, phrases, and sentences in their talk. Other learners come to Bae to ask questions, and if they are talking about something the other students are interested in, they also join in. Preparing for quizzes is a popular topic. Bae quietly talks about how he prepared for quizzes while he was learning English. He also writes items from previous quizzes on the blackboard for groups of students and asks them to talk through how they answered the items and how they prepared. Quite a few of them have good ideas. On one occasion, Bae notes with surprise that all the students have come to the board to watch. This board activity also allows students to ask specific questions about particles and on a whim, Bae writes "comparison" sentences with different particles, for example, and students point out those alphabetic differences. Bae types up these impressions into his weekly log.

Bae's second change is to still have learners do communicative tasks in class, but now learners do them twice (or in one case a third time at learners' request). Rather than teaching a grammatical form, then having learners do a task as practice, Bae has learners do the task first. They take a one-minute "stretch break" and then sit down to reconstruct what they said or wrote for the task. Then, Bae has learners review the lesson in the textbook and tell him the grammatical points. If necessary, Bae does some very brief direct teaching on the grammar points. He then has learners figure out how they would do the task a second time. Finally, learners do the task a second time. Sometimes they use the forms he wants them to, sometimes they do not. But he notices in one learner's online diary that she is writing down different ways to do tasks by writing her own little dialogs with variations between them. It is interesting to Bae that she has held in memory the grammar points and details of the task itself. He asks her permission to put the different dialogs on the board as anonymous samples and she agrees. Learners try both and say how they are different.

Bae also applies the "do something twice" rule to the little stories he writes for his students. Now, he simply has them read the stories in class. Learners read them twice, and the second time he reads them aloud. A few students, including the one female student, seem to be summarizing the story in English in their learner diaries, which means they are recalling the stories perhaps two to four days after the fact. Two or three learners use some Korean words and phrases to write part of the summary, even though Bae has not asked them to, and the words include the grammatical forms and words Bae has been trying to teach. All of this, too, goes into Bae's online log.

These changes have created a bit more work. Bae must really think through what he is doing and what effect that may have on learners' experiences. But at least he has made one decision about needing a new textbook after reviewing his weekly log. He will keep using the textbook he has and make changes to it for what he wishes to do. It is true the beginner-mid class is now moving through the textbook more slowly, but with doing tasks twice and having the self-study day, that is to be expected. See Table 6.3 for what Bae posits about theories of learning and learners.

As a result of his concerns about his learners and of his attendance at online teaching conferences, Bae makes some simple but potent changes in one of his Korean language classes. Some of these changes, such as repeating tasks with interventions, are best attributed to middle-level theories that Bae has been learning about, such as the Noticing Hypothesis, although he thinks there may be multiple explanations, based in learning theories, for learners' greater use of desired language forms the second time they do tasks. Bae feels no discomfort at the idea of multiple explanations, however, and he may be open to learning more about the theories as he continues his observations of learners. Whatever he learns may better inform his future actions. Bae has also been considering middle-level theories about how

Table 6.3 What Bae Posits about Theories of Learning and Learners

1. Communicative tasks are a means of practicing language forms. Practice is a means of learning.
2. It is desirable for learners to use the language forms intended by the teacher in tasks.
3. Learners are cognitive agents. They have thought processes.
4. A teacher should find out about learners' thought processes to help them.
5. Existing course structures such as online writing tools can be used to learn more about learners' learning and thought processes.
6. Doing tasks and other classroom activities twice seems useful. Two different middle-level theories, describing quite different learning processes, may explain it.
7. A teachers' own foreign language learning experiences and learning strategies may comprise course content.
8. Learners may have unexpected problems learning in class, such as having trouble reading a foreign language writing system for the purposes of learning. Intuitions on these issues should be followed up.
9. Learners may need time and guidance to develop study routines and successful learning. Using class time for this purpose is suitable.

Source: Authors.

learners' Metacognition can be developed, but at the same time he taps into his low-level teacher theory, in part shaped by his own foreign language learning experiences, to offer himself as a role model to learners. He decides to offer precious class time to develop learners' Metacognition, knowing from low-level teacher theory that he and the learners will not progress through the textbook quite as fast.

Reflective Projects

1. Bae makes a number of changes that shift the experiences of his beginning-mid learners. Name four to five of them (there may be more). Using your list, complete the table below. What are the theory sources for Bae's alterations of learners' experiences in the course?

What Bae does	Noticing	Metacognition	Bae's low-level theories

2. How effective do you think learning diaries are for understanding learners' thought processes? What does Bae do with the learning diaries? What could be changed with the diaries to make them more effective?

3. What if Bae had insisted that learners write in their diaries using Korean? How might that change learners' experiences with the diaries? How might that change the information Bae might get from the diaries?

4. Did Bae ever get any help at the two conferences about helping learners "hang on" to grammar for longer? What does Bae do to help learners? Where did he get the idea? From a middle-level or low-level theory? Both?

5. In this chapter, Bae is a teacher. At the same time, this chapter is about theories of learning and learners. Is Bae also a learner in this case? If so, what does he learn about? Can theories of metacognition be applied to teachers? How would you find other theories that account for how teachers add to or change what they know? What disciplines might have such theories?

6. Many learning theories, including metacognition theories, have components for both knowing and doing. Thus, growth in knowledge is posited but so is growth in ability to use knowledge. Assuming we can attribute these components to Bae, do you think his ten years of teaching experience made a difference to how he applied what he learned at the two conferences he attended?

7. Here is a basic task for English prepositions. Applying learning theories described in this chapter, how could the task be changed so learners learn prepositions?

   Last week in class you learned about the childhood adventures of teacher's grandmother. Together make a timeline of what she did using full sentences, based on the activities suggested in the word list: home, bicycle, school, lunchbox, ground, shop, candy, pocket, baby brother.

Then tell a classmate about the timeline of the little girl's day without showing him or her the timeline. Some of these verbs might be helpful: leave, go, ride, carry, drop, fall, stop, buy, put, return, give.

For an extra challenge, tell your classmate about the event out of order. Can he or she put them in the correct order?

CHAPTER SEVEN

Theories of Language and Learners

Why This Chapter?

This chapter focuses on the interaction of theories of language and second language learners. As in Chapter 4 ("Theories of Language and Teachers"), we believe theories of language means how language is characterized, studied, and commented and acted upon by scholars, administrators, teachers, and learners in second language education. In Chapter 4, we argued that what teachers know and believe about a second language comprises a significant impetus to their professional lives. Language is the content that teachers must handle. Now, in this chapter, we make the same argument; only we shift the focus to learners. There is a caveat: applied linguists and second language acquisition researchers have been theorizing learners' language knowledge for decades. The questions posed by these scholars have to do with whether learners have separate first language and second language systems and whether and how language use shapes learners' language knowledge structures, to name only a few (Hall, Cheng, and Carlson 2006). These remain significant and perennial questions and discussions, and as such they inform high-level theories such as Communicative Competence and Proficiency (Chapter 4) and multiple middle-level research agendas. In contrast, what we explore in this chapter is related to how learners experience language as content in classrooms. In other words, in educational contexts with institutions and textbooks and curricula and instructors, what are learners' views of language and what do they know about language, both upon arrival and once they have begun their study?

Learners' views or knowledge will shape their thoughts and actions as they grapple with the content of the course (the language) and the significant cognitive, cultural, and emotional challenges that ensue. Second language teachers can observe some of what their learners do. They are privy to some of learners' thoughts as learners ask questions or make requests for explanations or additional examples. In this chapter, we offer middle- and low-level theories to help teachers make sense of it. The middle-level theory area we explore is learner expectations. We call this a "theory area" because no one theory explains "learner expectations." There is no such thing as "the learner expectation model" (see Chapter 5). Rather, two or more theories, or areas of research, might be relevant to learner expectations of language taught in classrooms. The statement "might be relevant" refers to the idea that theories are circumscribed. In other words, they attempt to explain some things but make no attempt to explain others.

In this chapter, we describe how the High Middle Low Theory Model (Chapter 1) applies to middle-level theories relevant to language and learners. As with Chapter 4, we do this in two ways. First, we offer a table after each theory description suggesting what a particular theory posits, or proposes, about learners and language. In this chapter, we have a bonus with two additional tables that show the findings of published applications of two middle-level theories. Second, we highlight low-level teacher theories by portraying classroom artifacts through a teacher case study—that of learner cooperation and noncooperation. When learners come to classrooms, they have expectations about the course content (the language). They may have many reasons for resisting instruction or going along with what occurs in a second language course (Huang 2018). We think their expectations of the course content are part of that, and that the middle-level theories we describe in this chapter are relevant. Our case study introduces Anna, a novice Chinese foreign language teacher at a college. Our theory area of learner expectations, then, is experienced by Anna as learner cooperation and noncooperation. We outline Anna's low-level theories in two aspects. One is relevant to her own conception of language as a second language learner. She has studied English as a foreign language for many years and has an undergraduate degree in English language teaching. The second aspect is how she responds to her new professional role as a teacher of Chinese, her native language. We finish with reflective project ideas for readers to probe important concepts from the chapter.

How the High Middle Low Theory Model Applies to Theories of Learners and Language

We return briefly here to a significant theme we explored in Chapter 4, that of language seen as form, and language seen as use. We argue that both views, or treatments of language, are powerful traditions in second language education. These views of language form a context for the middle- and low-level theories we describe in this chapter.

Language Seen as Form

In the tradition of language as form, language is seen as a formal system, made up of sounds, vocabulary, phrases, sentences, and writing systems. The forms of language are treated as the course content and appear as such in course syllabuses. One example is a Chinese 1010 course ("Elementary Chinese") at the University of North Texas (retrieved December 8, 2020, from: https://facultyinfo.unt.edu/faculty-profile?query=Nanxi+Mengandt ype=nameandprofile=nm0330). For instance, in the Chinese 1010 course, the first seven lessons are taken up in "Phonetic Symbols" and "Useful Chinese Expressions." Following lessons are taken up in "Introduction to Chinese Writing," "Vocab and Characters," and "Text and Grammar." One lesson is taken up with "Compound Finals and Tones" (pronunciation) and other lessons are taken up with "Writing and Grammar."

Quizzes and "Unit Tests" for Chinese 1010 focus on "vocabulary," and "grammar," and the skills of "listening comprehension," "writing," and "reading." The mention of skills suggests a Proficiency orientation, in which learning vocabulary and grammar and pronunciation are seen as support skills for listening, reading, or writing (see Chapter 4; and Liskin-Gasparro 2003: 484). This suggests a view of language as use. Oral tests do take place in Chinese 1010. The syllabus also mentions that learners must hand in student-recorded dialogs as homework. Nonetheless, speaking is not mentioned in the daily course schedule and does not appear consistently as course content. Further, in the course outcomes, speaking is posed as a recitation of "short daily conversations in Chinese with memorized phrases and sentences." Arguably, then, the course focuses on language as form. Scrimgeour and Wilson (2009: 1) describe a Chinese language teaching foundation-generated curriculum in which "the document focuses primarily on presenting language as a code," "code" meaning "form." As a result of experiencing a course that focuses on form, learners may come to expect that knowledge of certain forms, and accuracy with them in minimal contexts such as single words and sentences, is what comprises second language study. Quizzes and tests that focus primarily on language as forms in minimal contexts may underscore that for learners (Moloney and Xu 2015).

Language Seen as Use

In a tradition where language is seen as use, the course content would be comprised of what learners do socially and cognitively with the second language (see the high-level theories of Communicative Competence and Proficiency; Chapter 4). One of the more recognizable content features of this tradition would be communicative functions, such as: (1) buying a train ticket from a ticket machine or a person at a train station; (2) ordering lunch at a restaurant; (3) following directions for making a pot of tea or a light snack; or (4) asking questions and trading opinions about a song or a poem. A course syllabus written in this tradition would name communicative functions, or perhaps situations ("first day at school" or "meeting friends") in which learners would use the second language to do things. Learners would be seen primarily as language users making and interpreting meaning (Swaffar and Arens 2005).

It is true that learners need to learn the forms of the second language, such as vocabulary, grammatical structures, pronunciation, and writing systems. It is likely these aspects of language will be mentioned in a course syllabus written in a tradition of language use, but they will not comprise the primary content of the course. Many textbooks follow a blended syllabus—the table of contents of a textbook is in effect a syllabus. Blended syllabus textbooks will have chapter headings and chapter activities that are posed as communicative functions or situations, with language forms being listed underneath as secondary or support content. In a language use-focused course with a blended syllabus, one activity might have learners hearing a recorded conversation or radio announcement and figuring out who is talking and what they are talking about. Learners might then listen additional times, noting new details, and/or noting the language forms they hear and perhaps inducing the rules of the forms' use in that particular text. But blended textbook syllabuses, and course syllabuses, can go another way and become form-focused. In a form-focused course, grammatical structures and vocabulary that are posed as supports for communicative functions can easily become the primary content of the course (Griffee 2012b). The communicative functions themselves might be reduced to two- or three-sentence dialogs, for learners to memorize and be tested on. See Chapter 4 on persistence of language seen as a system of forms.

Final to this brief section, the use of syllabuses for illustrative purposes here is not accidental. Syllabuses are "an important course communication tool," or even an operator's manual between teacher and student (Rumore 2016). A syllabus (called "course handbook" or "course guide" outside the United States) contains information that promotes student success and enhances learner communication with instructors (Calhoon and Becker 2008: 1). We think that learners pay attention to course syllabuses, even if they pay more attention to some syllabus parts (grading and absence policies) than others (Calhoon and Becker 2008). We will return to the topic of language course syllabuses in Chapter 9 on "Theories of Language and Institutions." Anna has been given a blended syllabus and a blended syllabus–type textbook to teach from.

Middle-Level Theories for Language and Learners

The theory area for this chapter is learner expectations (see also Chapter 5). We will explore learner expectations through Folk Linguistics and Knowledge about Language (KAL). These are middle-level theories as they are public and discussed in journals and at conferences and because they are concerned with specific domains of interest. In the case of Folk Linguistics, the domain of interest is what nonlinguists ("the folk") think and say about language, primarily about their everyday experiences with language that are available to conscious notice (Niedzielski and Preston 2003). It is relevant to what learners already believe about language, simply as language users and members of society, before they set foot in a second language classroom. In the case of KAL, the domain of interest is helping primary- and secondary-level students to become good communicators, usually through explicit instruction about the first language (grammar, lexis, phonology, levels of politeness, written versus spoken language, narrative or persuasive genres in written texts) (Constantinou 2019; Hawkins 2005). Some learners have taken second language classes, resulting in KAL with an emphasis on grammar, lexis, and morphology (Mitchell, Brumfit, and Cooper 1994; Roehr 2007). KAL is relevant in that while learners have a working relationship with their first languages as use, they may instead approach their second language as form in educational settings.

Learner Expectations

When learners first arrive at a college class for German or a post-secondary intensive program for English as a second language, they do not arrive as empty cups. They have expectations, even if unconscious, about the course content (language). They already have a first language, and they have a knowledge base of both schooled and unschooled concepts about language. They may have positive or negative responses to a particular language or to a language variety within their own first language (Montgomery and Beal 2011; Taylor and Marsden 2014). Learners also have expectations for academic settings (Lutz 1990; Tolman, Sechler, and Smart 2017). They know about course grades, and they may have formed some successful and unsuccessful approaches for getting a grade (Ivins, Copenhaver, and Koclanes 2017; Glick-Cuenot 2014). And once they have had experiences in a second or foreign language course, they have formed expectations about the course content (the second language), namely, about what aspects of language to spend time and energy on. Learners' expectations about language and language classrooms will have an impact on second language teachers as we will find with Anna, our Mandarin Chinese language teacher.

Folk Linguistics

Linguistics as a field seeks to apply science to build descriptions of the structure of languages. As Hoenigswald (1966: 20) stated, linguistics is the study of "what goes on" in language. Folk Linguistics is a subfield of linguistics and has its beginning in the 1960s at a linguistics conference where a presenter, Henry Hoenigswald, suggested that language users have views about their own language, their own speech community, and languages in general, and that these views ought to be sought and studied as data in their own right. Hoenigswald's use of the term "folk" simply meant users of language (ordinary people) who were not trained linguists. It was not meant that "the folk" are "ignorant, uneducated," or "backward" (Niedzielski and Preston 2003: xviii). Specifically, Hoenigswald (1966: 20) proposed: "We should be interested not only in (a) what goes on (language), but also in (b) how people react to what goes on (they are persuaded, they are put off, etc.) and in (c) what people say goes on (talk concerning language)." The account given by Hoenigswald is unusual in that the responses of his audience, themselves linguists, are reported. One attendee named Garvin said that folk commentary on language could be a means of linguists investigating themselves: To what extent do linguists themselves have unexamined folk beliefs about the language they are trying to explain? Yet another attendee, Ferguson, actually referred to "people who are in Applied Linguistics jobs" (21). He or she asked, should not they be aware of peoples' attitudes about a language so they can better plan education programs? We think our chapter here implies this very question and thus forms the basis for some of our Reflective Projects at the end.

Hoenigswald's proposal was controversial then and remains so today (Montgomery and Beal 2011). According to Trask (2007), some within mainstream linguistics see little value in asking nonlinguists about language. Such persons' knowledge about language is "minimal" and not aligned with what linguists wish to know about language (Preston 2005: 3). Further, many linguistic forms or usages are not noticed by language users themselves because they are focused on communicating meaning (11). In other words, their knowledge is use-based, or implicit. Of concern to linguists is that folk beliefs about language might be more than "innocent misunderstandings of language"—some folk beliefs can reveal "the bases of prejudice" of speakers of one variety of a language against speakers of another variety of that language, or against speakers of another language altogether (Niedzielski and Preston 2003: 1). An example of an "innocent misunderstanding" might be English speaker folks' negative reaction to a television newscaster saying, "Good night from Barbara and me" (305). Even though this construction is grammatically correct, one folk belief is that the newscaster ought to say "Good night from Barbara and I" because "I" sounds more polite. In this case, the grammatically incorrect version is a powerful convention in

Table 7.1 What Folk Linguistics Posits

1. Data collected from folk (nonlinguists) about their reactions to, and beliefs about, language provides insights on the structure of language, the uses of language in a speech community, and of languages in general.
2. Folk have variable levels of awareness of language and of their own language use.
3. Data on folk beliefs about language may reveal innocent misunderstandings of language or sources of prejudice toward speakers of different varieties of a language or toward speakers of another language.
4. Folks' beliefs about language may create a perceived reality that is unrelated to the actual facts of a language.

Source: Authors.

spoken American English. An example of a possible prejudice comes from the account of a Japanese linguist whose informant told her that Americans, as conversationists, diverged from her prescription (her expectations) of proper language. Americans were "insensitive" and did not think about "the needs of the interlocutor" (ix). Other examples are the beliefs of some folk that their own language is more "musical" or "logical" than other languages. Trask (2007: 92) notes: "Such beliefs rarely bear any resemblance to reality, except insofar as those beliefs *create* that reality" (original emphasis). See Table 7.1 for what Folk Linguistics posits.

How Folk Linguistics Was Studied by One Research Team

In the late 1980s, American linguists Nancy Niedzielski and Dennis Preston created an interview protocol, which is a list of questions with instructions on how to conduct an interview (see Griffee and Gorsuch [2016] on data collection protocols). They then supervised eleven linguistics graduate students, called "field workers" in the tradition of linguistics, to carry out interviews of sixty-eight adult respondents. Respondents were both male and female and "comprised a demographically diverse group" living in southeastern Michigan in the United States (Niedzielski and Preston 2003: 33). They came from multiple speech communities and ethnic groups. Some of the respondents had learned second languages but none were trained linguists. Thus, they were "folk."

Prompted by the interview questions, respondents commented on a wide range of topics. Two themes were: the first language and education, and first and second language learning. In terms of the first language and education, respondents were overwhelmingly concerned about "literacy," where the term seemed to mean the abilities of "reading, writing and spelling" taken together (Niedzielski and Preston 2003: 222). The ability to read seemed to respondents to depend on good spelling and thus "a knowledge of the 'sound values' of the letters" (222). Further, respondents believed that schools and family were responsible for ensuring young people could speak some version of "standard" English, even though respondents could not themselves remember any specific instructional techniques used in school to learn standard English. The price for not being able to speak or write standard English was high—many informants in the study associated "intelligence and standard English usage" (259). And, even though being able to use some standard form of English was highly regarded, informants seemed to take it as established fact "that many speakers control several varieties [of English]" that they could use according to the social situation (154). One informant told her field worker that she developed a conscious awareness of her own "variety shifting" while quite young (155).

Informants had much to say about first and second language learning. As folk (nonlinguists), they believed that first language learning happened "naturally" by children copying the language they heard adults speak. It was recognized that children could say "wild things" and make up their own sentences, but even then, some informants believed that children's "sentences (i.e., the structure patterns) are completely provided by the adult model" (Niedzielski and Preston 2003: 204). The researchers found that all respondents used phrases like children "pick it [language] up," with the implication that "the process is a natural one, perhaps even [an] effortless one" (204). Discussions in linguistics then current about innateness versus learnedness, which consumed scholars in the field, mattered not at all to informants. They were entirely unaware of the discussion. And, informants once again stressed the value of children learning "proper" language. If they did so, children would be "acquiring societal values as they acquire language" (209).

Informants' talk about second language learning was in contrast to their notions that a first language is learned naturally and effortlessly. When commenting on second language learning, informants had a "surprising level of concern . . . for linguistic structure in language learning" (Niedzielski and Preston 2003: 243). Some informants believed that learning pronunciation or sentence structure or morphology was easier in some foreign languages because a given language was "simpler" in that regard, or uniform, or "systematic" (246, 248). German, for instance, was hard to learn to pronounce because "they gurgle when they talk" (243), whereas Spanish pronunciation is easy to learn due to its "uniformity" (246). At the same time, one informant said that English was hard to learn as a foreign language because it is a "mish-mash of languages and seems to have only exceptions rather than rules" (248). In contrast, German was easier to learn overall than French because it is more "systematic," with the informants perhaps referring to sentence structure (248). Informants believed that a foreign language learned in a classroom was not "real" and would not result in communicative ability because only naturalistic learning promoted "learning and retention" (249). In the same vein, some informants believed that classroom learning would not be motivating to second language learners and that "without proper motivation, learning is doomed" (246). Finally, some informants believed that some people simply have a "talent" for second language learning (258), which underscores an overall respect on the part of respondents to the idea that the best language learning is "natural" learning (250). We point out here that we cannot state what Niedzielski and Preston (2003) have posited. There were not creating a theory. Rather, they were reporting results of their study into the Folk Linguistic beliefs of a group of English speakers at a particular point in time. They followed a theory to design their study. For instance, we note they designed a questionnaire based on theory so they could systematically collect data on linguistics topics of interest to them.

The Chinese language teacher in our case study, Anna, feels challenged when her students ask constant questions about language "rules" that take up precious class time. Then, they seem slow and resistant when she wants them to practice oral dialogs yet again, which is what Anna thinks her supervisor wants her to do.

Knowledge about Language

What is called "language arts" in the United States, *Yu Wen* (language and literature) in China, and *Guo Wen* (national language and literature) in Taiwan has long been a feature of primary and secondary education in most countries of the world. Constantinou (2019: 496) analyzed high stakes school exams in the United Kingdom, finding that exams from as early as 1867 required test candidates to read poetry passages aloud and to show mastery of "the rudiments of English grammar, including the analysis of sentences." In essence, language arts classes teach students' own first languages to them so they may learn some standard written and spoken form of their own language (Constantinou 2019). As an example of such course content, sixth grade students in Texas learn to "edit drafts using standard English conventions, including complete complex sentences" and learn English vocabulary by determining "the meaning, syllabification, pronunciation, word origin and part of speech [of words]" (Texas Education Agency 2020). The state of Ohio states that by learning about their own first language, children can "build a foundation for college and career readiness" and be able to read texts "of exceptional craft and thought whose range extends across genres, cultures, and centuries" (Ohio Department of Education 2017: 9).

While language arts classes have a long history, the term "Knowledge about Language" is more recent and can be defined as formal educational content that seeks to move young speakers' implicit knowledge of a first language (knowledge that is used without much awareness) to more "explicit understandings of language" where children can consciously talk about forms and uses of language (Mitchell, Brumfit, and Cooper 1994: 184; see also Andrews 2007; Hawkins 2005). By being schooled through "classroom talk about language" (metalanguage) (Mitchell, Brumfit, and Cooper 1994: 184), learners would be empowered by becoming more aware of "the social meaning of language variation and diversity" and how language functions as a system of forms and meanings (186). Generally, scholars working with KAL are concerned with whether *teachers* of language arts and of second languages have sufficient KAL to help learners develop KAL through metatalk and lessons (Andrews and McNeill 2005; Denham and Lobeck 2009; Fox 1993; Mitchell, Brumfit, and Cooper 1994; Wong 2010). But there remains sustained interest in *learners'* first language KAL and finding methods to develop it (for a US account, see Honda, O'Neil, and Pippin 2009; for a UK account, see Mitchell, Brumfit, and Cooper 1994; for an account from the Netherlands, see Van Rijt, Wijnands, and Coppen 2020). Mitchell, Brumfit, and Cooper (1994) also studied secondary-level second language learners' KAL, partly as a means of comparing learners' KAL in English, their first language, to their KAL as cultivated in French, German, and Spanish foreign language classes. The findings of the study are described below as an application of one KAL theoretical model.

One Theoretical Model of KAL

With the theorizing of language competence by Chomsky (1965), and ensuing discussion and theorizing by Hymes (1972) and others, Communicative Competence has had an influence on the theorization of KAL in first language education (Constantinou 2019), generally broadening a conceptualization of KAL from students being taught "sentence-level grammar" and "clause analysis" to putting greater emphasis on the "workings of whole texts and discourse genres" (Mitchell, Brumfit, and Cooper 1994: 186). Mitchell, Brumfit, and Cooper reported on LINC, a British-based language arts curriculum reform (187). LINC modeled KAL as having five components: (1) knowledge of language variety (between speech and writing; of accents and dialects; of functions, styles, and registers in speech and writing; variety in and connections between languages), (2) knowledge of language and society (speaker/listener, reader/writer relationships, for both interpersonal and mass use of language, with particular reference to the ways in which social power is determined by language use), (3) knowledge of language acquisition and development, (4) knowledge of the history of languages, and (5) knowledge of language as a system (vocabulary; grammar; phonology and graphology, including spelling patterns and scripts; textual organization and conventions; semantics—the sharing or mismatching of meaning between users). See Table 7.2 for what KAL posits.

Table 7.2 What Knowledge about Language (KAL) Posits

1. Young learners in formal K-12 schooling settings need to be taught their own first languages so they may use standard written and spoken forms of their language.
2. The goal of KAL instruction is to move learners from an implicit knowledge (unconscious knowledge) of their first language to explicit knowledge and awareness (knowledge available for comment).
3. KAL instruction takes place throughout learners' primary and secondary educations.
4. Conceptualization of KAL has expanded over time from building prescriptive knowledge of clause and sentence-level language to building awareness of language features in longer texts and broader societal contexts.
5. KAL is applicable to first language learners and teachers, and to second language learners and teachers.
6. One means of KAL learning in learners is having teachers use metalanguage (talk about language).
7. KAL has been theorized as having five components—knowledge of language variety, language and society, language acquisition, history of languages, and language as a system.

Source: Authors.

How Knowledge about Language Was Studied by One Research Team

In the early 1990s, Mitchell and her coauthors observed English schoolchildren's first language classes and their French, German, or Spanish foreign language classes. Classes were mixed ability and comprised multiple levels of experience in formal first and second language education classes. Classroom observations of KAL-related episodes were coded according to the five components of KAL described above, such as metatalk or activities on language variety, for example (Mitchell, Brumfit, and Cooper 1994: 190). Apart from class, and for research purposes, the children, aged eleven to sixteen, worked in small groups to do a series of problem-solving and discussion tasks. The tasks probed learners' KAL in terms of the five-component model described above. For instance, to probe learners' knowledge of language as a system, they were asked to unscramble "jumbled texts" and create sentences from "nonsense words" (198). To probe learners' knowledge of language variety, learners were asked to discuss "speech styles in English" (200) (how speakers of a language would vary what they said according to who they were talking to, and for what reason). One notable feature of Mitchell, Brumfit, and Cooper's research was that learners' KAL of their first language and a second language could be compared.

In classroom observations, there were striking differences in how KAL was treated. First language teachers focused on some, but not all, components of the KAL Model, using primarily longer written texts. In terms of language variation according to use, first language teachers asked learners to examine "the distinctive characteristics of language genres, literary and non-literary" (Mitchell, Brumfit, and Cooper 1994: 197). One teacher worked with a passage by Charles Dickens and drew learners' attention to the techniques the author used to give a descriptive account of an event. In contrast, second language teachers focused primarily on the KAL component of language as a system, and further did so "at the sentence level or below" (197). For instance, foreign language teachers taught learners metalinguistic terms such as subject, verb, and complement before giving examples of sentence-level language. Teachers would give explanations in English of the grammatical point and offered inductive-type activities where learners were shown a grammatical form and then asked "to formulate a grammatical point" (193).

Learners' problem-solving task talk with the research team suggested their first and second language KAL were different. In terms of the KAL component of language as a system, learners were quickly able to complete first language sentence-level tasks such as the sentence jumble but were then unable to explain the reasons for their decisions, suggesting strong implicit knowledge but weak explicit knowledge. This held true for learners' interactions with longer texts in the first language. They could explain generally that paragraphs were needed and that longer written texts required appropriate spelling and punctuation. Thus, learners had limited metalanguage (explicit KAL) with which to explain their first language. In terms of learners' second language, they demonstrated slightly more explicit KAL knowledge. Learners could use metalinguistic terms such as "tense, gender and number" with word- and sentence-level language tasks (Mitchell, Brumfit, and Cooper 1994: 198), although their descriptions of the grammatical rules were not detailed. The treatment of sentence-level language found in second language classroom observations was reflected in what learners could say in the small group tasks. Not surprisingly, a number of students in researchers' small group discussions said they had increased their understanding of "how sentences are put together" due to their French, German, or Spanish class experiences (198). Roehr (2007), a second language researcher, found that college-level learners of German in their fourth year did better on a test of sentence-level metalinguistic knowledge (explicit KAL) than learners in their first year. This suggests that the second language learners in Roehr's study had similar classroom experiences as second language learners in Mitchell, Brumfit, and Cooper's study. If second language teachers focus on sentence-level grammar and use metalanguage to describe a language's grammatical system, learners' explicit knowledge of KAL on those limited aspects of language may be developed.

For the KAL component on language variation, researchers found that learners had good "analytic ability" on first language speech styles (Mitchell, Brumfit, and Cooper 1994: 200). They seemed able to discuss specifics of "social variation in spoken English" (200). They could talk at length about their own speech practices in different settings and with different conversation partners. Learners' ability to talk about first language variation in written texts was less developed. They could differentiate between text genres but could not pick out features of the texts that marked them as particular genres. Learner data on second languages for the KAL component on language variation were not reported.

Finally, for the KAL component of language acquisition, learners closely connected what they could say about language learning processes to what they experienced in first and second language classrooms. They were able to comment that they found some classroom activities helpful for learning, and some teachers effective. However, they could not describe how their classroom experiences, or how their teachers developed their first and second languages. Learners were slightly more specific on their engagement in second language classes, saying that "systematic practice focusing on relatively 'micro' aspects of the language system (word lists, verb morphology, etcetera) was necessary for success" (Mitchell, Brumfit, and Cooper 1994: 199).

Our Chinese teacher Anna reluctantly bows to her students' demands to explain more about the "rules" of Chinese. But as will be seen Anna has a hard time explaining things about her own first language.

Low-Level Theories Concerning Language and Learners: A Chinese Teacher

This chapter identifies and describes low-level theories about language and learners held by a novice Chinese language teacher named Anna. First is a description of Anna's background, including her own second language learning experiences with English. Then, Anna's first semester as a teacher will be portrayed, focusing on her observations of and reactions to instances of learner cooperation and noncooperation. Finally, Anna's low-level working theories about language and learners will be identified in two tables: one is theories of language and learners in terms of Anna's own language learning experiences, and another is theories of language and learners in terms of Anna's beginning Chinese language students. Two tables are included because Anna is at a dynamic nexus in her professional life. She is at once a second language learner with a lot of recent formal education and a high degree of attainment, and at the same time a novice teacher of her first language for which she never had formal preparation.

Anna's Background

Anna is twenty-three years old, from Taiwan, and newly graduated from a university in Taipei where she majored in English language education. She wants to live abroad. Perhaps after a few years she can return to Taiwan to be a junior high school English teacher. She is qualified to do so by her undergraduate degree, for which she took classes in English grammar, English "expression" (translation), and test preparation for the General English Proficiency Test (Language Training and Testing Center 2016). Her final year included a combined teaching methods and teaching internship course. Anna and four classmates observed their supervisor teach English grammar to classes with forty-five fifteen-year-olds. The textbook was the same one Anna had used in high school, although updated with dialogs, some new oral picture description activities, and listening passages. But the same grammar points were covered. Anna remembers one listening exercise from her internship where the supervising teacher played a long passage of a girl telling a story. The supervising teacher made some changes, though. He played only one sentence at a time, while students wrote down missing words on a work sheet, as in:

I didn't want to read that book because I _____ _____ it before.

The missing words were *had read*. Students checked their answers. The supervisor then announced verb tense changes in the sentences and students had to make adjustments to the rest of the sentence, as in:

I don't want to read that book because I _____ _____ it before.

The missing words then became *have read*. Then, the supervisor played the next sentence of the girl's spoken story. He explained to Anna that the technique was good for showing how words change "according to context." The larger context presented by the listening passage as a narrative text was ignored.

Anna asked the supervising teacher how they might teach the new textbook pages on listening and picture descriptions, and he told her they *had* just worked on listening, with the single sentences, missing words, and changed verb tenses. The picture descriptions could be done later, "maybe if we have time," the teacher said. "The main thing you have to learn is how to teach grammar." Anna sighed. Grammar was never her thing. But Anna could almost see, and list, the vocabulary items from the high school textbook chapter by memory even seven years later. When she herself was fifteen, she spent a lot of time with vocabulary. She enjoyed it and found that memorizing and translating words and phrasal verbs such as *outtake* and *insist on* into Chinese (Chung 2006: 40) prepared her to do well on tests and quizzes.

Anna Arrives in the United States to Teach Chinese

Anna's college teacher tells her about a master's degree in applied linguistics in the United States. She explains that she can teach Chinese to US college students while she gets her degree. "It's not English, and a little out of your training, but still, it's your native language. It'll be easy for you to teach. You'll still get something out of it," she tells Anna. Anna would be abroad for two years. Anna applies to the university and is accepted. Upon arrival at the school, she takes a required three-week "workshop" just before the start of the new academic year. She and her classmates mostly talk about "good teaching" in small groups, and they teach ten-minute simulated lessons to each other. They give each other feedback on their pronunciation. Even though Anna is going to teach Mandarin Chinese, when her turn comes to teach a lesson, she teaches some tips for learning English vocabulary. Her talk boils down to memorizing words by saying aloud the English words and the Chinese equivalents, writing them in new sentences, and making her own English-Chinese flashcards.

As the workshop comes to an end, Anna is getting nervous. What will her students be like? And what is she going to teach? Has a textbook already been chosen? She hopes so. She has no idea what to teach about Chinese. She has taken many years of *Guo Wen* courses, but she hardly remembers them. She never had to think about Chinese the way she had to think about English. Even if she could remember, would it help her teach Chinese to foreigners? She is not sure. Anna finally hears from her supervisor. They agree to meet. At the meeting, which is just five days before classes begin, Anna meets another Chinese instructor. She is from China and is a second-year applied linguistics student. "Just call me Elizabeth," she tells Anna.

Anna's Teaching Situation and Her Students

Anna and Elizabeth's supervisor is a female applied linguistics faculty member who does not know Chinese. She hands Anna a textbook, a workbook, and a syllabus. Anna is greatly relieved. Now she has a textbook to work from! Classes meet five times per week, and Anna will have twenty-two beginning students in her class. "We want you to use Chinese as much as possible," the supervisor says. "Just keep repeating yourself and use actions to show what you want. Students should mostly be using Chinese in class. They study the grammar points and vocabulary in the textbook before they come to class. Class time is for using Chinese. Try not to use class time for explaining grammar." Anna studies the syllabus. It seems the first two weeks of classes are taken up with teaching *pinyin* and Chinese pronunciation. The *pinyin* surprises her as they do not use it in Taiwan; children just go straight to learning to read and write Chinese characters. But in China, she remembers, children learn *pinyin*, which is a Romanized alphabetic writing system to help in sounding out Chinese characters. Anna quickly learns *pinyin*, and she plans five days of lessons where students get quizzed on *pinyin* characters and practice writing out words and then saying the words aloud using the correct Chinese tones, which are indicated by small accent marks and shapes above the Romanized letters. Perhaps, then, *pinyin* is helpful for learning pronunciation.

Anna's students are a mixed group—half are male and half female. Most are first- or second-year undergraduates. A few have taken high school French or Spanish, but for most of them Chinese is their first foreign language. They are nineteen or twenty years old mostly, and a few talk to Anna enthusiastically about wanting to travel to China (not Taiwan, Anna notes). "Did you think there might be a study abroad program for Chinese?" asks one girl. "This class will be OK for basics, but I want to learn Chinese naturally," says another. A few of the boys ask her if they will study Chinese writing. "It looks so cool," one young man tells her. Through all this, Anna's own second language, English, is being stretched to the limit. The kids all talk so fast. Nonetheless, she does her best to explain to the students they need to study *pinyin* and the pronunciation explanations before they come to class. They need to be prepared to practice what Anna calls "oral drills" when they come to class.

At students' request, Anna spends a few minutes showing the *pinyin* in the workbook. Students asks her to pronounce *pinyin* words from the page, and she does so, saying each word once. Students make repeated requests to hear the words again, and ask about word meanings, but Anna tells them they should use the textbook website to hear the words more and practice on their own. Learning *pinyin* is kind of a waste of time anyway, she thinks. The quicker they can move on to Chinese characters, the better. Then she and the students can talk about word meanings. Perhaps if they know a lot of vocabulary, they will have an easier time figuring out the grammar of sentences on their own. Anna has a feeling, though, they will still want explanations of grammar. She is worried about that. She begins reading the textbook sections explaining Chinese grammar. But for every rule she reads, she can think of exceptions. Will not those be hard to explain? Anna starts out with twenty-two students, but by the end of the second week that number is down to seventeen.

Anna's Observations of Learners and Her Responses to Them

The first two weeks go well, Anna thinks. She is uncomfortable seeing students' puzzled faces when she speaks only Chinese, but she gets better at using actions to show learners what she wants. A few students try repeating her classroom instructions verbally and mimicking her actions in their chairs. Anna, intent to move class forward, just gives the next set of instructions.

After a few days of this, one student asks in English "Could you write down what you're saying in *pinyin?*" Anna nods her head, saying in Chinese, "At the end of class if we have time," and tapping her watch. She forgets to do it at the end of class and there is no time, anyway. The next class, a French class, comes in the door right when she finishes. One female student who has been waiting for Anna to write down her classroom commands, slaps down her notebook in annoyance. A few students laugh.

Elizabeth helps Anna make some *pinyin* quizzes. Students take the quizzes, which focus on single words, and Anna returns them the next day with each mistake circled carefully. At the end of the two weeks, Anna has the idea to spend some of a class going over the last quiz. A few learners have asked her how they can succeed in class. "Chinese is just so hard," one says. So, Anna thinks the students will like her plan to go over the quiz. They can check their own progress. She has learners pronounce the words from their corrected quiz papers and demonstrates what the words sound like with the wrong spelling or tone marks. She uses a little English, and then there is a flood of questions from learners. "What's this word mean?" one female student asks, pointing at a word. As students' questions continue to pour in, Anna answers in English, and she is surprised to see that an entire class period has gone by. She is not sure if students have gotten the message that practicing and focusing on quizzes will help them get a good grade.

In the following month, the class begins studying later chapters in the textbook. The class syllabus only says "Chapter 2" or "Chapter 3" for a given week. But when you look at "Chapter 3" in the textbook, there are pages and pages of things to do. There are two pages of grammar explanations in English, and a list of vocabulary, in English and in *pinyin*, that students are supposed to learn before class. Then there is a listening passage and a dialog in *pinyin* to do on the topic of "Getting to School." It is about two foreign exchange students going to their first Chinese language class at a school in southern China. Then there are two pages where learners are supposed to put their pre-studied vocabulary into the dialog and replace some of the words in the dialog and then practice saying the "new" dialog. Then there are five more things to do like learning new Chinese characters that are embedded into yet another dialog. Learners are then supposed to practice writing the new Chinese characters on their own.

A number of these things create problems in class, Anna thinks. First, students are supposed to know the grammar points and the vocabulary lists for when they come to class to practice using the dialogs. This very point is causing conflict. It seems the students still have questions about grammar and they want to ask questions about it. Anna directs them back to the book. The explanations in the book are supposed to be complete. They should be enough. When she does this, there is a wall of noise. Students move their chairs and begin talking all at once. When Anna calls them together to begin practicing another oral dialog, students seem slow to respond and keep talking to each other in English. At the end of one class, a student asks,

"How are we going to be tested? Are you just going to give us sentences to complete, or something?" The student next to the first student asks, "Will we be tested on all the grammar points, or just some of them?" Anna replies that students ought to know all the grammar points and vocabulary and that if they try, and work at it every day, they will master them. The second student says, "Oh."

Second, the listening passage is deeply puzzling to Anna. It seems long, and even though it contains some of the grammar points and vocabulary introduced in the chapter, there are some new, unknown words and sentences. Anna thinks it is too hard for beginners and too much of the language code to process in detail. There are some colloquial phrases used by a bus driver that are not "standard" Chinese. If Anna plays the listening passage line by line, students will just have more questions, and it will take too long. So, she just plays it all the way through. She pays little attention to the textbook questions on the passage, which really are simple. They just ask students to identify how many speakers there are, and where the speakers are and what they are trying to do and whether they succeed. There is even a question for students to identify and write down any words or expressions they have not heard before. A few students have already listened to the passage and answered the questions. One raises his hand and asks if he can confirm his answers. Would Anna say what the correct answers are? Anna wants to move on to other things, but she relents and simply asks students to quickly get together in pairs and check their answers together. Another student asks if they can hear the listening passage again. Anna has already logged off the website with the listening passage, but with a sigh she reopens it and plays the listening passage again. She wants to get to the dialogs, and so when another student asks to hear the passage one more time, she looks at her watch and tells the student he needs to do it at home. He says, "Okay, but will there be something like this on the test?" Anna is not sure. Her supervisor has not shown her the test yet. Anna cannot imagine having students listen to a long passage on a test and then answering simple questions on meaning that might have ambiguous answers. How will that help to know whether the learners have mastered the course content?

Third, it looks to Anna like learners are supposed to mostly recite memorized dialogs in class. And so they do. Anna coaches learners to say the dialogs exactly right with the correct tones. Sometimes they get it right and sometimes they do not. Some students seem to pay close attention and work quite hard at it. Others seem to get frustrated when they forget a word or say the wrong tone. So students can see more progress with their work, Anna creates a new scoring sheet where she grades learners' pronunciation of tones, whether they use the expected words, and whether they spoke the words in correct order. She gives students their scores at the end of each week. Some students look at their scores, but others just put them in their backpacks without looking at them. Anna finds some of them thrown in the garbage at the building entrance.

Finally, some of the students ask questions about what they should say in different situations. They have noticed in the listening passages that some of the characters are using colloquial phrases. Learners think one of the phrases is a greeting, but they are not sure. They want to know what this or that phrase means and when they should use them. Is this greeting used with bus drivers? Shopkeepers? What about with a teacher? Anna tells the students briefly when they are used but then she says, "It's important for you to use polite Chinese. So, let's just learn it first and then the local language can come later when you have a higher level." Most of the students are quiet after such exchanges but a few students just keep asking questions anyway. When Anna invites them to visit her office hours, they do not come.

An Intervention

After the first month of classes, Anna's supervisor contacts her and they have a meeting. She shows Anna an updated attendance list. Only twelve out of twenty-two students are still enrolled. Anna had noticed fewer students were coming. She is horrified to learn that her students have complained that she is not giving them the additional explanation they need on grammatical structures. They want time to talk about vocabulary, too. And it is not clear to them, just from the dialogs they seem to practice so much, how the words and sentences could be changed for a different situation, or to mean something different. Anna is also surprised that her students are disappointed they are spending so little time in class on writing in Chinese and learning to read. Apparently, two students said that they registered for Chinese because they think the writing system is artistic and cool.

Anna's supervisor tells Anna she can put aside ten minutes at the end of each class to take learners' questions on grammar and other matters. And perhaps they can set aside one day of the week for writing and reading practice? Can students just bring their workbooks and work in them quietly, and can Anna circulate and answer questions? Anna agrees to this, and her supervisor says she will get back to Anna with a revised course syllabus to take into account the extra time that will be needed for the reading and writing workday. This sounds fine to Anna. She thinks more about what to do about the other complaints her students made. She remembers her teaching supervisor in Taiwan using a listening passage to show how to change a sentence from the passage into another sentence to change its meaning. Anna could try that, but are her students advanced enough? And the part about explaining grammar ten minutes per class? She is a bit terrified of that. Can she explain her own first language? The textbook might help a little, but students do not understand the terminology that is sometimes used: noun phrase, verb phrase, modifier, subject, and object. She knows the terms for her own learning of English, but she has no idea how to explain them to students. And is that her job? What is she going to do?

Table 7.3 What Anna Posits about Language as a Second Language Learner

1. Language is a system of forms.
2. Grammatical structures and vocabulary are the building blocks of language and the main forms of language. These then comprise the content of second language classes.
3. Learning a language is learning the grammatical structures and vocabulary of the language.
4. Longer texts such as narratives can be processed as single sentences for the purpose of instruction and learning.
5. The grammatical structures and vocabulary of a language can be memorized through a variety of means.
6. To master this body of content (the language) takes effort. Effort pays off.
7. A textbook provides the grammar and vocabulary of a language.

Source: Authors.

See Table 7.3 for Anna's low-level theories about language from her perspective as a second language (English) learner.

We do not think Anna's theory of language is simply the sum of her responses as a learner. She is now a teacher and her perspectives have changed. See Table 7.4 for what Anna posits about language and learners in her Chinese language class.

Anna still sees language as form as a novice teacher, but now the content areas of language form have expanded to include pronunciation, for example. She is gripped by shifts in her low-level theories. She is aware her students expect certain things, and some of these are further pointed out by Anna's supervisor in the intervention. We believe, however, that at this stage of her professional life, Anna is not yet informed by middle-level theories. Nonetheless, theories such as Folk Linguistics and KAL might help explain some of Anna's experiences. For instance, some of her learners describe Chinese as "artistic," and others say that classroom learning is "OK for the basics" but that "natural learning" has to be done in a country where the language is spoken. Anna has a hard time processing these unexpected ideas. But of greater concern to Anna is that her students seem to struggle with the idea that learning Chinese will take effort. What Anna observes may be expressions of learners' own unexamined Folk Linguistic ideas, which, right or wrong, may account for their expectations. As a native speaker of Chinese, Anna has her own legacy with her first language to deal with. She has strong implicit knowledge of her language, and she experiences Chinese

Table 7.4 What Anna Posits about Language and Learners in Her Chinese Language Class

1. Language forms comprise the course content.

2. What learners need to know about language is in the textbook and workbook. This is the course content.

3. What constitutes the language forms (the course content) has been expanded from grammatical structures and vocabulary to include the content areas of pronunciation and writing *pinyin* and Chinese characters. Anna struggles with how to think about and teach these content areas.

4. Learners discover the language forms (grammatical structures, vocabulary, *pinyin*, Chinese characters, etc.) on their own from the textbook and workbook. Anna wonders whether learners know they are supposed to do this.

5. To master language forms is to be accurate with them. Oral drills in class and writing practice at home are ways of increasing accuracy.

6. Course content can be graded for difficulty. This is new for Anna, and she is not sure how to "grade" language forms. But beginning learners should only be exposed to forms appropriate to their level.

7. Polite, standard language forms are most appropriate for beginning learners.

8. A good knowledge of vocabulary can assist learners' self-study of grammatical structures.

9. Learners want to know grammar rules, but they want explanations Anna is not sure how to give.

10. Unambiguous answers are best.

11. Anna is unclear how to explain grammar rules and word meanings in ways that avoid ambiguity.

12. Learners do not know terms for describing language forms, and Anna does not know how to explain the terms.

13. Anna is puzzled by learners' perception that Chinese is "artistic."

Source: Authors.

as use. This means she does not have explicit, formal knowledge of Chinese, or that she knows how to explain Chinese, which she must now learn to do as a novice language education professional. In terms of KAL, we think Anna's learners may have an uneven grasp of metalinguistic concepts that would make it easier for her to explain language as a system as she thinks she must do. And this presumes Anna knows the metalinguistic terms herself in terms of her own native language.

Reflective Projects

1. In your own words, define "learner expectations." Consider learner expectations in the context of a second language course. What kinds of things might second language learners have expectations about? Make a list. What will happen if a course is different from what learners expect? What might learners do or think? Would these actions or thoughts be positive? Or negative? Or perhaps both?

2. For point 1 above, did your list of things that learners might have expectations for include the language being studied? Based on your experience as a second language learner or teacher, what do you think learners expect of the language being learned? How do they think about the language? Do their expectations seem to have more to do with language as form? Or do their expectations seem more related to language as use?

3. What are examples from the chapter of student noncooperation? What about learner cooperation? Can you think of other examples from your own experiences as a second language learner or teacher?

    Consider now the two middle-level theories described in this chapter—Folk Linguistics and Knowledge about Language (KAL). These theories were proposed as explanations of learner expectations about language. Complete the table below.

	Explained by Folk Linguistics? How?	Explained by Knowledge about Language? How?
Examples of learner cooperation in this chapter:		
Your own examples of learner cooperation:		
Examples of learner noncooperation in this chapter:		
Your own examples of learner noncooperation:		

Use the table to assess whether the two theories provide explanations, and how much. Is there another middle-level theory that can be explored to explain learners' ideas about of the language they are learning? How might you learn more about the theory? How would you assess the theory for whether or how it explains learners and their treatment of language in classrooms?

4. Even if Folk Linguistics and Knowledge about Language explain well learners' theories or views of language, how could the theories be used to solve problems such as those Anna is experiencing?

5. If you wanted to learn more about learners' views or perceptions of language, or their Knowledge about Language, how would you go about doing it? How would you use the information?

6. Anna was surprised by her students' Folk Linguistic comments about Chinese and language learning. Are these innocent misunderstandings? How might these kinds of ideas be countered? Should they be countered?

7. The model of Knowledge about Language described in this chapter posits five areas of knowledge: language variety, language and society, language acquisition, history of languages, and language as a system. Define in your own words these areas.

Choose one area that is not typically dealt with in second language courses. How would you approach teaching students about it? What do you want students to know, and why? How might a course textbook be used as a resource?

PART THREE

Institutions

CHAPTER EIGHT

Theories of Teaching and of Learning, and Institutions

Why This Chapter?

This chapter focuses on two areas, theories of teaching and theories of learning, in interaction with institutions. By theories of teaching, we mean an explanation of how language teachers teach knowledge and skills to foreign/second language learners. As described in Chapter 2, teaching theories may be present as middle-level theory (Gravells and Simpson 2014; see also Chapter 4 on the Proficiency Movement) and/or as low-level theory (Chapters 1, 2, 4, and 9). This chapter follows up with a teacher we met briefly in Chapter 4, Felicia, a teacher of German at a university in Colorado, who has a working awareness of high-, middle-, and low-level teaching theories. By theories of learning, we mean any middle-level theory that accounts for how humans form knowledge, awareness, and competence in a second language (Larsen-Freeman 2012). In Chapter 6, middle-level theories of learning appear in teachers' thinking and practices (Noticing and Metacognition). And, as described in Chapter 7, learners and teachers alike have low-level theories about learning languages, even though the theories held by learners and those by teachers may be very different. As two distinct stakeholder groups, learners and teachers have different purposes, experiences, needs, and values.

In the present chapter, the institution is presented as yet another significant stakeholder in second language education. Administrators, as the human agents of institutions, are portrayed here as having distinct priorities and purposes. The other chapters in this book focus on theories of teaching or theories of learning or theories of language, taken as single areas in interaction with teachers, learners, or institutions. In this respect, the current chapter is a departure in that teaching and learning are taken up together. In all other respects, the structure of this chapter is the same as other chapters. We will outline how the High Middle Low Theory Model (Chapter 1) applies to institutions and theories of teaching and of learning. We do this in two ways. First, we offer a table after our high-level and middle-level theory descriptions suggesting what the theories posit, or propose. For this chapter, our high-level theory area is Evaluation (Griffee and Gorsuch 2016) and our middle-level theory is the language use description framework *Common European Framework of Reference* (*CEFR*; Council of Europe 2001, 2018). Strictly speaking, neither Evaluation nor *CEFR* prescribes anything about teaching or learning (Madaus and Stufflebeam 2000; Council of Europe 2018). But it is by viewing the institution as a unique stakeholder, a view that both Evaluation and *CEFR* affords us, that we see institutions and administrators do care about the results of teaching and learning, even if they sometimes do not seem to have overly nuanced views of how these occur (Gevara et al. 2015; Liviero 2017; see however Bush and Glover 2012).

Second, we highlight middle- and low-level theories about teaching, and about learning, by portraying local artifacts through a teacher case study. The artifacts for this chapter will be a job interview between Felicia and three stakeholders at a school, and a Course Logic model that Felicia sketched out after meeting her students and learning about an external exam that is incredibly important to many stakeholders in her new context. For, as it happens, Felicia has moved to England for one year to be near her daughter, who is attending graduate school there. Felicia is familiar with the ACTFL *Guidelines* (American Council for the Teaching of Foreign Languages 2012a), an American-based language use description framework (Chapter 4), and so *CEFR* is new to her. She gets to know it better, as she has gotten a part-time job teaching German at a secondary school in England. We finish with reflective projects for readers to probe important concepts from the chapter.

How the High Middle Low Theory Model Applies to Theories of Teaching and of Learning, and Institutions

In this chapter, we explore a high-level theory area, that of Evaluation, and a middle-level theory, that of the language description framework *CEFR* (Council of Europe 2001, 2018). Evaluation as a high-level theory area encompasses every element of an educational program, including stakeholders, learning outcomes, the curriculum (Chapter 9), and assessments (Genesee and Upshur 1996; House 1993; McDavid and Hawthorn 2006; Norris 2008; Rea-Dickins and Germaine 1998). Evaluation also potentially accounts for and documents the circumstances that make an educational program necessary and give it shape (Griffee and Gorsuch 2016; Stake 2000; Stufflebeam and Shinkfield 2007). The process of evaluation, which is to estimate the worth of any aspect of a program, is often carried out by administrators although teachers may also evaluate to great benefit (Griffee and Gorsuch 2016; Kiely and Rea-Dickins 2005) as Felicia's experiences will show. CEFR, as described in Chapter 4, is comprised of theorized and publicly available documents and websites that attempt to create a common understanding of second language ability "by having prose descriptions of learners' abilities using the language set on an intuited, continuous, linear scale" (Gorsuch 2019a: 423). CEFR is a significant element of second language education in the United Kingdom and Europe (Diez-Bedmar and Byram 2018; Figueras 2012; Leung and Lewkowicz 2013) and shapes programs and the experiences of teachers and learners alike.

Evaluation

Evaluation is a process in which information about a program is collected and interpreted to assign worth to that program, or parts of the program (Griffee and Gorsuch 2016; Kiely and Rea-Dickins 2005). Those judgments of worth are then used to make decisions (Cronbach 2000; Stufflebeam and Shinkfield 2007). Example decisions are whether to continue a program (McDavid and Hawthorn 2006), whether new materials or teaching techniques are worthwhile (Riazi and Mosalanejad 2010), whether a program is doing enough to build learners' self-efficacy (Gorsuch 2009), or whether a program needs to change its focus in accordance with new information about learners' needs (Rogers, LeCompte, and Plumly 2012).

Decisions made as a result of Evaluation can be roughly divided into two types: Summative decisions and formative decisions (Stufflebeam and Shinkfield 2007). Summative decisions are made for reasons of accountability. Summative decisions are "yes/no" in their scope: "Do we hire someone or not?" "Do we continue a program or not?" These are the types of decisions that administrators and education officers need to make. Thus, they are summative, institutional decisions. As can be seen, for the purposes of this chapter we are including people (assistant teachers, teachers, administrators, etc.) as objects of Evaluation (Donaldson 2010; Scriven 2000; see however Stufflebeam 2000). Formative decisions are made to improve, revise, or refocus (Griffee and Gorsuch 2016; Stufflebeam and Shinkfield 2007). Formative decisions might be more limited in scope and yet more detailed and constructive: "What can we do to improve the use of our existing course materials?" "Can we identify the reason why learners are not improving their listening? If so, what do we do about that?" Related to people in a school, an example would be: "What training programs are available that might support Teacher M to use more pair and group work in class?" "What are better questions to ask during interviews for prospective teachers?" While these decisions are often associated with teachers, school administrators also need to make formative-type decisions.

Evaluation as a High-Level Theory Area

We identify Evaluation as a high-level theory area for two reasons. First, Evaluation is a field in its own right, with a universe of theoretical, research, and ideological traditions. Evaluation exists outside second language education and is present in fields as diverse as nursing education, anti-poverty programs, and public health initiatives (Madaus and Stufflebeam 2000; Stufflebeam and Shinkfield 2007). Evaluation workers may be called upon to evaluate any or all of these types of programs, without necessarily being specialists in those disciplines. Rather, their specialty is Evaluation (Stufflebeam 2000). Accreditation, the official means by which an entire school will be periodically evaluated to show overall worth, is an example of such an external evaluation (Scriven [2000] called it "inspection" in England; e.g., Long, Danechi, and Loft 2020). Evaluation workers may also be specialists in the area they evaluate. For instance, second language education specialists have made good use of Evaluation traditions and models to the benefit of second language teachers, learners, courses, and programs (e.g., see Berwick 1989; Brown 1995; Kiely and Rea-Dickins 2005; Norris 2008; Zhu and Flaitz 2005). Second, Evaluation processes depend on pulling into relationship theoretical and methodological models, potentially from more than one discipline. For instance, to explain the difference in learning results between two different instructors teaching the same course, learner time on task (from psychology) must be considered in relation to middle- and low-level teaching theories (from education and second language education; Griffee and Gorsuch 2016: 20). In order to offer evidence of student learning to education officers external to a school, evidence of positive classroom and learning processes (from education) must be considered in relation to quantitative and qualitative measurement principles (from psychology and education) (Mitchell 1992).

Evaluation Models

It will help to understand the phrase "pull into relationship" by viewing two visual models of Evaluation. Recall from Chapter 1 that a visual model is simply one form, or representation, of a theory. One research tradition in Evaluation is Program Theory (Bickman 1996; Rogers 2000; Rossi, Lipsey, and Freeman 2004; see also Gorsuch [2019b] and Griffee and Gorsuch [2016] for second language education examples). In this tradition, the questions asked are: "How does a program work? How does it achieve its outcomes? Is the curriculum sufficient to support learners to achieve the

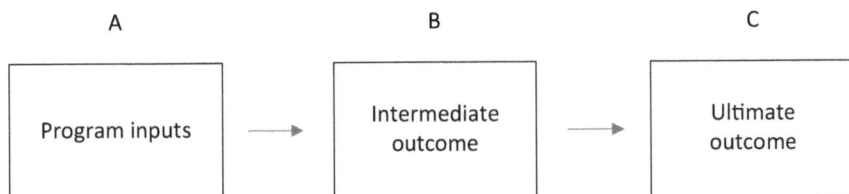

FIGURE 8.1 Simple causation model for Program Theory (adapted from Rogers 2000: 223; used with permission).

program or course outcomes?" The goal then is to define each assumption of how a program works, and then to investigate each assumption. "Is an assumption sound? Does it make sense? Is there theoretical backing for it? Is there some lack in the reasoning behind the assumption? Is the assumption a possible focus for improvement? Does something need to be revised?" To identify what to investigate, evaluators need a model (Stufflebeam and Shinkfield 2007). Thus, the first step is to make a model of assumptions that cause some effect, in other words, a causal model. See Figure 8.1 for a "simple causation model" offered by Rogers (2000). The orientation of the model is from left to right. The model posits that the program inputs (A) cause intermediate (or immediate) outcomes (B), which in turn cause ultimate outcomes (C).

An application of this model, adapted to just one aspect of a language course, can be seen in Figure 1.2 (Chapter 1) as an example of teacher theory. The teacher believes that having learners read short and easy stories and having learners answer comprehension questions and do grammar exercises in pairs (course inputs or "A" in Figure 8.1) will result in an intermediate outcome ("B") of learners spending more time on task that will in turn result in an ultimate outcome ("C") of learners getting better quiz scores. Causal models are also called Program Logic or Course Logic as such visual models seem to probe the logic or a program or course. As will be seen below, our teacher, Felicia, sketches out a Course Logic model. She finds it useful to think about her teaching ("inputs") and then to consider the effects on students' learning ("outcomes").

Here is an elaboration of the Program Theory model in Figure 8.1 from early childhood education where teachers at a school conduct home visits to their students. This model speaks to what teachers believe they do, and what school administrators believe should happen, during home visits that result in improved student learning. See Figure 8.2.

Again, the orientation is from left to right. Upon questioning teachers and administrators in the program, the evaluators constructed this causal model. The desired outcome ("C") is improved student learning in classrooms. The program input ("A") is teachers spending a moderate amount of time simply

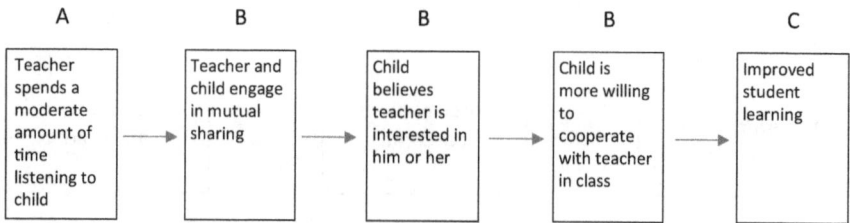

FIGURE 8.2 Program Theory of an innovation in early childhood education (adapted from Rogers 2000: 215; used with permission).

listening to the child during the home visit, rather than the teacher conducting a rigid sort of interview. The first intermediate effect of the teaching and child engaging in mutual understanding (the leftmost "B") is believed to be caused by teachers listening ("A"). That intermediate understanding is then thought to cause the child to believe the teacher is interested in him or her (the middle "B"), and so on. Any number of educational or psychological theories for both teaching and learning brought into relationship might underpin this assumed causal chain, for instance, Attachment Theory from sociology (Jarvis and Creasey 2012) and Instructor Immediacy from biology education (Cooper et al. 2017).

A second tradition in Evaluation is the use of visual models to describe relationships between functional elements of a program or course. The model is then used to focus on an evaluation study. We offer as an example the SOAC, or the Stakeholders Outcomes Assessments, and Curriculum Model (Griffee and Gevara 2011; Griffee and Gorsuch 2016). While originally designed for second language education, we argue it can be applied to any educational setting. See Figure 8.3.

The "Evaluand" component is the part of a program or course that is being evaluated and thus appears in the center of the model. Examples are a new teaching method, materials used by learners, a course scheduling plan that affects how often and for how long learners are in class, and class size. The "World" is something that makes the program necessary, such as an education system and a society that believes foreign language courses are necessary for secondary-level students. Young people need to have a competitive edge as future workers in a global economy, something in which British policymakers have had a recent and active interest (Hagger-Vaughan 2020; Jack 2021; Johnstone 2014; Long, Danechi, and Loft 2020). "Stakeholders" are "persons or groups interested in the existence and results" of a program (Griffee and Gorsuch 2016: 26; Kiely and Rea-Dickins 2005). These would be teachers, students, supervisors and administrators, parents, future employers, textbook publishers, politicians, and education authorities. The existence of stakeholders is a key concept for this chapter in that various stakeholders at the school and education authority level must

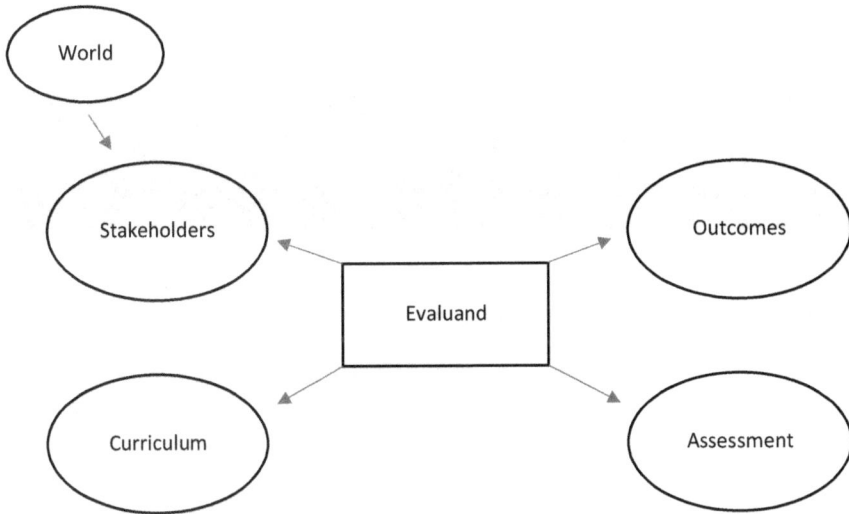

FIGURE 8.3 The SOAC (pronounced "soak") Model.

Sources: Griffee and Gevara (2011); Griffee and Gorsuch (2016).

interview Felicia and evaluate her teaching qualifications to decide whether they can hire her. "Outcomes" are learning goals and formal statements of what a course or program intends to accomplish (Stufflebeam and Shinkfield 2007). As will be seen, *CEFR* is used in Felicia's new school as a resource for discussions on outcomes. "Assessments" are tests, quizzes, questionnaires, diaries, and classroom observations that are used to determine whether learners have met course outcomes. Finally, "Curriculum" is any aspect of a program used to support learners to reach learning outcomes, including teaching, exercises, textbooks, handouts, lectures, home visits (Figure 8.2), school facilities, and relevant high-, middle-, and low-level theories used by teachers or administrators at a school (Griffee and Gorsuch 2016; see also Chapter 9 in this volume).

Any two or three of the SOAC model components, say "Outcomes" and "Stakeholders," can be drawn into relationship with each other, depending on what evaluators want to learn about the Evaluand. Which SOAC components evaluators want to bring into relationship to probe the Evaluand may depend on whether they wish to make a summative or formative decision based on what they learn. See Table 8.1.

As can be seen in Table 8.1 only when different components of a program or course are brought into relationship can a specific type of evaluation study be adequately modeled and thus focused. SOAC allows for relating different program parts to guide different evaluation studies depending on what is needed. In addition to the examples in Table 8.1, a formative evaluation study is suggested when Curriculum is brought into relation

Table 8.1 Sample Evaluation Studies Suggested by the SOAC Model

SOAC Model Components Brought into Relationship	Evaluation Study and Examples	Summative or Formative Decision
The World, Stakeholders, and Outcomes	Outcomes Validation Study *Asks*: Are the outcomes of a program or course relevant? Are they worthwhile? *How outcomes might be investigated*: Evaluator does a literature review. Evaluator does a document retrieval (syllabuses, websites, mission statements) of previous outcomes at the school. Evaluator interviews stakeholders. *Example*: A college-level Japanese language teacher probes course outcomes he inherited.	Summative and Formative (From the example: Some outcomes were dropped, some were retained, and some were revised.)
The World and Stakeholders	Needs Analysis *Asks*: What do learners need from a program or course? *How learner needs might be investigated*: Evaluator consults results of an outcomes validation study. Evaluator defines what is meant by "need." Evaluator does a literature review of published analyses of trends from the field. Evaluator interviews stakeholders and/or distributes questionnaires. *Example*: An instructor in an EFL teacher preparation program describes additional needs for grammar instruction to expand learners' (future EFL teachers) ability to read current teaching literature and resources.	Formative (From the example: Needs recast as new outcomes for the program.)

SOAC Model Components Brought into Relationship	Evaluation Study and Examples	Summative or Formative Decision
Curriculum and Outcomes	Program Logic, Course Logic *Asks*: Is the curriculum sufficient to support learners to achieve the program or course outcomes? *How curriculum might be investigated*: Evaluator makes a program or course logic model (Figures 1.2 and 8.2 in this volume). Evaluator investigates the course inputs by interviewing stakeholders, examining materials, teaching, etc. (whatever is suggested by the program logic model). *Example*: A college-level Spanish language teacher finds that three course inputs: (1) learner online preparation, (2) in-class treatments of online preparation, and (3) additional online materials are deemed sufficient by teachers but insufficient by learners to bring about an intermediate outcome of improved spoken communication (Alarcon 2018).	Formative (From the example: Evaluator suggests more reading and listening activities to be done in class, and increasing the amount of class time allotted to speaking practice.)

Source: Authors.

with Stakeholders. Test Validation (analyzing the trustworthiness and appropriateness of a test for a given program or course) is suggested when Curriculum and Assessment are brought into relation. Liviero (2017) brings into relationship Assessments (the GCSE—General Certificate of Secondary Education—examinations, a focal point of foreign language education in England), Curriculum (secondary-level teachers' grammar teaching practices), and Stakeholders (education authorities, head teachers, and teachers) to conduct a summative evaluation study. In her study, she finds that teachers do indeed teach to the test, noting that "five out of eight teachers adopted a similar approach to teaching grammar . . . providing students with ready-made sentences that satisfied exam requirements, including . . . a range of verbal tenses and/or connectives" (37–8). At the same time, this test, as Liviero suggests, does not assist learners, or teachers, to develop learners' metalinguistic knowledge. Yet building learners' metalinguistic knowledge (their ability to explain language structure and use) has been a priority of stakeholders at the national level in England since the 1990s (Liviero 2017; see also section on "Knowledge About Language" in Chapter 7).

Stakeholders

Evaluation as a theory area calls into existence the notion of stakeholders. This is important because it allows us to see a program from points of view outside our immediate concerns as teachers, which is to teach and work directly with learners. In this chapter, this means being able see teaching and learning from the point of view of the institution. This "outside" view may reveal unexpected and useful insights such as: (1) why teacher qualifications are required, (2) why administrators ask the questions that they do in teacher job interviews, (3) why some programs prefer to use (or say that they use) language use description frameworks such as the ACTFL *Guidelines* and *CEFR*, and (4) why institutions care about learner achievement, but then sometimes use assessments that do not seem of immediate value to teachers, such as large-scale, pan-program proficiency tests.

Stakeholders in an educational setting are any human actors who have an interest, or "stake," in the outcomes of learners' engagement in a school (Dunkerly and Wong 2001; Griffee and Gorsuch 2016; Stake 2000; Stufflebeam and Shinkfield 2007). Stakeholders in an institution or school are, of course, teachers, learners, and parents. Additional stakeholders of interest in this chapter are head teachers of content areas, coordinators, department chairs, deans, and principals, who make up the human face of an institution. Stakeholders external to schools but who are nonetheless responsible for supporting the educational mission are school inspectors, accreditors, local education authorities, elected school board officials, and education authorities at the county, state, or national levels (Long, Danechi, and Loft 2020). The various titles used here depend on the education level of a school (primary versus secondary versus tertiary) and the way a society or nation has organized its education system. Some stakeholders' roles are quite potent in the sense that they may value exams or other measures of school quality (learner retention, acquisition of monetary grants, etc.) with which they make summative decisions (Mitchell 1992). Later in this chapter, our case study German teacher, Felicia, will learn that stakeholders at her new school in England are deeply concerned about learners earning their GCSEs. Learner results on these tests and qualifications bring into relationship a school's curriculum and assessment (external tests) and would be used to make very broad summative-type decisions such as: Did the school measure up? Does corrective action need to be taken at a school? How can teachers be better supported so students do better on GCSE exams? Should we cut our German programs if our learners can't pass GCSE exams in that subject anyway? Such use of external exam scores is common but is also accompanied by probing criticism (Hagger-Vaughan 2020). See Table 8.2 for what Evaluation as a high-level theory area posits.

Table 8.2 What Evaluation Posits

1. Any kind of program can be evaluated.
2. Any aspect of any program can be evaluated at nearly any level of specificity.
3. Evaluation posits the existence of stakeholders.
4. Stakeholders have different interests, experiences, needs, and points of view.
5. Evaluation can benefit any stakeholder group.
6. Evaluation models (theories) are necessary to guide and focus an evaluation.
7. Some Evaluation models bring into relationship processes within a program.
8. Some Evaluation models bring into relationship program processes and stakeholders.
9. Some Evaluation models bring into relationship theories from different disciplines.
10. Some evaluations done at the institutional level are summative for reasons of accountability.

Source: Authors.

The Common European Framework of Reference

CEFR (Council of Europe 2001, 2018) is a language use description framework (Gorsuch 2019a). It is a collection of publicly available documents that applies the high-level theory of Communicative Competence to second language program and classroom planning and practice (Council of Europe 2001: 9). The three primary sources from the Council of Europe are: *Common European Framework of Reference for Languages: Learning, Teaching, Assessment* (2001) with 265 pages and *Companion Volume with New Descriptors* (2018, 2020) with 235 and 274 pages, respectively. As described in Chapter 4, language description frameworks attempt to create a common understanding of second language ability by putting descriptions of learners engaged in language use on a scale from low to high. These common understandings can be then used by stakeholders internal or external to a school to discuss foreign language education outcomes (Council of Europe 2001, 2018; Deygers et al. 2018; Figueras 2012; Lowie 2012; McLelland 2018; see however Diez-Bedmar and Byram 2019; Harsch 2018). For instance, a learner at the *CEFR* A1 level (see Table 8.3) can, when listening to a conversation between other speakers, "understand some words and expressions when people are talking about him/herself, family, school, hobbies, and surroundings [and can] understand words and short sentences when listening to a simple conversation (e.g. between a customer and salesperson in a shop), provided that people talk very slowly and very clearly" (Council of Europe 2018: 56). It is intended that learners as well as teachers use the *CEFR* descriptors to formulate their own outcomes and mark states of progress (43).

From 2001 to the present, *CEFR* has developed self-assessment "Can-Do" descriptors to be used by learners (e.g., see Council of Europe 2020: 177). These are written in the first person and are somewhat simpler than descriptors used by teachers and administrators. For instance, a listener at the A1 level is told: "I can recognize familiar words and very basic phrases concerning myself, my family and immediate concrete surroundings when people speak/sign slowly and clearly" (177). Self-assessment "grids" for language learners to add to a "portfolio" (see below) are available in thirty-two languages (Council of Europe 2022).

The two overall aims of *CEFR* are: to promote "European stability and . . . the healthy functioning of democracy" (Council of Europe 2001: 4); and to "aid European mobility" by attuning stakeholders in second language education to learners' needs (1). Knowing multiple languages is seen as indispensable to European language learners at all ages and across all walks of life as a means of experiencing the personal enrichment of "otherness in language and culture" (1). Learning foreign languages is seen as a means "for opportunity and success in social, educational and professional domains" (Council of Europe 2018: 25). To accomplish this, learners must determine what they "have to learn to do in order to use a language for communication" (Council of Europe 2001: 1). In practical terms, this means "providing a common basis for the explicit description of objectives [outcomes]" for language education (1). Stakeholders such as teachers, learners, parents, and school administrators may then enjoy transparency of discussion and planning for "courses, syllabuses, and qualifications" (1; Council of Europe 2018: 42). *CEFR* has gotten attention outside of Europe and is trialed and researched outside the European context (e.g., see Asdar 2017; Runnels and Runnels 2019; Tono 2019).

CEFR has a seven-point scale from Basic User to Proficient User (see Table 8.3). It posits four modes of communication (reception, production, interaction, and mediation) upon which multiple tables of descriptors for each are based (Council of Europe 2018: 32). For instance, under "reception" appears two "overall" descriptor tables for listening comprehension and reading comprehension. But then there are an additional ten descriptor tables that identify more specific areas of receptive language use. "Understanding conversation between other speakers" is differentiated from "Listening to announcements and instructions," and "Reading correspondence" is seen as different than "Reading as a leisure activity." It is here that the theoretical basis of Communicative Competence for *CEFR* becomes apparent. Communicative Competence posits language use as a social and cognitive event that involves an interaction between (1) learners' language knowledge,

Table 8.3 *CEFR* Scale Structure

Level	Sublevels
Basic User	Pre A-1
	A1
	A2
Independent User	B1
	B2
Proficient User	C1
	C2

Source: Authors.

(2) their ability to plan and monitor, and (3) the characteristics and demands of the language use situation (see Table 4.3; Chapter 4 in this volume; and Gorsuch 2019a). In essence, the different descriptor tables represent general language use situations (point 3), which place different demands on learners' language knowledge (point 1) and which invoke learners' planning and monitoring (point 2). It is this diverse offering of language use situation scales that allows for a greater focus on learners' language use needs. "Which language use situations do we wish to help learners develop ability in?" In other words: "What are our course/study outcomes?" See Table 8.4 for definitions of the four modes plus descriptor table titles for each.

Also found in *CEFR* 2018 and 2020 are descriptors for "strategies" within the four modes (Table 8.4). To explain: *CEFR* posits language use as "the actions performed by persons who as individuals and as social agents develop a range of competences, both general and in particular communicative language competences" (Council of Europe 2001: 9; see also Piccardo, North, and Goodier 2019). The "range of competences" include world knowledge and the ability to learn, among other competences, and also Communicative Competence, which comprises linguistic competence (knowledge of language as a system), sociolinguistic competence ("sensitivity to social conventions" of language use), and pragmatic competence ("functional use of linguistic resources") (Council of Europe 2001: 13). "Strategies," then, may stand in for the competence of "ability to learn" and Communicative Competence itself. Strategies, as presented in Table 8.4, are used by learners to: (1) extract information from a communicative event, perhaps beyond learners' present abilities ("monitoring and repair," "asking for clarification"), and (2) enhance communication ("compensating," "cooperating"). Point 1 might be considered more primarily a cognitive process and point 2 more primarily a social process. That strategies are

Table 8.4 *CEFR* Modes, Definitions, and Descriptors

Mode	Definition	Descriptor Tables
Reception	Oral and/or written language input that a language user receives and processes	Overall listening comprehension Understanding conversation between other speakers Listening as a member of a live audience Listening to announcements and instructions Listening to audio media and recordings Overall reading comprehension Reading correspondence Reading for orientation Reading for information and argument Reading instructions Reading as a leisure activity Watching TV, film and video *Communication strategies* Identifying cues in inferring (spoken, signed, and written)
Production	Language produced by a language user in spoken or written form, which is received by an audience	Overall spoken production Sustained monologue (describing experience) Sustained monologue (giving information) Sustained monologue (putting a case) Public announcements Addressing audiences Overall written production Creative writing Written reports and essays *Communication strategies* Planning Compensating Monitoring and repair
Interaction	Language use episodes in which a language user acts alternately as speaker and listener, and reader and writer	Overall oral interaction Understanding an interlocutor Conversation Informal discussion (with friends) Formal discussions (meetings) Goal-oriented cooperation Obtaining goods and services Information exchange Interviewing and being interviewed Using telecommunications Overall written interaction Correspondence Notes, messages, and forms

Mode	Definition	Descriptor Tables
		Online conversation and discussion
		Goal-oriented online transactions and collaboration
		Communication strategies
		Taking the floor (turn-taking)
		Cooperating
		Asking for clarification
Mediation	Language user interprets and/or translates spoken or written messages	Overall mediation
		Relaying specific information in speech
		Relaying specific information in writing
		Explaining data in speech
		Explaining data in writing
		Processing text in speech
		Processing text in writing
		Translating a written text in speech
		Translating a written text in writing
		Note-taking
		Expressing a personal response to creative texts
		Analysis and criticism of creative texts
		Collaborating in a group (facilitating interaction with peers)
		Collaborating in a group (collaborating to construct meaning)
		Leading group work (managing interaction)
		Leading group work (encouraging conceptual talk)
		Facilitating pluricultural space
		Acting as intermediary in informal situations
		Facilitating communication in delicate situations
		Communication strategies
		Strategies to explain a new concept (linking to previous knowledge)
		Strategies to explain a new concept (adapting language)
		Strategies to simplify a text (amplifying a dense text)
		Strategies to simplify a text (streamlining a text)

Table original to this book; information sourced from Council of Europe (2018, 2020); used with permission.

named, and described at different ability levels, present teachers and learners alike significant food for thought when planning learning outcomes. For one thing, naming such strategies recognizes learners as social beings who can reason and learn to use a second language within accepted social rules. Stakeholders will need to think through how a learner would appropriately show "cooperation" in a second language and cultural setting.

For instance, learners at an A2 level (high basic; Table 8.3) "can indicate when they are following" (Council of Europe 2020: 89) whereas slightly more able learners at a B1 low level "can repeat back part of what someone has said to confirm mutual understanding and help keep the development of ideas on course" and "can invite others into the discussion" (89). As will be seen in our case study, Felicia, our German teacher, takes interest in "cooperating," an interaction strategy, levels A1 to B1. Such descriptors suggest that learners are engaged in a discussion, or some other similar task such as a dictogloss, something that Felicia gets Rick, our French teacher in Chapter 4, interested in trying (Wajnryb 2012). The strategy described here, should learners be guided to learn and use it, could be both cognitively and socially enriching.

Teaching and *CEFR*

As noted above, *CEFR* does not prescribe specific teaching methods. To do so would impose "one single uniform system" (Council of Europe 2001: 7). Rather, teaching should be based on learners' needs "and must relate to a very general view of language use and learning" (9). Pursuant to the idea of language use, *CEFR* does suggest that teaching (and learning) involves "strategies, tasks, texts, an individual's [general] competences, communicative language competence, language activities [and] language processes" (10). Once again, it becomes apparent that *CEFR* has as its theoretical basis Communicative Competence, which posits the importance of a learner's world knowledge, personal attributes, and an understanding of a language use situation (Chapter 4). *CEFR* makes a curious suggestion along these lines that teachers should not assume that language learners have pre-knowledge about the world. Topics worth teaching should help learners learn language but also learn world knowledge (11; see also Piccardo, North and Goodier 2019). If any teaching method is to be used, it must "strengthen independence of thought, judgment and actions, combined with responsibility" (Council of Europe 2001: 4).

CEFR suggests that teachers need to encourage learners' autonomy by asking learners to collaborate together and creating classroom structures that offer learners insights on what they do well and what they need to improve (Council of Europe 2018: 27, 49). If teaching is consistent with Assessment and Curriculum (Figure 8.3 above), then tests and portfolios ought to offer teachers important information with which to give learners formative feedback (49). Thus, classroom tests and learner portfolios are examples of classroom structures (practices) that raise learners' awareness and cultivate autonomy (Sidhu, Kaur, and Chi 2018). The term "portfolio" has a somewhat *CEFR*-specific meaning as a dossier that documents learners' abilities and language use experiences in terms of *CEFR* Can-Do descriptors (e.g., see Goullier 2006). Learner portfolios are a form of learner self-assessment (Little 2006: 170–1).

The phrase "teaching and learning" appears frequently in *CEFR* documents, suggesting the central importance teaching is seen to have for second language learning outcomes. Second language teaching, and the teachers themselves, are seen as key assets to promote the aims of the Council of Europe to create in Europe a "greater mobility" for European citizens, along with "more effective international communication" between individuals of different backgrounds (Council of Europe 2001: 5).

Learning and *CEFR*

The Council of Europe describes a number of learning processes their authors believe are compatible with the use of *CEFR* descriptors and Can-Do statements. The processes they describe can be summarized as those of situated learning, "the ecological approach and approaches informed by sociocultural and socio-constructivist theories" (Council of Europe 2018: 29–30). Situated learning is a view that rejects learned knowledge as something separate from the social and physical setting in which that knowledge is learned. Thus, the cognitive processes that learners engage in to learn are shaped by context (see Social Development Theory, Chapter 3). Brown, Collins and Duguid (1989: 33), American psychologists, use the example of someone learning to use a tool. They note that the learning process, its length, frequency, manner, and perceived aims, is shaped by "each community that uses the tool, framed by the way members of that community sees the world" (33). Learning is seen as an apprenticeship, a collaboration, in which more knowledgeable individuals work with less knowledgeable individuals as a means of learning (Council of Europe 2001: 33; see also Vygotsky, Cole, and John-Steiner 1979). No wonder that *CEFR* suggests learning is promoted by interaction between teachers and learners but also "between learners themselves" (Council of Europe 2018: 27). Thus, learners should be engaged in "communicative language activities and [using] strategies" (30).

CEFR authors also emphasize that learning should be self-directed by learners. One means of this is by learners becoming more aware of their own learning and progress through self-assessment (Council of Europe 2001: 6). Learners take center stage and should be engaged in language use tasks and activities "enabling learners to act in real-life situations" (Council of Europe 2018: 27). Tasks, activities, and collaborative projects highlight learners as "social agents" who are "acting in the social world and exerting agency in the learning process" (26). Cultivating learners' self-images as having social agency in the foreign language will increase learner motivation and confidence (Council of Europe 2001: 5). The best way to encourage learner development of this kind is to ensure learners experience an institutional alignment of "needs . . . objectives . . . content . . . selection or creation of materials . . . teaching methods . . . evaluation, testing and assessment" (7; 2018: 23). See the Stakeholders Objectives Assessments and Curriculum Evaluation Model (Figure 8.3; Griffee and Gorsuch 2016), which can be used to investigate such alignments.

Later commentators on the use of *CEFR* in schools underscore learner self-assessment as a means of learning: Learner autonomy is "synonymous" with *CEFR* (Cook and Rutson-Griffiths 2022). Asdar (2017), Sidhu, Kaur, and Chi (2018), and Cook and Rutson-Griffiths (2022) offer specific examples of and techniques for learner self-assessment. Learners told Asdar (2017) that self-assessment was preferable if teachers explained it and they could use a form with which to self-assess. Learners who worked with self-assessment longitudinally saw more benefit the longer they did it (Cook and Rutson-Griffiths 2022). *CEFR* Can-Do materials themselves can be used to enhance learners' confidence to self-assess (Cook and Rutson-Griffiths 2022).

CEFR and institutions

One aim of *CEFR* is to "assist learners, teachers, course designers, examining bodies and educational administrators to situate and coordinate their efforts" in foreign language education (Council of Europe 2020: 22). These are, of course, stakeholder groups. If we very briefly set learners aside, two potent stakeholder groups remain: school administrators who work in schools, including education officials who work outside schools; and teachers themselves (Mitchell 1992). These stakeholder groups together comprise institutions. This is an oversimplification, but for the purposes of this chapter, we suggest the following four points:

1. Administrators are concerned with providing classes, teachers, and materials to learners (Meredith 2002).
2. They are concerned with the outcomes of teachers' and learners' efforts (Donaldson 2010, 2013; Hagger-Vaughan 2020; Long, Danechi, and Loft 2020; Meredith 2002).
3. They are concerned with upholding and interpreting policies of education officials external to the school (Hagger-Vaughan 2020; Liviero 2017; Price 2012).
4. The other stakeholder group, teachers, are concerned with creating learning environments, and with creating relationships with

learners, teacher colleagues, and administrators to maintain or enhance those learning environments (Barton 2014; Brisard and Menter 2008; Burke 2011; Liviero 2017; Price 2012; Tyack and Tobin 1994).

This is not to say that teachers are unconcerned or uninformed about education policy (Diez-Bedmar and Byram 2019; Heriansyah et al. 2021; Liviero 2017). Rather, for the purposes of this chapter, their immediate concerns simply have a different focus from those of administrators.

CEFR is used differently by different institutional stakeholder groups (Lowie 2012; see Diez-Bedmar and Byram 2019 [CEFR used for textbook selection and syllabus planning]; Figueras 2012 [CEFR used for designing teacher professional development projects], McLelland 2018 [CEFR used for setting language learning outcomes]; Moonen et al. 2013 [CEFR used for textbook selection]; Ohio Department of Education 2014 [equating CEFR with statewide tests]; Pavlovskaya and Lankina 2019, Shackleton 2018, Sidhu, Kaur, and Chi 2018 [CEFR descriptors used for designing in-school tests; and Tono (2019) [different levels of CEFR used for creating written and spoken texts used for learner input]). One might get the idea that CEFR has fully infiltrated all curriculum processes, including teacher planning and teaching, learner planning and learning, writing syllabuses, selecting textbooks, writing in-school tests, and preparing learners for external high-stakes tests. But curriculum innovation, a significant subfield of the high-level theory area of Curriculum (Chapter 9), predicts that an innovation, no matter how well founded in theory and research, will have uneven impacts on schools, and on teachers, teaching, learners, and learning (for CEFR-specific commentary, see Hunke and Saville 2019; Jones and Saville 2009; Runnels and Runnels 2019). Second language education as a field has long been researching what promotes and constrains curriculum innovation in schools (see Holliday 1992, 1994; Markee [1997] for classic and still-relevant commentary).

Given the different roles and priorities of stakeholder groups, an uneven impact of an innovation such as CEFR in a single institution should not be surprising. It is nonetheless useful to consider some specifics. For example, second language teachers and learners alike may be more responsive to high-stakes external tests than they are to in-school tests. External tests are highly valued by administrators to use for summative-type decisions (Barton 2014; Hagger-Vaughan 2020; Liviero 2017; Long, Danechi, and Loft 2020; see however Graham 2021). Unfortunately the student-as-communicator and social agent ethos promoted by CEFR (Council of Europe 2020; Piccardo, North, and Goodier 2019; Shackleton 2018) does not necessarily prepare learners for the test content and test item types found in external general proficiency tests, including England's GCSE exams (e.g., see Department for Education 2021; Woore et al. 2020; see Cook and Rutson-Griffiths 2022 for an example with CEFR and popular general proficiency tests in

Japan). Second, a school may lack teacher/administrator teams who have internally cohesive professional ties, even though teacher and administrator collaboration on curriculum planning is associated with better learner experiences (Brisard and Menter 2008; Printy and Liu 2020; Thoonen et al. 2011). Third, to use any innovation, both teachers and learners need support (Diez-Bedmar and Byram 2019), which may be hard to get, given full course schedules and a lack of resources (Hai and Nhung 2019; Sidhu, Kaur, and Chi 2018) or even awareness that support is needed. See Little (2006) for examples of teacher support projects. Finally, second language teachers may simply see language as form, focusing their teaching on sentence-level grammar and lists of vocabulary (see Chapter 4; Grenfell and Harris 2014; Johnstone 2014; Piccardo, North, and Goodier 2019; Tedick 2009). Learners themselves may see language as form due to prevailing folk beliefs about language, and incomplete Knowledge about Language. They may pressure teachers to spend precious class time on grammar and vocabulary explanations (see Chapter 7). Language may not be seen as use, as is promoted by *CEFR*. To the extent that administrators are aware of *CEFR* and what it entails, it may not matter. Administrators must work with the resources they have, including teachers. Teacher development is slow and costly (see Chapter 9 on a Saudi government initiative to transform their labor pool of second language teachers). See Table 8.5 for what *CEFR* posits.

Low-Level Theories Concerning Teaching, Learning, and Institutions: A Teacher of German

This chapter identifies and describes low-level theories about teaching, learning, and institutions held by an experienced German-language teacher named Felicia. First is a description of Felicia's experience and professional training. Second, Felicia's interview for a temporary part-time teaching job will be described. We will meet school administrators and a local education official at the interview and get an idea about their institution-oriented concerns. Third, we will see Felicia's first encounters with her students and colleagues. Through these different stakeholder groups, Felicia gets some understanding of institutional priorities. Finally, Felicia's low-level working theories about teaching, learning, and institutions will be identified and presented in a table.

Felicia's Background

Felicia is fifty-five and has been a full-time instructor of German language and culture at a private college in Colorado. Aside from living in Augsberg,

Table 8.5 What the *Common European Framework of Reference (CEFR)* Posits

1. A significant means of personal, educational, and professional enrichment is knowing multiple language and cultures.
2. Language use is learned.
3. A common understanding of learners' language use at different levels of ability should be established.
4. Establishing common understandings of learners' abilities is best done through descriptions of language use.
5. Descriptions of language use can be used by any stakeholder.
6. Stakeholders' central focus should be learners' language use needs.
7. Language use situations should be treated as different from each other.
8. Language use invokes multiple learner competencies, including Communicative Competence, their world knowledge, and their ability to learn.
9. Language learners have social identities. Their language use is shaped by their understandings of social rules and norms.
10. Language learning and content/world knowledge learning may be inseparable.
11. Communication strategies are both cognitive and social in their nature and function. As such, strategies may be seen as expressions of situated learning.
12. Language teaching should promote learners' language use.
13. Formative tests and feedback, and learner self-assessment, promote learner autonomy and language learning processes.
14. Teacher-learner and learner-learner collaboration promotes learner autonomy.

Source: Authors.

Germany, for two years, she has lived in Colorado her entire life. In her early forties, after a divorce, she returned to university to get a doctorate in German at a large state university in Colorado. One of her instructors specialized in Evaluation, and from him, Felicia learned to make Course Logic models (Figure 8.1) to uncover the assumptions of what makes a course tick, or how it is supposed a course works. For her doctoral dissertation she expanded her work with Course Logic models to explore what teachers of German were thinking about the "engines of learning" (the inputs) in courses they were designing. She learned that many of her research subjects, all high school teachers of German, believed that the main inputs for their courses were German grammatical forms and

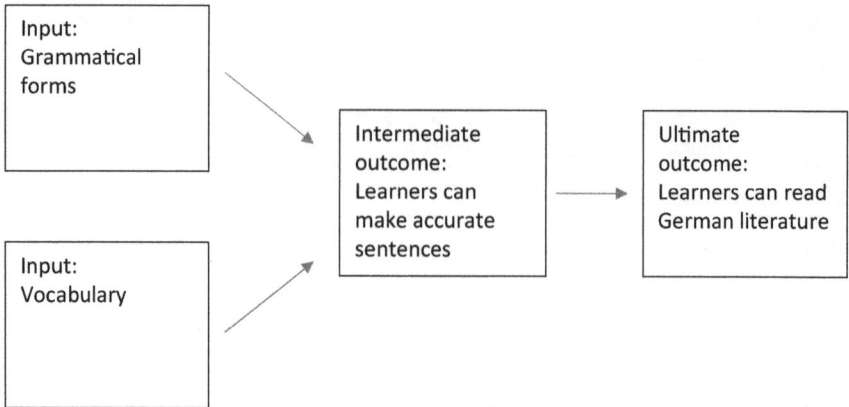

FIGURE 8.4 Logic Model of Felicia's Research Subjects (Teachers of German).
Source: Authors.

vocabulary. They hoped these inputs would help learners make accurate sentences in the short term (an intermediate outcome), which would thus enable learners to read German literature in the long term (an ultimate outcome). Felicia sketched out a Logic Model to express what she was hearing. See Figure 8.4.

Felicia felt this logic was faulty. Learners needed texts longer than sentences and actual reading practice as inputs if the ultimate outcome was to be reading German literature. Felicia remembers spending half her time in Augsberg reading books, newspapers, sales leaflets, and public announcement signs. As a result, she became a good reader. Yet, as she continued to talk to her research subjects, she began to see that most of the resources available to them, such as state education agency websites, textbooks, and summer "refresher" seminars offered by universities, all supported a primary focus on grammatical forms and vocabulary. Even if her research subjects attended ACTFL seminars, which their school districts sometimes had money for, Felicia found that the teachers placed a lot of emphasis on speaking and writing descriptors, particularly those parts that had to do with grammar and vocabulary. One teacher even pointed out a writing descriptor for Novice High: "able to recombine learned vocabulary and structures to create simple sentences on very familiar topics . . . due to inadequate vocabulary and/or grammar, writing at this level may only partially communicate the intentions of the writer" (ACTFL 2012a: 14). When Felicia pointed out the other parts of the same descriptor, such as: "Writers . . . are able to meet limited basic practical writing needs using lists, short messages, postcards, and simple notes" (14), the teacher simply said, "If learners' vocabulary and grammar aren't good enough, they can't write messages or notes." When Felicia pressed the teacher on why reading descriptors were not being consulted (24), he replied that speaking and writing were the best ways to know whether learners were being accurate with grammar and vocabulary. Reading was like a "black box," the teacher thought. You would never really know what learners understood unless the student produced spoken or written language. Felicia understood, through her dissertation, that teachers had their own theories that shaped what they thought and did (seeing language as form), regardless of alternate theories presented them from prestigious professional organizations such as ACTFL (seeing language as use). She thought about this again and again as she befriended Rick, a French language teacher in another state. He saw language as form (Chapters 4, 6, and 9), and it was hard to persuade him that learners could engage with language as use.

Felicia's two children have grown, and one of them has been accepted to graduate school in England, in a large city in the Northeast. Felicia decides to take a year off from her school in Colorado and be in England with her daughter, who has problems with depression and anxiety. Once Felicia arrives, however, she finds her daughter is doing well. Felicia has a lot of time on her hands after visiting museums and traveling within the city. At a party with her daughter's academic department, Felicia learns that an urban secondary school near her rented apartment is looking for a part-time temporary teacher of German. She contacts the school, completes the paperwork they send her by email, and then gets asked for an in-person interview. The man on the phone tells her: "It will take just an hour. It will be me, one of our other foreign language teachers, and an officer from our local education authority."

The Job Interview

Felicia arrives at the school, which is large, brick, and modern-looking. The low buildings are stained with rain and look a little scruffy. The school day is ending, and there are crowds of students leaving through the central gate. They are young, just barely teenagers, and come in every size, shape, and color, just like any American junior or senior high school. The only difference is they are wearing uniforms, which are worn in every state of repair and disrepair imaginable. Felicia enters a room for the interview. Three people face her, two men and one woman. One man introduces himself as the head teacher (which Felicia learns means school principal). The second man is a French teacher, and the woman is an officer from the local education authority. Each committee member takes an active part in the interview, and by the end of it, Felicia is tired.

The interview goes something like this:

Head teacher (HT): We have looked over your vita and we have noted your graduate degrees. Could you tell us about them?

Felicia (F):	Yes, the MA was at the University of Northern Colorado. They have an MA in world languages with a strong teaching component. Most of my student teaching was at a high school.
French teacher (FT):	How much student teaching did you actually have?
F:	One school year. I went in four days a week, all morning for two semesters.
FT:	Semester?
F:	Two of your "terms," I suppose, of five months apiece?
	Education authority officer (EAO): Yes I think we can all agree Ms. Caswell's graduate degrees are excellent. I noticed, however, that your doctorate is in German studies. Is that actually German language, or is it something else, like cultural studies? What I mean is, how is your German?
F:	My German is quite good. We had two years of intensive German along with six courses per year in teaching and learning theories. My final year was spent in courses on Evaluation. My dissertation was on high school teachers of German and how they theorized their teaching and content coverage.
HT:	Evaluation?
F:	Yes. How to judge the worth of a program?
EAO:	Yes, yes. But how is your German? Have you been to Germany?
F:	In speaking, listening, and reading, I'm judged to be "Superior" and in writing I'm judged to be "Advanced mid-high."
FT:	Is that some kind of qualification you use in America?
F:	Yes it's ACTFL. The American Council for Teaching Foreign Languages.
HT:	[using the internet on his cell phone] Oh yes I see. [to his colleagues] That's CEFR C2 for speaking, listening, and reading and C1 for writing.

EAO:	What about study abroad? I'm trying to get an idea about your cultural experience.
F:	I lived in Augsberg for two years after I finished my MA. I have family there.
EAO:	Ah.

From this point, the head teacher asked about her work as an instructor at her college. He was interested in how long she had been teaching, what level the students were, and how learners were tested. The French teacher wanted to know about her colleagues in Colorado. How did they decide their course outcomes? Did they work together? How did they choose textbooks (Chapter 9)? Felicia felt refreshed to hear that all foreign language teachers (Spanish, French, German, Italian, and Hindi) met weekly and worked together closely using something they called "CEFR" as a discussion point. Felicia made plans to spend the week looking at any *CEFR* documents she could find. The education officer asks no further questions after remarking that after a check of Felicia's "dossier," she would "be in touch." She says, "We must ensure you have what we call Qualified Teacher Status." To Felicia, this meant the officer would be contacting her college in Colorado and doing some checks into her graduate degrees.

Felicia Explores CEFR

Felicia spends the next two days looking for *CEFR* materials online. She is delighted to learn that the Council of Europe, the corporate author of *CEFR*, has a lot of free, downloadable materials. Some appear to be book length. How to decide which to read first? She checks some recent articles about *CEFR* she found in online academic journals and finds that even articles written in 2021 mention the 2001, 2018, and 2020 *CEFR*. This suggests that this older "2001" *CEFR* is still relevant, perhaps foundational for the latter two publications. She starts with the 2001. She learns that 2001 is indeed foundational, and as she reads, she sees that *CEFR* has multiple tables for different language use situations. She sees that the "descriptors" in each table all characterize language use, and that learner abilities can be judged by what they seem to do as they use language. Felicia wonders if this means that learners' performances on that single language use task are then taken as their level of ability. This would not happen with the ACTFL *Guidelines* where stakeholders are admonished to not see learners' performances on in-class tests and tasks as "true" indicators of their proficiency (Chapter 4).

Felicia sees a "self-assessment grid" with a section on spoken interaction for learners to use. From the 2001 publication, she is intrigued that the authors took on "interaction" and worked to develop it as a concept. It would be a tough topic, where most teachers or textbooks or scholars in 2001 would simply talk about "speaking." She thinks that the mark of a robust concept is whether it can be developed over time and whether it persists. When she checks the 2018 *CEFR* she learns that "interaction" has been expanded to spoken, written, and online interaction. Spoken interaction alone now has nine descriptor tables for "conversation" (Table 8.4). But then she sees something of real interest to her, "goal-oriented cooperation" and then in particular a "strategies" table on "cooperating." Felicia has long worked to get her college learners to do tasks together using as much German as they can, or at least a mixture of German and English. She is all for teaching strategies and then encouraging their use. She wants to use *CEFR* for pointing out to her students what their efforts to use strategies might look like. Rather than be discouraged and unclear about their stumbling, English-mixed German, they will see they are at a certain stage in their development. She also hopes learners will learn to better use their metacognition and their ability to plan and monitor (Chapter 6). She sees that *CEFR* mentions these processes are part of language use (Council of Europe 2020: 112).

Felicia Meets Her Students

Felicia gets the job, and two weeks later she is teaching two classes per day, three days per week. One class is a group of eleven fifteen-year-olds and the other is a group of eight fifteen-year-olds. Both groups have studied German for about two and a half years. A few of them are quick to tell Felicia they want to focus on passing their upcoming GCSEs. "How will you help us do that?" one young man asks. Felicia thinks about this and answers, "We can spend part of each class reviewing what you already know." One girl groans. Felicia laughs and continues, "We will spend the biggest part of class learning how to *use* what you know." And with that she takes out a small blue rubber ball and says in German, "Wie heißen sie?" (What's your name?). She tosses the ball to a girl to her right. Felicia smiles and gestures encouragingly, and the girl answers in German "Ich heiβe Jenny Jones" (My name is Jenny Jones). Jenny tosses the ball back to Felicia and to Felicia's delight, asks "Wie heißen sie?" (What's your name?). Felicia answers "Ich heiβe Felicia Caswell" ("My name is Felicia Caswell"). Felicia tosses the ball to another student, this one a boy, and asks again in German "What's your name?" The boy answers. The next time the ball comes to Felicia she tosses it to another person, who answers and then Felicia tosses it right back to the same person and continues the conversation by saying: "Wie geht es dir?" (How do you do?). The girl is a little surprised but then answers, "Mir geht's gut. Oh! Uh . . . Wie geht es dir?" (I'm well. Oh! Uh . . . How do you do?). She self-corrects when she guesses that her second utterance is more appropriate for a first meeting with someone.

```
┌─────────────────────┐
│ Input:              │
│ Learners' existing  │
│ linguistic,         │         ┌────────────────────┐      ┌────────────────────┐
│ sociocultural and   │         │ Intermediate       │      │ Ultimate outcome:  │
│ textual knowledge,  │         │ outcome:           │      │ Increased learner  │
│ and knowledge of    │         │ Enhanced learner   │─────▶│ confidence with    │
│ learning resources  │         │ collaboration,     │      │ language use       │
└─────────────────────┘         │ reconstruction, recall│   │                    │
                                 └────────────────────┘      └────────────────────┘
┌─────────────────────┐
│ Input:              │
│ Communicative       │
│ functions           │
│                     │
│                     │
│                     │
└─────────────────────┘
```

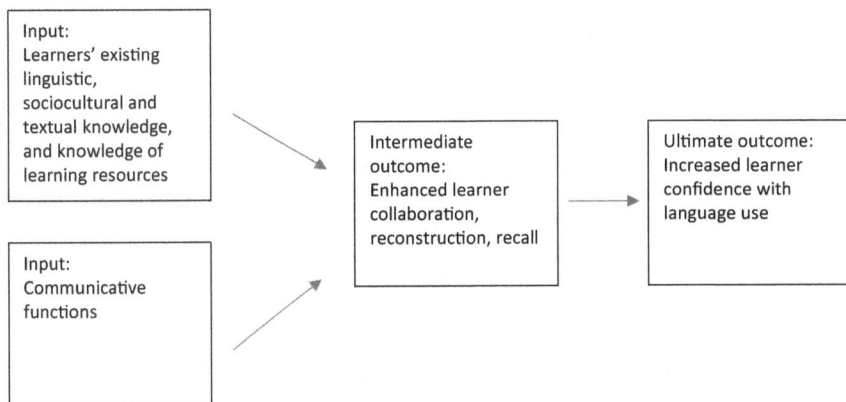

FIGURE 8.5 First Logic Model of Felicia's German course with secondary students.

Source: Authors.

The next time Felicia tosses the ball to a student, she asks "Wohnen sie hier?" (Do you live near here?). This conversational gambit was a new expression for most students, and the student holding the ball looks around at her classmates for help. Felicia says in German, "It's OK if you all want to look at your book and help her out," and she mimes picking up her book and looking through it. A boy looks through his coursebook quickly and tells the girl "Wohnen sie hier? She's asking if you live near here." This goes on, until Felicia and the learners construct a whole conversation, with about ten lines, of what would be an ordinary interaction between new neighbors working in a community garden. During this, Felicia encourages students to look through their books for help with what to say. The coursebook is grammar oriented, and not oriented to situations (greeting a new neighbor) or communicative functions (exchanging information), but the students can piece together what they need, even though they make some mistakes. Felicia does not correct their pronunciation at this point. The next time Felicia meets the students she gets them to work in groups of three to reconstruct the ten-line conversation. She then asks them to make any corrections or other changes they might like to their reconstruction. One student asks if older German speakers might use different language than younger ones, and Felicia says "Das ist eine wichtige frage" (That is an important question). She uses both German and English to answer the question and then invites learners to create a second "new neighbor" conversation to reflect a different social need. After her first week, Felicia sketches out her Course Logic so she can think about what she is doing so far.

The Teachers' Meeting

Felicia attends the weekly teacher's meeting. It takes an hour. There are twelve teachers there: five of Spanish, four of French, one of Italian, one of Hindi, and Felicia. There were two topics: The upcoming GCSE exams for their fifteen- to sixteen-year-olds; and using *CEFR* to propose outcomes for that same group. The French teacher who was at Felicia's job interview explains, "We don't want to have students spend their final year with us just doing exam preparation. That would just be more grammar and vocabulary review, with practice dictations, translation exercises, reading passages and answering questions, and the like. They use the language doing that, of course, but it's not terribly authentic." A Spanish teacher, who is head of the foreign languages group, announces they have forty-nine students who want to try for the GCSE exam in a foreign language. "That's seven more than last year," says the foreign language group head. She projects a website from the UK Education Ministry on the wall; it outlines the content for modern foreign languages (MFL), which includes sections for Spanish, French, and German. The bulk of the website is taken up specifying word lists to be mastered and grammatical forms to be covered. Felicia thinks that grammar and vocabulary appear to be taken as the content of language study. In the German section of the website, she sees familiar subheadings such as "reflexive use of verbs" and "adjectival phrases." She sees no mention of *CEFR*.

The talk turns to *CEFR* and Felicia learns that the teachers hope their fifteen-to sixteen-year-olds, in addition to passing their GCSE exams, will attain a *CEFR* A2 level with maybe a few learners getting B1. Felicia figures this to be novice high to intermediate low in ACTFL terms. That is pretty good for secondary school learners who have studied only for a few years. Another Spanish teacher reviews the *CEFR* descriptors they have been talking about recently, including "overall listening comprehension," "listening to announcements," "overall spoken interaction," "conversation," and "obtaining goods and services" (Table 8.4). She draws everyone's attention to descriptors that focus on what seems to be a kind of transition from A2 to B1 where learners can comprehend or handle "familiar" topics (A2) to being able to interact or listen without much preparation to verbal language that may involve less familiar topics (B1). The Spanish teacher adds that it would be easy to use authentic recordings for listening that would motivate learners and to devise situations for learners to buy things they needed. A high A2 learner, she explains, "can interact in predictable everyday situations (e.g., a post office, a station, a shop) using a wide range of simple words and expressions," while a B1 learner "can cope with less routine situations in shops, post office, bank, for example, returning an unsatisfactory products" and "make a complaint" (Council of Europe 2018: 89).

Felicia speaks up and talks about how *CEFR* descriptors for "goal-oriented cooperation" and the strategy "cooperating" have attracted her. She says she has been working on ways for learners to collaborate on tasks in a way that helps them with language use *and* focus on grammatical forms. She mentions how learning grammar implicitly is a popular topic at language teaching conferences in the United States where learners can learn grammar by using it in reading, writing, listening, and speaking activities; learners can be encouraged to talk to each other about what they think the rules are; teachers can help learners figure out the rules by asking questions or giving hints; and teachers can also ask learners to compare the new grammar rules to the grammar rules of their first language. Felicia says her thinking has evolved on this topic and that she has found an easy-to-use technique called a dictogloss to get learners to collaborate.

"Oh yes," says a Spanish teacher, a man in his forties from Eibar, Spain. "I know dictogloss. Where pupils read or hear a passage perhaps with five lines, containing some grammatical point of interest? Then perhaps you dictate it repeatedly and they write it down while helping each other get down the correct version?" Felicia nods. The teacher continues, "Then the pupils get together later and reconstruct the passage, and then spend some time analyzing and correcting their little texts?" (Wajnryb 2012: 7). Felicia says, "Yes."

The Hindi teacher speaks up: "But what does that have to do with *CEFR*?" Felicia smiles and says, "There are two tables of descriptors for cooperation. I'm thinking that I can help learners use at least some German while they collaborate and then use the cooperation descriptors to help them see that their efforts are part of their own development of strategies. To me, cooperation, using even mixed L1 and L2 is the essence of language use." Felicia asks the section head if they have time to look at the cooperation tables, and he says they do. She puts them up on the projector so everyone can see. First, she shows "Cooperating" as an interaction-type communication strategy, where A2-level learners "can indicate when they are following." Low B1 learners "can invite others into the discussion" (Council of Europe 2020: 89). Then, she shows "goal-oriented cooperation" descriptors where a "low" A2 learner "can communicate in simple and routine tasks using simple phrases to ask for and provide things, to get simple information, and to discuss what to do next." A "high" A2 learner "can discuss what to do next, making and responding to suggestions, and asking for and giving directions" (77). The teachers talk for a few minutes among themselves. Then the Hindi teacher says, "I don't see how pupils can learn how to use German to do these things. How can you possibly anticipate what a particular passage will require pupils to be able to do?" Felicia answers,

Table 8.6 What Felicia Posits about Institutions, and Theories of Learning and Teaching

1. "Institutions" are more than individual schools. They might be better termed "institutional cultures" made up of individual schools, education authorities, publishers, higher (teacher) education, and professional organizations, among others.

2. Institutions collectively shape teaching and learning.

3. Administrators are not a homogeneous stakeholder group, depending on their roles.

4. Administrators seem concerned with teachers' qualifications as measured by academic degrees, teaching experience, and language abilities.

5. Teachers seem concerned about details of teaching and learning.

6. For institutional and school purposes, levels in a language use description framework may be readily accepted as descriptive of learners' and language users' (teachers') language ability.

7. Language use description frameworks develop over time. It is worthwhile to observe and consider long-term changes in published language use description frameworks.

8. Teachers may selectively accept and use elements of language use description frameworks for exploration of teaching and learning aims.

9. Language use descriptors may themselves be parsed, split up, and used selectively according to a teacher's theory of teaching and learning, and his or her view of language as form or as use.

10. Language use descriptors may be selected as a means of consensus.

11. Language use description frameworks and descriptors may be used to broaden teachers' conceptions of possible course outcomes at a school.

12. Learners' language use should be encouraged.

13. Learner collaboration is a significant means of learning how to use language.

14. Learner collaboration is both a social and a cognitive act.

15. Learners need to learn how to use both social and cognitive strategies.

16. Language as form and language as use outcomes can be bridged through careful attention to course logic.

17. Learners have an idea that language use is shaped by social needs.

18. There are multiple ways a required textbook can be used by students.

19. Learners may not be deemed by teachers as capable of using the second language to carry out collaborative tasks.

20.	Teaching communicative functions needed for collaboration may assist students to use the second language in collaborative tasks.
21.	Learners can be asked to account for what they could not do and yet still needed to do with the second language while engaged in collaborative tasks.

Source: Authors.

I agree that what we ask learners to do when they collaborate will change the language they use. But I think that if consideration is given to what they need to do in terms of communicative functions, I can give them a working language. Asking for instructions might be seen as one communicative function. And maybe I can even get them to make an account of what they could not do using German to cooperate and what they needed or wanted to be able to say? I will say it bothers me a little that *CEFR* descriptors for cooperating do not mention mixing L1 and L2, so I do not know what the authors think growth looks like in that regard. But perhaps this is because I don't know *CEFR* well enough yet.

Felicia then says, "Sorry I took up so much time with this." The meeting ends, and Felicia and three other teachers agree to meet for coffee later that day to talk more. See Table 8.6 for what Felicia posits about institutions and theories of learning and teaching.

Felicia is an experienced teacher with two graduate degrees. As a result, she is comfortable thinking about her teaching in terms of high-, middle-, and low-level theory and can slip in and out of, and between, these theory categories. What may have started out as a low-level theory (language should be used) became a subtly different working theory when Felicia got to know middle-level and high-theories (learning strategies and Communicative Competence) better. At some point in the past, Felicia realized learners needed to go through a process of learning how to use language, and that learning strategies and all elements of Communicative Competence, among other things, would be sustainable resources from which she could devise inputs for courses.

Joining a school in a very new institutional context has jostled Felicia a bit, but in a good way. She sees institutions and schools with fresh eyes, and she thinks she understands at least the outlines of significant institutional priorities. Her graduate course work in Evaluation has helped with that. Further, due to her comfort with high-, middle-, and low-level theories, she feels confident she has ways to combine her own teacher theories and priorities with institutional priorities.

Reflective Projects

1. Identify stakeholders in your institutional context. Identify their
    various roles. What do they care about? What is your evidence?
    How would you investigate?

Stakeholder	Role	What the stakeholder cares about

2. The authors suggest that administrators and institutions may not
    seem to have nuanced ideas about how teaching and learning
    occur. Yet the authors leave this open by not providing evidence.
    Considering your specific school context, what do you think?
    What's your evidence?

3. Can two course logic (causal logic) models exist for two teachers
    at the same school who teach the same course? Consider the case
    of Aisha (Chapter 9). Choose two stakeholders attending the pre-
    semester teachers' meeting mentioned in the case study. Sketch
    out a course logic model for each person with inputs, intermediate
    outcome, and ultimate outcomes. How are the two models
    different?

4. Focusing on Felicia's case study in this chapter, identify summative
    and formative decisions made by stakeholders or discussions or
    processes they engage in that might lead to a decision.

Stakeholder(s)	Summative or formative decision/discussion

For each decision or discussion, what sources do stakeholders draw on as a basis?

5. Is there anything missing from Table 8.2 on what Evaluation posits? In other words, is there anything that is implied in the chapter section on Evaluation that does not appear in the list of proposals in Table 8.2?

6. If *CEFR* was designed for stakeholders in Europe, what accounts for it attracting interest in other parts of the world? Can a language use description framework such as *CEFR* be transplanted? Why or why not?

7. The authors offer a number of reasons for *CEFR* not being fully implemented at a school (whether in Europe or not). What are they? Considering your own institutional situation, which of these reasons are compelling? Can you think of how you might "solve" non-implementation?

8. Looking at Felicia's course logic model (Figure 8.5), what theories are brought into relation? Consider applying the High Middle Low Theory Model as a means to clarify your response.

CHAPTER NINE

Theories of Language and Institutions

Why This Chapter?

This chapter focuses on the interaction of theories of language and institutions. By theories of language, we mean how language is thought of and studied and acted upon by administrators, teachers, and learners in the second language education field. In Chapter 4, we explored what teachers know and believe about language, and how their knowledge and belief systems shaped their lessons and quizzes. In Chapter 7, we focused on learners and how their unschooled and schooled knowledge and beliefs about language changed their expectations of classroom instruction. In this chapter, schools (institutions) take center stage.

It is in schools where the significant, neglected, and richly generative high-level theory of Curriculum is most present. Curriculum is a family of general and applied theories about content (Flinders and Thornton 2013a), involving ongoing practical reasoning and inquiry (Bobbitt 1924; Reid 1999) about tests, instruction, and materials and textbooks. As language is the content of second and foreign language classes, theories of language are deeply implicated in whatever curriculum processes take place in a school. Three questions might be posed: (1) *How is the second language experienced by learners at a school?* In textbook chapters with lists of vocabulary and explanations of sentence-level grammar? In dialogs highlighting known and unknown vocabulary? In naturalistic listening extracts where learners identify a sequence of events? (2) *What units of teaching are used?* A series of tasks? A set of dialogs? 500-word texts? Projects? Practice tests? (3) *In what sequence do learners experience the units that are used?* Are dialogs most needed for survival in a foreign country treated first? Or are dialogs needed to make friends treated first? Do the 500-word stories appear in a larger narrative order? Or are the stories unrelated one-offs designed to highlight whatever sentence-level grammatical forms or vocabulary are presented?

Underlying the three questions posed here are the schools themselves, which "structure learning in ways that reflect some wider reality" (Reid 1999: 97). We can then pose yet a fourth question: (4) *What would the wider reality be for a particular school?* Do the prevailing politics of the school's country suggest that young citizens should study a second language as a means of internationalization? Have business interests defined specific workforce needs that require some kind or some level of second language ability? Do learners' families want content instruction to be given in a second language as a means of upward social or economic mobility?

The four questions probe the significant issues that administrators and educators consider while engaging in second language curriculum processes at a school. One of the most consequential curriculum processes is the evaluation and selection of course textbooks. Course textbooks that teachers select comprise a significant element of learners' and teachers' experiences with the second language at a school. Further, textbook evaluation and selection processes bring teachers into close contact with each other, both intellectually and professionally. Such contacts flavor the institutional culture and directly impacts teachers' working lives.

Schools are also the seat of socially accepted ideas of what constitutes accomplishment in learning (Reid 1999). It is not surprising that tests are important to schools as a means of identifying milestones (learner readiness and end states for example) relevant to their program. One university-based English-language institute in the Middle East notes on its website (King Abdul Aziz University 2021):

> The intensive ELIE track is for incoming students intending to major in English in the Department of European Languages and Literature at the Faculty of Arts and Humanities. Students are required to score at least 28 on the Cambridge English Placement Test, which corresponds to the Common European Framework Reference (CEFR) proficiency level of high A2 and take a writing placement test that demonstrates the ability to write at a CEFR high A2 level. It's a two-semester academic English course taking students from high A2 CEFR to low B2 CEFR.

Both internal and external tests are mentioned, and the tests are linked to external standards, in this case the *Common European Framework of Reference* (*CEFR*; Council of Europe 2001, 2018; see also Chapter 8). *CEFR* assumes that a common understanding of learners' language ability can be established and set on a linear scale. Inherent in tests used to place learners on such a scale is a theory of language. In this chapter, internal tests administered at a school are used to place learners into ability groups. They are thus a key feature of the formalized school curriculum.

In this chapter, we describe how the High Middle Low Theory Model (Chapter 1) applies to high- and low-level theories relevant to language and institutions. As with Chapters 4 and 7, we do this in two ways. First, we offer a table after our theory description suggesting what the theories or theory areas propose, or posit. Stating what theories posit promotes inquiry in that readers can compare the proposals to what they have read in the descriptions and teacher case studies in the chapter, and to their reading from other chapters and sources, as well as to their academic and workplace experiences. Second, we feature low-level teacher theories by describing school artifacts using a teacher case study. The institutional practices or artifacts we focus on in this chapter are textbook selection and learner ability grouping practices. We feature Aisha, an experienced teacher who works in an English as a foreign language (EFL) preparation program at a women's campus of a university in Saudi Arabia. The period preceding an academic term is terribly busy at Aisha's school. It does not help that the university is transitioning into an English-medium school. The department head and the teachers must together evaluate and select textbooks for new classes they must offer and make placement tests to place incoming and continuing learners into the three ability levels the university president believes should exist. In other words, they must engage in curriculum processes. Having completed a master's degree in applied linguistics, Aisha is familiar with middle-level theories within Curriculum. We follow her during preterm school activities, and become privy to the interplay of middle-level theories and low-level teacher theories in her thinking, actions, and words as they relate to Aisha's understanding of language in the context of her school. We finish with reflective project ideas for readers.

How the High Middle Low Theory Model Applies to Theories of Language and Institutions

We return to a significant theme explored in Chapters 4 and 7—that of language seen as form, and language seen as use. Language seen as form has deep historic roots in foreign language education (Johnson 1982). In contrast, language seen as use has compelling theoretical roots (see Chapter 4; Dubin and Olshtain 1986; Johnson 1982). To the language seen as use tradition, we add in this chapter a new frame of thinking about language, that of mentoring learners as language users in communities of practice as a means of forming identity. This is Multiple Literacies, also referred to as Multiliteracies.

Language Seen as Form

This tradition may operate "under the radar," meaning that teachers and administrators encounter this theory of language as a default, or unconscious, way of thinking. In this tradition, language is seen as a system of forms, made up of sounds, vocabulary, sentences, and writing systems. It is this formal system ("formal," meaning focused on linguistic forms) that comprises the content of a course, and learners learn the system through memorization, teacher lectures, individual study, and drills (Alrashidi and Phan 2015; Mitchell and Alfuraih 2017). The tradition of language as form appears as "language" content in textbooks using a "blended syllabus" (see Chapter 7). One textbook widely used in Saudi Arabia, *English Unlimited A2 Elementary Coursebook* (Tilbury et al. 2010), has a blended syllabus with four components: "goals," "language," "skills," and "explore" (publicly available table of contents retrieved from: https://www.cambridge.org/files/7313/7294/3057/9780521697729pre_p001-006.pdf). The Chapter 1 "language" component focuses on form and highlights "grammar" (possessive 's, *be* present tense, *be* past tense), "vocabulary" ("people you know," "talking about jobs," "how you know people"), and "pronunciation" ("syllables").

In the high-level theory of Communicative Competence, the language as form sensibility corresponds to a narrow conception of linguistic competence where "the sentence patterns and types, the constituent structure, the morphological inflections, and the lexical resources" (Celce-Murcia, Dornyei, and Thurrell 1995: 16–17) of the second language are given primary focus, and awarded the most classroom time on task (Gorsuch 2019a: 419). In a language as form tradition, the most attention may be given to the "language" component of a blended syllabus type textbook even though this may not be the intention of the textbook authors, the teachers, or the school. This practice may be reinforced if preparation for internal and external tests used in a school is construed as learners engaging with the second language as a formal system, narrowly conceived.

Language Seen as Use

In a language as use tradition, language would be seen as a means to accomplish social acts, and as a way to communicate with others. Language use is also a system (Celce-Murcia, Dornyei, and Thurrell 1995; Hymes 1972; Johnson 1982; New London Group 1996; Wong and Zhang Waring 2021). Thus, learning a second or foreign language in the tradition of use would involve not only using language as a means of learning but also having students overtly learn the socially appropriate or commonplace ways of communicating in a culture (New London Group 1996; Swaffar and Arens 2005). Language conceived as course content in this tradition would appear as communicative functions, texts, and tasks (Austin 1962; Ellis 2003; Nunan 1989; Schechtman and Koser 2008; Wilkins 1976). Examples given earlier in this chapter are naturalistic listening extracts where learners identify a sequence of events, and 500-word texts appearing in successive narrative order, such as short chapters in a novella. In such short narrative texts, learners might be asked to identify the language used by the author that suggests a story character is up to no good, and then to consider how a different language choice would change the meaning of the text (Maxim 2006). A narrative text in a language-as-use classroom would not be presented for the sole purpose of highlighting whatever sentence-level grammatical forms are being taught that week, even though a teacher may find ways for learners to notice the forms and then later use the forms to make a podcast or to write a review of the novella on a book seller's website.

Textbooks with a blended syllabus may have elements of language as use (Johnson 1982). For instance, in the *English Unlimited A2 Elementary Coursebook* table of contents mentioned earlier in this chapter (Tilbury et al. 2010), the "goals" section mentions how to "introduce people" and "say who people are" and "say how you know people" while hosting a guest at home. The communicative functions, or social goals, then, include "introducing people." These communicative functions are used in a "target activity" in the chapter, which is to "talk about someone you know well" and to "ask people to repeat" (publicly available table of contents retrieved from: https://www.cambridge.org/files/7313/7294/3057/9780521697 729pre_p001-006.pdf). With a blended syllabus, the "language" forms (the grammar and vocabulary) are to support learners as they engage in language use (*use* being called "goals" and "skills" in the *English Unlimited* coursebook presented here. This is a familiar pattern seen in the Proficiency Movement (Chapter 4). But it is still an open question what elements of the syllabus teachers and learners will award the most time and attention to (see Chapter 7). Some of this will depend on curriculum processes (decisions) taking place at the school.

Language Use in Communities of Practice—Multiple Literacies/Multiliteracies

Multiple Literacies is a middle-level theory that proposes that foreign language education should have the goal of helping learners function in another language and thereby expand their "critical language awareness, interpretation and translation [ability], historical and political consciousness, social sensibility, and aesthetic perception" (Pratt et al. 2008: 290). This tradition is alternately referred to as Multiliteracies and is simply termed

Multiple Literacies in this book for the sake of consistency. Multiple Literacies operates out of a tradition of language as use. The teaching implied by this theory leads teachers to mentor learners to work with multiple texts on specific topics over successive class meetings and repeated engagement with the texts (for teaching descriptions, see Kern 2008; Maxim 2006; Michelson 2019). "Multiple texts" means print sources, online sources, audio files, and visual images (multimodalities) that learners select and consume as a process of discovery of not only language but also literary and cultural content (Gaspar and Berti 2019: 277; Kress and van Leeuwen 2021). Teaching as mentoring is significant here. Teachers and also more expert peers (classmates) are to assist learners in completing projects and engaging in personal discovery by scaffolding, offering feedback, and guiding learners through processes of "forethought, design, and reflection while reading, writing, listening, and speaking" the L2 (Gaspar and Berti 2019: 276). Because the teacher-student and student-student relationships are based on mentoring, learners create their own community to which they can increasingly contribute with growing expertise (Gee 2021; see also Social Development Theory, Chapter 3). Such processes are necessary for learners to form their own identities and competence in preparation for a work world of multiple social communities using multiple forms of given languages (New London Group 1996).

Looking at language use in terms of Multiple Literacies has implications in terms of the basic curriculum questions posed at the beginning of this chapter: (1) *How would learners experience the second language?* (2) *What are the basic units of teaching?* (3) *In what sequence would the units of teaching be arranged?* (4) *What is the wider reality a school is responding to?* In terms of question 1, learners would experience the second language through multiple forms of texts with multiple treatments of the texts on multiple occasions. In terms of question 2, the units of teaching would be series of tasks and longer projects (see Gaspar and Berti 2019; Michelson and Anderson 2021). For question 3, the sequence in which learners work, this would depend on the projects chosen and the texts selected. For question 4, our case study teacher Aisha believes that her students, who are young Saudi women, face a future in a rapidly changing society and in a rapidly changing world in which a foreign language, English, is widely used. As it transpires, Aisha's school administration shares this assessment of a wider reality but has different ideas on how to respond to this reality. As will be seen, teaching in a Multiple Literacies framework will not conform easily to the syllabuses implied in most available course textbooks that most teachers and institutions adopt in the Saudi market. Aisha, our teacher in the case study, has to think carefully about textbook selection. She is on the selection committee, and she wants to work with projects and texts while at the same time select a textbook that will satisfy her colleagues.

A High-Level Theory for Language and Institutions

The high-level theory area for this chapter is Curriculum. Textbook evaluation and selection will be explored as a component of curriculum. Curriculum comprises high-level theory. It is public and discussed at conferences and in journals, newsletters, and list-servs. It is ever-present in schools and is actively discussed in all disciplines taught and learned in schools (e.g., see journals such as *Chemistry Education Research and Practice*, *Language Arts*, *Curriculum Studies in Health and Physical Education*, and *Mathematics*). Curriculum is comprised of multiple traditions of inquiry and scholarly comment. Curriculum as we experience it in second language education has significant and continuing overlap with the field of Education, for instance.

Curriculum

In this section, we define Curriculum. We then describe the basic function of curriculum processes and present two ways that Curriculum theorizes. In this book, Curriculum is defined as a family of theories about content (Flinders and Thornton 2013a), involving ongoing practical reasoning and inquiry (Bobbitt 1924; Reid 1999), resulting in decision-making about the experiences learners ought to have (Bobbitt 1924; Johnson 1989a; Pinar 2012). In basic terms, these decisions are about what learners will learn, in what basic sequence, using what resources are available (Berwick 1989; Nation and Macalister 2010; Rodgers 1989). The terms curriculum decision-making and curriculum processes will be used interchangeably.

The basic function of Curriculum is to answer the question of how "round" content gets arranged into a linear shape that comprises learners' experiences. In other words, how do we get from language (content) to something that learners experience in a classroom or course that is bounded by time, having a beginning, a middle, and an end? There is no beginning, middle, or end to language. Yet institutions (schools) must program content in such a way so there is a beginning, a middle, and an end (Johnson 1982). Within those new, squashed, linear shapes comprising experiences, it is hoped learners will learn. This image leads to the first area that Curriculum seeks to theorize.

Theorizing Content and Learning

The first way Curriculum theorizes is to define what a Curriculum theory must attempt to do. According to Bode (1927: 193), an early American Curriculum scholar, a theory of Curriculum must theorize what is worth knowing (content), and how people learn. Curriculum theory as described here can be generally stated or stated with more specificity with the purpose of applying the theory. More general theorizing would take place at the level of nations, ministries of education, or professional teaching associations, such as ACTFL (Chapter 4). More specific theorizing and deliberation, and application, would occur in schools, programs, and courses.

General Education commentators theorize content in broad terms, where decisions about content are seen as a practical response to the need for societies to organize themselves, usually through mass education, for whatever present and future is wished for (Eisner 2013; Flinders and Thornton 2013a; McIntosh 2013; Pinar 2012; Reid 1999). Thus, while some high- and middle-level theories presented in this book describe knowledge (Communicative Competence) or phenomena (Folk Linguistics) or propose a process (Multiple Literacies/Multiliteracies), Curriculum theory as construed here is a predictive tool for planning and bringing about a desired result.

Three Examples of How Content and Learning Are Theorized

As a first example worthwhile content is theorized to be "wider social insight" and preparation for adult life (Bode 1927: 87) or "professional knowledge" in preparation for work in industry (Bobbitt 1924; Flinders and Thornton 2013a: 4). In terms of theorizing learning, Bode (1927: 147) theorizes learning as taking place while learners engage in projects, described as "a wholeheartedly purposeful activity carried on in a social context," much like tasks and projects in a tradition of language as use and Multiple Literacies. Examples are building a radio to learn about physics or raising corn to learn about biology (149). To Bobbitt (1924: 35), another influential and early American Curriculum theorist, learning takes place by identifying what learners lack through diagnostic testing and then focusing scarce instructional resources on those specific areas. The mention of diagnostic testing, with the implication that learners ought to be grouped in some manner ("the gifted, the average, the sub-average"; 61), will become relevant in this chapter's teacher case study.

A second example focuses on language education. The Council of Europe theorizes content both generally and specifically. Generally, content is theorized as foreign language competence that will serve European citizens professionally and personally in a manner of their own choosing (Council of Europe 2001: 1–2). In 2018, worthwhile content was theorized as "enabling learners to act in real-life situations, expressing themselves and accomplishing tasks of different natures" (Council of Europe 2018: 27). Specifically, content is theorized as the components of Communicative Competence, including linguistic competence (109), sociolinguistic competence (118), pragmatic competence (123), and functional competence (125). Even more specifically, the "content" of pragmatic competence is theorized in part as "discourse competence," which in turn is comprised of the "ability to structure and manage discourse" and to design texts in terms of "how stories, anecdotes, jokes, etc. are told" (Council of Europe 2001: 123). In terms of theorizing learning, the Council of Europe authors are careful not to name specific language learning theories but rather generally describe multiple positions concluding with a mainstream theorization: "learners do not necessarily learn what teachers teach and [learners] require substantial contextualized and intelligible language input as well as opportunities to use the language interactively" (140).

The third and final example is specific to second language education in Saudi Arabia where the case study for this chapter takes place. Worthwhile content here is generally theorized to be learners learning how to learn English for their own purposes, becoming adept at problem-solving for future professional needs, and increasing their digital literacy (Elyas and Badawood 2017). More specifically, foreign language ability is theorized as "basic English skills" and "linguistic competence required in different professions" (Elyas and Badawood 2017: 78). At one English preparation program, worthwhile content is stated to be "skills in academic writing/reading and academic listening/speaking" for high beginning learners (King Abdul Aziz English Language Institute 2021: 18). Content is further defined as units in a required textbook and "language items" that "are to be presented and practiced during specified timeframes" (21). The textbook, which is commercially published, has a "blended syllabus" (see definitions and examples earlier in this chapter and also in Chapter 7). The content described, then, is "reading skills," "vocabulary," "grammar," "critical thinking," and "writing" (Ostrowska 2014: 4–5). The theory of learning how to write appears to have three components: (1) building skills (2) for particular writing task "types" ("write descriptive sentences"), (3) using an assigned writing task (5). The author further posits that the book's "grammar syllabus" provides the basis of learning how to write through having learners develop good "sentence structure" (11). This theorizing of foreign language writing content and learning reappears in our teacher case study of Aisha, who has a different theory of language and a different theory of Curriculum for academic writing.

Theorizing Components

A second way Curriculum theorizes is through identification and theorization of curriculum components. This perspective emphasizes Curriculum as a system (Markee 1997; Ornstein and Hunkins 2012), wherein the components are (ideally) aligned with each other, and test results can show (or not) that the hoped-for learning has occurred. The curriculum components that are generally agreed upon are: learners, needs analysis, measurable goals and stated outcomes, assessments, syllabuses, materials, schools and classrooms, curriculum guides and policy statements, and teachers and instruction. See Table 9.1 for definitions and examples of how the categories are theorized. These are in essence statements of what Curriculum theorists posit, or propose. Thus, the theorizations in Table 9.1 are debated, discussed, investigated, and tested.

The table is not comprehensive. There are likely more theorizations and proposals within the curriculum components, many of which are representative of ongoing, practical curriculum decisions taking place at schools. One other striking feature of the curriculum theorizations in Table 9.1 is that some commentators work in general Curriculum (Bobbitt 1924; Flinders and Thornton 2013b; Pinar 2012) while others work in second language education Curriculum (Breen et al. 1989; Markee 1997; Nation and Macalister 2010). Active inquiry in Curriculum is both historical and ongoing in both disciplines.

The components in Table 9.1, particularly materials, will appear in Aisha's case study. She knows a textbook evaluation checklist she wants to use to prepare for an upcoming meeting. She thinks this will help her win collegial support to select a textbook with a blended syllabus–type table of contents that gives some treatment to developing learners' reading and writing of extended texts, while still conforming adequately to her colleagues' unstated teacher theory (and unstated program goal) that learners work with sentence-level linguistic forms. As we will learn, her strategy to inject middle-level theory into a low-level theory curriculum process (textbook selection) is only partly successful.

What seems equally important here is how curriculum components may operate as a system, where there has been a conscious effort to align materials, outcomes, and assessments, for example (Brown 1994). Such alignments seem rational in that the arrangement allows teachers and school administrators to evaluate whether materials are effective and whether outcomes are appropriate by using data from learner test scores, and from learner and teacher feedback. Then, the logic goes, changes could be made based on data and not just an administrator's feeling (Griffee and Gorsuch 2016). Certainly, many administrators and teachers observe an interconnectedness of curriculum components. For instance, teachers asked to use a new book ("Materials" in Table 9.1) will be sensitive as to how well the materials support how they wish to teach, or how they feel it is "safe" to teach ("Teachers and Instruction" in Table 9.1) (Martin 2005). Administrators who are pressured to reduce in-class learner time and increase class size as a means of budget control ("School and Classrooms" and "Syllabus" in Table 9.1) will be concerned how these measures may cause declines in learners' test scores ("Assessments" in Table 9.1). The key here is how the components only *may* operate as a rational and formalized system.

Table 9.1 Definitions and Examples for Theorized Curriculum Components

Curriculum Component	Definition	How Component Is Theorized
Learners	The learners who are admitted to a school or program	A curriculum is constrained by learners' abilities, previous experiences, and attitudes (Johnson 1989b; Nation and Macalister 2010; Richards 2001).
		Learners should take diagnostic tests (Bobbitt 1924; Flinders and Thornton 2013b) and placement tests (Nation and Macalister 2010) so teaching will be more efficient.
		Educators should assume there are three levels of learners for content areas a school plans to offer: "sub-average ability, middle ability, and high-ability" (Bobbitt 1924: 71).
		Schools tend to put learners into homogeneous groups (Bolotin Joseph, Mikel and Windschitl 2011; Reid 1999).
Needs analysis	A collection of data on learner needs from stakeholders	Learner needs are defined by the values of stakeholders such as learners, teachers, administrators, parents, and education authorities (Griffee and Gorsuch 2016; Ornstein and Hunkins 2012; Richards 2001).
		One source of learner needs is commentary from curricular or content specialists (McIntosh 2013).
		Primary questions in a needs analysis examines who the learners are, who the teachers are, and why a course is necessary (Dubin and Olshtain 1986).
		Learner needs can be grouped into categories such as lacks, wants, necessities, objective and subjective needs, language and skills needs (Nation and Macalister 2010).

(continued)

Table 9.1 (continued)

Curriculum Component	Definition	How Component Is Theorized
Measurable goals and stated outcomes	What a school or program wishes learners to accomplish in general terms (missions, aims, or goals) and specific terms (outcomes, objectives)	Course outcomes are statements of how larger course purposes or goals are accomplished. They should be specific enough so that achievement test items or tasks can be designed from them (Gorsuch and Griffee 2018). Outcomes linked to assessments increase accountability (Eisner 2013; Pinar 2012). Outcomes should state a standard of achievement (Bode 1927; Eisner 2013). Standards are based on what competent adults can do (Bode 1927). Standards attached to learning outcomes are based on the values of those who write the outcomes (Eisner 2013; Flinders and Thornton 2013b). Specific objectives should be formulated by teachers while more general goals or aims can be articulated by principals or school superintendents (Bobbitt 1924).
Assessments	The tests (classroom tests and standardized tests), quizzes, questionnaires, observations, and so on and the data collection protocols used with them to evaluate learners' progress and achievement on stated outcomes	One approach to student assessment is a monitoring approach in which learners get feedback from multiple test types for a course, including diagnostic tests, short-term achievement tests, end-of-course achievement tests, and standardized proficiency tests (Nation and Macalister 2010). Diagnostic tests will increase teaching efficiency (Bobbitt 1924). An emphasis on standardized tests signals to learners and to other stakeholders that standardized test scores are the only way learning can be demonstrated (Eisner 2013). Linking standardized tests and a curriculum may limit local curriculum content choices (Pinar 2012).

Syllabuses	A course-based document that specifies learning content and sequence for the content	There are different types of syllabuses, including notional-functional, process, structural, grammatical, language as form, language as use, situational, comprehension, skills, task-based, negotiated, communicative (Dubin and Olshtain 1986; Johnson 1982; Markee 1997; Munby 1978; Nation and Macalister 2010).
		Working syllabuses for a course can be a blend of syllabus types (Dubin and Olshtain 1986; Johnson 1982).
		"Syllabus" in some contexts means a course outline stipulating course regulations, but in curriculum syllabus means a working, extended statement of what a specific group of learners will learn and how they will learn it (Dubin and Olshtain 1986).
		Syllabuses should take into account learner levels and course time constraints (Dubin and Olshtain 1986).
		Syllabuses should provide continuity in the form of contiguous narratives, reviews, use and reuse of grammar (Dubin and Olshtain 1986), and revisiting topics, vocabulary, and grammatical items in new contexts (Nation and Macalister 2010).
		Guidelines for syllabus sequencing may be grammatical simplicity, what learners need first, what communicative functions can be grouped together to form longer learner discourses (Johnson 1982), what learners need to know to do a larger task, how generalizable a rule or lexical item is, the degree of cognitive load, how much learner interpretation or decoding is needed (Markee 1997).

(continued)

Table 9.1 (*continued*)

Curriculum Component	Definition	How Component Is Theorized
Materials	The textbooks, workbooks, worksheets, websites, and computer programs, and so on that learners and teachers use for teaching and learning in a course	Materials have the greatest influence on what occurs in classrooms (Johnson 1989b). Materials and instruction may be taken to be *the* curriculum (Littlejohn and Windeatt 1989). Textbooks inform learners what language learning is taken to be (Littlejohn and Windeatt 1989); this may conflict with the ways teachers are expected to teach (Elyas and Badawood 2017). Materials may be regulated by authoritarian regimes (Pinar 2012) or used to create uniformity in teaching (Ofori-Attah 2008). Commercial textbooks may be the de facto syllabus of a course (Dubin and Olshtain 1986). Structural syllabuses compared across commercial textbooks are strikingly similar; this may comprise a kind of generic syllabus (Johnson 1982). Teachers may need training to use more approaches to using textbooks, even for textbooks of their own choosing (Breen et al. 1989). Textbooks and materials should be critically evaluated and criteria and checklists are available for this (Dubin and Olshtain 1986; Nation and Macalister 2010; Richards 2001).
School and classrooms	The environment where a curriculum is enacted, typically buildings, classrooms, libraries, computer labs, but also the culture of a school and personnel in a school	Available physical resources at a school (audio and video equipment, provision of textbooks, etc.) constrain a curriculum (Nation and Macalister 2010; Richards 2001). Simply having access to information technology resources does not guarantee student learning (Pinar 2012). Schools are a collection of stakeholders, including principals, heads of departments, and teachers all of whom have social roles (Markee 1997). Schools have a culture with norms, habits, and values (Bolotin Joseph, Mikel and Windschitl 2011; Richards 2001). Schools may be seen as businesses that need to be made efficient (Pinar 2012). Large class sizes and how much time is scheduled for a course will constrain a curriculum (Nation and Macalister 2010). Stakeholders are not internally homogeneous. Some individuals may be early adopters of a new curriculum idea (Markee 1997).

Curriculum guides and policy statements	Documents used to regulate teachers' and administrators' curriculum decision-making for accountability purposes	Curriculum guidelines represent the official curriculum (Bolotin Joseph 2011). Policy statements are general and represent administrative or governmental directives (Baldauf 2006; Johnson 1989b). Curriculum guidelines offer a program's educational philosophy, sources of materials for teachers, and standards for assessment of learners (Markee 1997).
Teachers and instruction	The teachers who initiate, manage, or facilitate the activities, tasks, homework assignments, and other acts of instruction that learners experience	Instruction is defined as teaching methods such as the Project Method (Bode 1927), task-based teaching (Markee 1997), four strands-focused and fluency-focused, comprehension-focused, and communicative language teaching (Nation and Macalister 2010; Richards 2001). Instruction is an expensive resource and therefore must be made efficient (Flinders and Thornton 2013a). Materials and instruction may be taken to be *the* curriculum (Littlejohn and Windeatt 1989). There is a current tendency to see teachers as technicians for test preparation or "covering" a syllabus, or simply agents of higher authorities (Baldauf 2006; Mikel 2011; Pinar 2012). Teachers' roles and relationships with learners may be challenged by curriculum policy statements on "new" types of desired outcomes such as learner digital literacy (Elyas and Badawood 2017). Teachers need to take into account the nature of spoken versus written language in their speaking and writing task management (Burns 1990; Dubin and Olshtain 1986).

Source: Authors.

Table 9.2 What Curriculum Posits

1. Curriculum is practical theorizing and reasoning that results in ongoing decisions about learner experiences.
2. Curriculum decision-making involves contested stakeholder views of wider realities and contested views on how to meet those wider realities.
3. Curriculum decisions range from general to specific; sometimes this is a function of stakeholder roles.
4. Curriculum focuses on decision-making about what content is worth learning, and in what manner or order.
5. Curriculum must take into account the nature of content and the nature of how learners learn.
6. Curriculum is constrained by the resources available in a school, including limited time.
7. Curriculum components are interconnected even if they are not rationally planned as being so.
8. Curriculum decisions may be more or less rational and more or less data driven.

Source: Authors.

Many curricula in schools may simply be comprised of general ability tests and commercially available textbooks, neither of which administrators or teachers have direct input into or perhaps comprehensive understanding of (Gorsuch and Griffee 2018). See Table 9.2 for what the theory area of Curriculum posits. See also Table 9.1 for specific propositions made by Curriculum scholars.

Textbook Evaluation and Selection

A key component of the theory area of Curriculum is materials. Materials are "class exercises, textbooks, handouts" (Griffee and Gorsuch 2016: 29). This chapter will focus on textbooks, as they are "commonplaces" of a curriculum (Bolotin Joseph 2011: 9). What makes this theory area relevant to theories of language is that embedded within second language textbooks are theories of language held by the authors and then mediated (shaped) by textbook and software publishers. See discussions on blended syllabuses that comprise the table of contents of many commercially published textbooks (Chapter 7, and earlier in this chapter in the "Language seen as form" section). Publishers are in turn influenced by competition for buyers, who are administrators, teachers, and learners (Affordable Learning Georgia 2018), who have different priorities in selecting textbooks (Angell, DuBravac, and Gonglewski 2008; Nimehchisalem and Mukudan, 2015).

Textbooks are part and parcel of teachers' and learners' classroom experiences. Textbooks are seen as *the* curriculum in many respects (Angell, DuBravac, and Gonglewski 2008; Garinger 2002; Mahmood 2011; Nimehchisalem and Mukudan 2015). They are key resources for teachers, both novice and experienced, to provide learners with language presentation, explanations, practice, and engagement with authentic language samples (Affordable Learning Georgia 2018; Dubin and Olshtain 1986; Gorsuch 2012; Rahimpour and Hashemi 2011; Skierso 1991). Many textbook selection decisions take place at the program level (Angell, DuBravac, and Gonglewski 2008), while some second language teachers have individual authority over textbook selection. Regardless of how textbook selection is done, there is convincing commentary that points to the need to objectify and systematize selection as much as possible, rather than to rely on impressionistic judgments (Ansary and Babaii 2002; Skierso 1991; Tomlinson 2013). The main means to do this is through theorized criteria for textbook evaluation, often in checklist form (although see also designedly non-theorized checklists such as Ansary and Babaii 2002).

As mentioned in Chapter 1, one aspect of theory is to make sense of some phenomenon or some characteristic of an object of interest and then putting into words an explanation or description so it can be conveyed to other persons. Theorized criteria for a textbook evaluation checklist can be seen as an example of this aspect of theory. To make sense of the important process of textbook selection, anyone theorizing a checklist would engage in multiple processes such as introspection (Tomlinson 2013), reading and reasoning through previous commentary (Mahmood 2011; Skierso 1991), and surveying teachers, textbook authors, and learners (Affordable Learning Georgia 2018; Mahmood 2011). A second aspect of theory is that it is tested using evidence, meaning that any proposed textbook checklist should be used and tested. For example, do the theorized criteria mean the same thing to multiple users? Does using the checklist result in the local practical reasoning that makes up the backbone of curriculum processes at a school? Does the checklist help to select a useable textbook that promotes students' learning and success to attain course goals?

Skierso's (1991) procedure and checklist for textbook evaluation and selection remains much cited (e.g., Ellis 1997; Garinger 2002; Mukudan and Nimehchisalem 2012; Mahmood 2011; Nimehchisalem and Mukudan 2015; see Ansary and Babaii [2002] for a list of additional checklists). Skierso argued that language teachers needed to learn to evaluate textbooks systematically for practical and professional reasons—"practical" because teachers needed to know how to compensate for a selected textbook's weaknesses or to better use its strengths; "professional" because teachers may be asked to evaluate textbooks for administrative purposes both before and after a textbook's use (Skierso 1991: 432; see also Rahimpour and Hashemi 2011). In essence, Skierso was asking teachers to rely more on middle-level theory and less on low-level theory.

Skierso (1991) further theorized that a checklist or survey instrument should be used in a two-step procedure. The first step is to analyze the existing curriculum and the second step is to systematically evaluate a given textbook in reference to the curriculum (see also Garinger 2002). The first step involves collecting specific information on the learners (age, language background, level), the teachers (language background, level of preparation), the course syllabus (content, emphases given to different content, and tasks for which specific content areas are needed), and the institution (aims, class size, class scheduling practices, textbook budget) (Skierso 1991: 432–4). Thus, Skierso firmly conjoins Curriculum (Table 9.1) with textbook evaluation. The "Curriculum" section of her instrument has thirty-four items. Many items show a theorization of language as use, specifying content as language skills but also specifying what tasks the skills are used for. Skierso theorizes Curriculum content as "language areas" such as "grammar," "vocabulary," and "pronunciation," which could be taken as a focus on form. But her theorization of language as use comes through in her additional questions about percentages for emphasis according to the course syllabus, and more importantly, what percentage of "grammar" will be used for "reception" and for "production" (443). Under "Institutional Data" checklist users are asked to reflect on "Institutional or National Objectives." These include boxes for "language reception," "language production," "cultural recognition," and "global/cross-cultural awareness," among others (444).

One of the reasons Skierso's checklist remains salient is because of its comprehensiveness. Once the checklist user has completed the first step and collected information on the curriculum, a textbook-specific ninety-three-item checklist follows, to be completed for a given textbook (see Skierso [1991] for the full checklist). For each item (each criterion), the teacher would rate the textbook on a five-point scale with 4 = "Excellent" to 0 = "Totally lacking." Each criterion is then weighted according to the relevance of the criterion to a given curriculum. Thus, for a given criterion: "Register: To what extent does the text teach the register appropriate for the needs of the students (e.g., formal or literary style vs. conversational style vs. technical style)?" the score of 4, 3, 2, 1, or 0 would be assigned and then weighted A = "Required," B = "Preferred," or N = "Not applicable." The score for each criterion would then be added up for a total score. The criterion on register just named here is relevant to our case study with Aisha. She wants a textbook that clearly shows the difference between written and spoken language, whereas her boss and colleagues assume that any language presented in a textbook, spoken language included, will resemble decontextualized written language because only grammatically "correct" or "polite" language will help learners learn linguistic forms. This bias is common in second language textbooks (Aronsson 2014; Wong and Zhang Waring 2021) and in teaching (Burns 1990).

There are eleven subtests in the whole ninety-three-item checklist, including "aims and goals [of the textbook] regarding language skills and cultural understanding" and "vocabulary and structures: grammar" (Skierso 1991: 445–6). Of the ninety-three items (criteria), only eighteen directly query about linguistic forms, such as "grammar," which is theorized in four parts relevant to textbook selection: "number and sequence appropriacy," "accuracy [of information]," "clarity and completeness," and "meaningful context."

Skierso (1991) consulted sixty-five sources to theorize her curriculum and textbook evaluation criteria. Later adaptors Mukudan and Nimehchisalem (2012) seemed to believe that at least some of Skierso's criteria were valid, but for a variety of reasons, elected to write individual criteria to be more specific and limited in scope. They adapted Skierso's (1991) instrument, reducing the thirty-four items in the curriculum section to five items, simply querying the extent to which the textbook matched the course syllabus (one item) and the extent to which the textbook matched the learners' backgrounds (four items). The remaining forty-five textbook-related criteria in their checklist use a five-point scale (4 = "Always true" to 0 = "Never true") that queries users as to the "physical and utilitarian attributes" of a textbook (six items, including "It is durable"), "learning-teaching content" (eight items, including "The situations created in the dialogues sound natural and real"), and "writing" (three items, including "Models are provided for different genres") among other theorized areas (Nimehchisalem and Mukudan 2015: 775–6). When they asked language teachers to rate textbooks using both Skierso's and their checklist, they found statistical overlap between teachers' ratings, again suggesting that they found her theorizations to some extent compelling.

Nimehchisalem and Mukudan argued their instrument was theoretically valid and yet could be completed more quickly by a busy teacher than Skierso's (1991) procedure and instruments. Missing from their adapted checklist, however, is the comprehensive treatment of learners, teachers, the course syllabus, and the institution. This means missed opportunities for a theorized analysis of the curriculum itself, and a practical connection between commonly accepted components of a given curriculum, such as outcomes, teachers, and materials (Table 9.1). This is not to criticize. Rather, the differences between the checklists point to differences not only in what the researchers wanted to measure but also, more fundamentally, differences in their theorizations of textbooks and Curriculum. One might ask similar questions about checklists that are condensed from multiple published checklists, usually by means of finding common criteria the checklists share. In attempting to make a textbook evaluation checklist "easier" to use, or more applicable to a variety of teaching situations, are the theorizations used to create the original criteria then lost or broken? Does the condensed checklist have conceptual clarity? In other words, will different users understand the criteria in similar ways? Does using the checklist result in the localized practical reasoning that comprises what Curriculum is? Does the checklist result in textbook selections that promote students' learning and attainment of program outcomes? See Table 9.3 for what the theory area of textbook evaluation and selection posits.

Table 9.3 What the Theory Area of Textbook Evaluation and Selection Posits

1. There are compelling practical and professional reasons for teachers to engage in textbook evaluation even if they are not tasked with textbook selection.
2. Textbook evaluation and selection has multiple practical, professional, and administrative purposes.
3. Textbook evaluation and selection should be objective and systematic.
4. One means to achieve relative objectivity and systematicity is through theorizing and developing checklists and procedures for using them.
5. Theorizing textbook evaluation checklists is done through introspection; reading previous commentary; and surveying teachers, learners, and administrators.
6. Textbook evaluation and selection checklists should be used, tested, and improved.
7. Textbook evaluation and selection checklists arguably depend on a theorized analysis of the existing curriculum. Textbooks and other curriculum components are interlinked.
8. Like curriculum, textbook evaluation and selection checklists may theorize both what constitutes worthwhile content and how people learn content.

Source: Authors.

Low-Level Theories Concerning Language and Institutions: A Teacher of English

This chapter identifies and describes low-level theories about language and institutions held by an experienced EFL teacher named Aisha. First is a description of Aisha's experience and professional training. Second, Aisha's workplace will be described with a focus on the weeks preceding the beginning of a new school term. Finally, Aisha's low-level working theories about language and institutions will be identified and presented in a table.

Aisha's Background

Aisha has just turned thirty. She is Saudi and has graduated from a top women's university. At her freshman year, her university started teaching all content courses in English, and it was a terribly hard time for both her and her classmates. Even though they had all done pretty well in English classes in their earlier schooling, nothing prepared them for reading, listening, speaking, and writing in English for their psychology, literature, and computer science classes. By the second year, some of her friends had dropped out. Aisha stuck with it, and with the help of a female tutor from Germany her father found, she finished her undergraduate degree in English language translation. Her teachers at the college, and her tutor, a middle-aged woman teaching English for a year at a commercial language school, encouraged Aisha's interest in reading and writing English. They encouraged her to find texts to read from many sources on topics interesting to her, including books, magazines, and the internet. They also worked with her to write for different purposes, such as letters to friends, personal and business emails, short book reports, instructions for installing computer software, cooking recipes, and reflective essays. They encouraged Aisha's awareness that different grammatical forms appeared in different texts, and that the different forms were appropriate for different writing purposes. The different writing projects they set for Aisha called for deliberate vocabulary selection, as well as certain phrases. For instance, short reflective essays might use phrases like "My general impression is that" and "There are some problems with this argument" whereas cooking recipes would not use such phrases, nor would letters to friends. Aisha found learning the phrases interesting because they were bound to genre, but not necessarily to specific national cultures. It was as though the different texts she read and writing tasks she did had their own language use cultures. She enjoyed her growing precision in saying exactly what she meant to say for a different rhetorical purpose. It gave her choices and self-expression.

In her mid-twenties, Aisha found a job as a teaching assistant at another women's college in a medium-sized Saudi city. It was a newer school that did not yet have an English-medium program. The Saudi government wanted to increase young Saudis' ability to compete for jobs and academic study opportunities internationally, and to become literate in computer technology and science. The way to do this, the government reasoned, was to make young Saudis more proficient in English. Like it or not, English was *the* global language nowadays. One strategy, then, was to "re-tool" Saudi higher education and to improve it from within. If young, keen Saudis were sent on full scholarships to American, British, European, and Australian universities for advanced degrees in English and in other subjects, they could return to Saudi universities with their new expertise *and* English competences. The administration at Aisha's school recommended her for a master's program in applied linguistics scholarship. She would be in the United States for two years, expenses paid, and upon successful completion of her degree, she would return to a guaranteed teaching job back at her school with a promotion.

Aisha's Master's Program Testing Course and Materials Design Course

Aisha focused particularly on courses on Conversation Analysis, testing, and materials design. She chose the last two topics because she wanted to be better at understanding the curriculum decisions administrators and teachers made at her school in Saudi Arabia. The placement tests given at her school in Saudi Arabia were a pressure point between students and teachers. Teachers spent a lot of time talking to students and students' families about test results they disagreed on. Textbook selection decisions, on the other hand, were a huge pressure point between the school administration and the teachers. Whatever textbook was chosen, teachers complained about it—the textbook did not provide enough practice in the grammar points they knew would appear on end-of-semester tests, or the one-off textbook chapter themes did not seem to keep students' interest, nor were the themes interesting to the teachers, although no one said that too loudly.

While studying about proficiency and placement tests in the testing course, Aisha was reminded of one girl at her school in Saudi Arabia, who thought she should be in a high ability group, not the low group, which is where that year's placement test put her (students at Aisha's school back in Saudi Arabia seemed to fall into two groups every year). The girl said, "I answered all the multiple-choice questions perfectly!" Aisha and her boss had dug up the girl's test paper. The multiple-choice questions focused on grammar points and vocabulary embedded in single sentences, and the girl had done well on them. But, in fact, she had not done well on the article reading and essay response section and had written only a single paragraph with disconnected sentences all lined up perfectly to the left like a poem. She had likely not understood the short, easy article she needed to read to write her essay. Aisha wondered whether the two parts of the placement test ought to be combined the way they were to make a single decision of "low group" or "high group." Could not the girl be put into a high ability group just for grammar review or vocabulary building courses, but then be put into a low ability group for a reading and writing class where learners actually learned different text features and used language to express themselves? Would not that make teaching more efficient, anyway? But then, she was not sure about that, either. Was not reading and writing coupled with grammar and vocabulary choices? Would not attention in one area create learning in the other?

Aisha, despite struggling with yet even greater reading and writing challenges in her master's program, still loved to read and write. She wanted to create a new reading and writing course at her school back in Saudi Arabia. She thought that when the time came, she might know how to argue for such a course. She had taken not only an American but a British proficiency test, both of which had reading and writing subtests. If her school in Saudi

Arabia wanted students to do well on these big international tests, they had to be better prepared for them, and being good at single sentence grammar and decontextualized vocabulary knowledge would not help students, not entirely.

In her materials design class, Aisha studied textbooks first. She selected one that was widely used in Saudi Arabia, but not yet at her own school. She had not realized that the table of contents of a textbook was in fact a syllabus that spelled out content but then also sequencing of content as in "Chapter 1," "Chapter 2," and so on. But she noticed that none of the "theme" parts of each chapter carried through to other chapters. There was no actual sequence. Further, as a result, the "vocabulary" sections of each chapter simply dealt with small new lists of words related to the theme. Very little vocabulary was recycled. With a textbook evaluation checklist in hand, she set out to estimate what percentage of a given textbook chapter dealt with reading, writing, speaking, and listening. She found this hard to do because there seemed to be a lot of overlap between writing and speaking. Students did a lot of writing sentences and sentence completion, and composing short paragraphs, but then these same sentences and basic patterns were used to do speaking practice.

Aisha also estimated how much time each section of a chapter would take her to teach. She then added up all teaching times for all sections in a chapter. She found that any given chapter would take twenty-two hours of class time, that is, if she and her students had unlimited time. But when she recalled how much time her school had scheduled for a given chapter in another book, only ten hours were available. This was a real eye-opener. She then guessed, based on her memory, that the grammar, vocabulary, and perhaps some of the writing sections, if they were thought to help with practicing grammar and vocabulary, might be covered in class while the rest would be assigned as "homework." The textbook she studied for her master's program course did have a few pages on writing. But when looking across chapters, she noticed the same small-scale generic writing tasks being used. They were editing tasks of existing short essays, or paragraph writing assignments, but nothing longer. There was no real sequencing of different, and increasingly complex, writing tasks, such as reading and commenting on cooking recipes, then giving advice on a recipe, then writing a script for a video-recorded recipe demonstration. Unless teachers created their own tasks, students might not have much of a repertoire of self-expression.

Aisha Back at Work

Having finished her master's course, Aisha was back in Saudi Arabia and ready to participate as a regular teacher at her school. A month ahead of the new semester, the head of her department had a special meeting for all teachers. They were handed four textbooks under consideration for the following school year. One of them was the textbook Aisha had evaluated in her master's program materials design course. The teachers were to return in one week to select which textbook to use for the following semester. "I know it's late notice," said the department head, "but something's come up." She then announced that the school was transitioning to an English-medium school the following year. She said, "We need to improve our current students' language skills in all four areas in the next year to come. They must be ready to complete their second or third year doing everything in English. The students who will be fourth years are exempt. Basically, we have to build an 'English preparation intensive course' from scratch." This announcement was met with stunned silence. The department head then said, "These four textbook series are the ones you have to choose from. Each title has three levels that the publishers say are *CEFR* levels A1, A2, and B1." "Three levels? No longer two?" one teacher asked. "Yes, three levels," the department head answered. "Our school president says we will prepare classes for three levels."

The Textbook Selection Meeting

At the meeting the following week, Aisha was ready to argue for her choice of textbook series. It was the same book she had evaluated in her materials design course. She felt it had real drawbacks, but that it would accommodate the grammar practice and vocabulary practice she thought her colleagues would insist on. At the same time, she thought she could adapt the early reading and writing sections so that learners would need to read the short passages in a chapter multiple times during a given week and pay attention to different features each time. She also thought that she could begin to add longer supplementary reading passages and have students look for the elements of the texts that were unique to the purpose a reading passage had been written for, such as vocabulary and phrases. She felt she could think of more varied writing assignments than the book called for, and then link them to the supplementary reading passages the learners would engage with. Best of all, the book had multiple review chapters, with one appearing after a "unit" of three chapters. Aisha knew her department head would have to organize making new placement tests, or at least she hoped she would. How else would they create three learner ability groups? Perhaps the review chapters could be good sources for test items.

The meeting did not go quite as Aisha planned. On one hand, the teachers adopted the textbook series she had hoped for. Aisha would have to work to find the right supplementary reading materials and fit them to the writing tasks she had planned, but she thought she could make it work. On the other hand, one of the teachers had seen the faculty handbook for another, established English prep program, and talked about how the handbook stipulated what pages had to be covered in the required textbook by what dates in the semester. "We need to do the same," the teacher said. "It's the only way to make sure everyone covers the same materials. Everyone needs to be on the same page." Aisha sighed in frustration. She could guess which pages would be stipulated—those containing the "core" grammar and vocabulary portions of each chapter. The other sections on listening, reading, and writing would be given short shrift, or assigned as homework. Aisha jumped into the discussion. She said that an English prep program would meet more hours per week than what they were used to. There could be more flexibility with time. Further, if they wanted students to do well in an English-medium campus, they had to work on reading and writing, with texts that were longer than sentences and paragraphs. She ended with, "Our students are young women, who are living in a changing society. We need to help them find self-expression. Perhaps we can do this by working with their reading and writing, so they may find new viewpoints and learn to express themselves in different ways." One teacher answered, "They can do that by just getting a degree! They don't need our help beyond that." The meeting ended without any firm decision on adopting a strict timetable for completing textbook pages. Aisha thought her department head was leaning against the idea.

A New Placement Test

In the next weeks, Aisha worked with the department head and two of her colleagues on a placement test. They included items from the review chapters of the textbook series, many on grammar and vocabulary, but Aisha also helped select items testing students on reading and listening passages, taken from a teacher's workbook that came with the textbook series—33 percent of the items were taken from the lowest level book, 33 percent came from the middle level book, and 33 percent came from the highest level book, claiming to bring learners to the *CEFR* B1 level. She had no idea how well the test would work to place students into three groups, but she felt there was a chance it would work well enough. She was far less sure whether the students in the school would actually comprise three groups of low, middle, and high ability. She was not sure where her school president got the idea of three groups. She suspects that her school's students really fall into two groups—low and middle. Only a few of the young women would be in a high-level group at a *CEFR* B1 level because they had studied abroad or had private tutors. But Aisha thought she would keep an open mind depending on the test results.

Aisha did not succeed in persuading her department to also test students' writing, and thus would not have a chance to teach the special writing course she had wanted to offer. "One step at a time," her department head told her. See Table 9.4 for what Aisha posits about language and institutions, and also about textbooks.

Table 9.4 What Aisha Posits about Language as a Teacher and Institutional Stakeholder

1. Language forms at the word and sentence level and in longer texts change according to what language is used for.

2. Second language use can be a means of learning second language forms.

3. English-medium study demands language use skills beyond what grammar and vocabulary study can do. In other words, an English-medium program curriculum requires new decisions about content.

4. Different genres of written texts can be learned, both through reading written texts and doing writing tasks.

5. Many stakeholders in a second language program will want to continue seeing content as primarily second language forms.

6. Limited time is a constraint to a language program's curriculum. In some situations, time constraints may force a conception of language as forms.

7. It is possible to adapt second language textbooks to increase learners' language use.

8. Textbook adaptation can be creative and fulfilling.

9. Knowing a textbook very well will help teachers' adaptation efforts.

10. Textbook evaluation checklists, depending on what they ask, can change how a textbook is evaluated. If textbook evaluation checklists query on language use or what learners are learning the language for, it changes how a textbook is evaluated.

11. Students can gain powers of choice and self-expression through getting experience with a variety of second language texts and tasks.

12. Textbook series available in multiple levels *might* be useful to creating placement tests with items in different content areas, and at different levels of difficulty.

Source: Authors.

This moment in Aisha's professional development shows middle-level theories beginning to inform her low-level working theories. For example, in using a textbook evaluation checklist informed by a theory of language as use, Aisha was able to come to new conclusions about the second language as content in a curriculum. She began to see texts and tasks as the teaching units of the curriculum. This would very much change how her students experienced the second language in classes. Even as she was able to do so, she noted that other qualified teachers were quite capable of coming to entirely different conclusions as to what constituted worthwhile content (words and sentences). Even as she used middle-level theories to inform her practical reasoning about the curriculum, she used her own experiences as an English language learner, and a learner of content, as low-level teacher theories. Simply using middle-level theory from a textbook evaluation checklist might not account for how quickly she was able to plan her adaptation of the textbook series she persuaded her colleagues to adopt. In addition, she had developed low-level teacher theory from her observations of learner ability groups, believing instinctively there were two ability groups at her school, and not three. At the same time, she tapped into middle-level theory to arrive at a method of lifting the new placement test items from the textbook series her school adopted. High-level Curriculum theory informed her that the different components of Curriculum were interconnected, and that they could be rationally planned to become moreso.

Reflective Projects

1. On the first two pages of this chapter, four basic questions are posed:
   - How is the second language experienced by learners at a school?
   - What units of teaching are used?
   - In what sequence do learners experience the units that are used?
   - What would the wider reality be for a particular school?

   Answer these questions for a teaching situation you know.

2. What Curriculum decisions are made in the teaching situation you describe in project number 1 above? Use components from Table 9.1 to help you answer.

3. What is the prevailing wider reality for the school/teaching situation you described? How specifically does that change Curriculum decisions that take place at the school?

4. Looking at Table 9.1, find events or ideas from Aisha's case study that correspond to the proposed curriculum components.

5. In Table 9.1, some of the components may overlap. Where do they overlap? What is the nature of their overlap?

6. Find a textbook evaluation and selection checklist from a teaching journal. Evaluate the checklist. Is the checklist theorized? Where does the author get the procedure and the items for the checklist? What are the specific theories the author mentions? Are their theories evident to you, but not mentioned by the author? What are they? Match them to specific checklist items.

7. One way Curriculum is theorized is to account for how worthwhile content is decided on, and how learners are to learn that content. In textbooks, curriculum statements, faculty handbooks, and so on that you may know (look at Table 9.1 for ideas), can you find evidence of how the author(s) of these documents arrived at their decisions about worthwhile content, and what they believe is the nature of language learning?

REFERENCES

Abend, G. (2008), "The Meaning of Theory," *Sociological Theory*, 26(2): 173–99.

Abrams, D., and M. A. Hogg (2004), "Metatheory: Lessons from Social Identity Research," *Personality and Social Psychology Review*, 8(2): 98–106.

Achinstein, P. (1965), "Theoretical Models," *British Journal for the Philosophy of Science*, 16(62): 102–20.

Adair-Hauck, B., and R. Donato (2002), "The PACE Model: A Story-Based Approach to Meaning and Form for Standards-Based Language Learning," *French Review*, 76(2): 265–76.

Affordable Learning Georgia (2018), "Quality Standards for Open Educational Sources," retrieved July 15, 2021, from: https://www.affordablelearninggeorgia.org/find_textbooks/selecting_textbooks

Ahmadian, M. (2012), "The Relationship between Working Memory Capacity and L2 Oral Performance under Task-Based Careful Online Planning," *TESOL Quarterly*, 46(1): 165–75.

Ahmadian, M., and M. Tavakoli (2010), "The Effects of Simultaneous Use of Careful Online Planning and Task Repetition on Accuracy, Complexity, and Fluency in EFL Learners' Oral Production," *Language Teaching Research*, 15(1): 35–59.

Ahmadian, M., and M. Tavakoli (2011), "Exploring the Utility of Action Research to Investigate Second-Language Classrooms as Complex Systems," *Educational Action Research*, 19(2): 121–36.

Alamarza, G. (1996), "Student Foreign Language Teacher's Knowledge Growth," in D. Freeman and J. C. Richards (eds.), *Teacher Learning in Language Teaching*, 50–78, Cambridge: Cambridge University Press.

Alarcon, L. (2018), "A Course Logic Study for a New Multi-Audience Beginning University Spanish Course," unpublished manuscript.

Allana, S., and A. Clark (2018), "Applying Meta-theory to Qualitative and Mixed Methods Research: A Discussion of Critical Realism and Heart Failure Disease Management Interventions Research," *International Journal of Qualitative Methods*, 17: 1–9.

Allport, G. (1979), *The Nature of Prejudice*, New York: Perseus.

Alrashidi, O., and H. Phan (2015), "Education Context and English Teaching and Learning in the Kingdom of Saudi Arabia: An Overview," *English Language Teaching*, 8(5): 33–44.

Al-Shammari, Z., H. Al-Sharoufi, and T. Yawkey (2008), "The Effectiveness of Direct Instruction in Teaching English in Elementary Public Education Schools in Kuwait," *Education*, 129(1): 80–90.

American Council for the Teaching of Foreign Languages (2012a), "ACTFL Proficiency Guidelines 2012," retrieved March 22, 2020, from: https://

www.actfl.org/publications/guidelines-and-manuals/actfl-proficiency-guideli
nes-2012

American Council on the Teaching of Foreign Languages (2012b), "Performance
Descriptors for Language Learners," retrieved March 22, 2020, from: https://
www.actfl.org/publications/guidelines-and-manuals/actfl-performance-descript
ors-language-learners

American Council on the Teaching of Foreign Languages and Council for the
Accreditation of Educator Preparation (2015), "ACTFL/CAEP Program
Standards for the Preparation of Foreign Language Teachers," retrieved May 31,
2022, from: https://www.actfl.org/sites/default/files/caep/ACTFLCAEPStandard
s2013_v2015.pdf

American Council on the Teaching of Foreign Languages and National Council
of State Supervisors for Languages (2018), "Can-Do Statements Introduction,"
retrieved December 10, 2018, from: https://www.actfl.org/publications/guideli
nes-and-manuals/ncssfl-actfl-can-do-statements

American Psychological Association (2020), *Publication Manual of the American
Psychological Association* (7th ed.), Washington, DC: Author.

Anderson, J. R. (1983), *The Architecture of Cognition*, Cambridge, MA: Harvard
University Press.

Anderson, J. R. (2005), *Cognitive Psychology and its Implications* (6th ed.),
New York: Worth.

Anderson, N. (1999), *Exploring Second Language Reading: Issues and Strategies*,
Boston, MA: Heinle and Heinle.

Andrews, S. (1994), "The Grammatical Knowledge/Awareness of Native-
Speaker EFL Teachers: What the Trainers Say," in M. Bygate, A. Tonkyn,
and E. Williams (eds.), *Grammar and the Language Teacher*, 69–89, Hemel
Hempstead: Prentice Hall.

Andrews, S. (2007), *Teacher Language Awareness*, Cambridge: Cambridge
University Press.

Andrews, S., and A. McNeill (2005), "Knowledge about Language and the "Good
Language Teacher,'" in N. Bartels (ed.), *Applied Linguistics and Language
Teacher Education*, 159–78, Verlag: Springer.

Angell, J., S. DuBravac, and M. Gonglewski (2008), "Thinking Globally, Acting
Locally: Selecting Textbooks for College-Level Programs," *Foreign Language
Annals*, 41(3): 562–72.

Ansary, H., and E. Babaii (2002), "Universal Characteristics of EFL/ESL
Textbook: A Step towards Systematic Textbook Evaluation," *Internet TESL
Journal*, 8.

Archer, A. L., and C. A. Hughes (2011), *Explicit Instruction: Effective and Efficient
Teaching*, New York: Guilford.

Arnold, J. (2000), "Seeing through Listening Comprehension Exam Anxiety,"
TESOL Quarterly, 34(4): 777–86.

Aronsson, B. (2014), "Prosody in the Foreign Language Classroom: Always
Present, Rarely Practised?" Unpublished manuscript, Umea University,
Sweden, retrieved July 24, 2021, from: https://www.researchgate.net/publicat
ion/271729402_Prosody_in_the_Foreign_Language_Classroom_-_Always_Prese
nt_Rarely_Practised

Asdar (2017), "Students' Self-Assessment on Their Spoken Interaction Using CEFR," *The 1st Education and Language International Conference Proceedings*, Pakistan, Center for International Language Development of Unissula, retrieved April 9, 2022, from: http://jurnal.unissula.ac.id/index.php/ELIC/article/downl oad/1222/931

Auestad, L. (2015), *Respect, Plurality, and Prejudice: A Psychoanalytical and Philosophical Enquiry into the Dynamics of Social Exclusion and Discrimination*, London: Karnac.

Austin, J. L. (1962), *How to Do Things with Words*, Oxford: Clarendon.

Austin, J. L. (1975), *How to Do Things with Words* (2nd ed.), Cambridge, MA: Harvard University Press.

Ausubel, D. (2000), *The Acquisition and Retention of Knowledge: A Cognitive View*, Dordecht: Kluwer Academic.

Bachman, L., and A. Palmer (1996), *Language Testing in Practice: Designing and Developing Useful Language Tests*, Oxford: Oxford University Press.

Bachman, L., and A. Palmer (2010), *Language Assessment in Practice*, Oxford: Oxford University Press.

Baldauf, R. (2006), "Rearticulating the Case for Micro Language Planning in a Language Ecology Context," *Current Issues in Language Planning*, 7(2–3): 147–70.

Bandura, A. (1997), *Self-Efficacy: The Exercise of Control*, New York: W.H. Freeman.

Barrs, M. (2022), *Vygotsky the Teacher: A Companion to his Psychology for Teachers and Other Practitioners*, New York: Routledge.

Bartels, N. (2005), "Applied Linguistics and Language Teacher Education: What We Know," in N. Bartels (ed.), *Researching Applied Linguistics in Language Teacher Education*, 405–24, Boston, MA: Springer.

Barton, A. (2014), "Making Progress in Languages Issues around Transition," in P. Driscoll, E. Macaro, and A. Swarbrick (eds.), *Debates in Modern Languages Education*, 163–73, London: Routledge.

Bartunek, J. M., and M. K. Moch (1987), "First-Order, Second-Order, and Third-Order Change and Organization Development Interventions: A Cognitive Approach," *Journal of Applied Behavioral Science*, 23(4); 483–500.

Bellarmine, R. (2019), "The Teacher's Sense of Plausibility in Development and Teacher Training," in A. Maley (ed.), *Developing Expertise through Experience: Ideas for Continuing Professional Development*, 25–6, London: British Council.

Beretta, A. (1991), "Theory Construction in SLA: Complementarity and Opposition," *Studies in Second Language Acquisition*, 13(4): 493–511.

Berwick, R. (1989), "Needs Assessment in Language Programming: From Theory to Practice," in R. K. Johnson (ed.), *The Second Language Curriculum*, 48–62, Cambridge: Cambridge University Press.

Bickman, L. (1996), "The Application of Program Theory to the Evaluation of a Managed Mental Health Care System," *Evaluation and Program Planning*, 19(2): 111–19.

Binns, A., and S.-K. Johnston (2021), "Impact of Assistant Language Teachers on English Education in Shizuoka," in P. Ferguson and R. Derrah (eds.), *Reflections and New Perspectives: JALT Proceedings*, retrieved January 1, 2022, from: https://doi.org/10.37546/JALTPCP2021-11

Bjork, C. (2015), *High-Stakes Schooling: What We Can Learn from Japan's Experiences with Testing, Accountability, and Education Reform*, Chicago: University of Chicago Press.

Black, M. (1962), *Models and Metaphors*, Ithaca, NY: Cornell University Press.

Blease, D. (1983), "Teacher Expectations and the Self-Fulfilling Prophecy," *Educational Studies*, 9(2): 123–9. Published online: July 6, 2006. doi: 10.1080/0305569830090206

Bloom, S. J., P. Airasian, K. Cruikshank, R. Mayer, P. Pintrich, J. Raths, and M. Wittrock (2001), *A Taxonomy for Learning, Teaching, and Assessing: A Revision of Bloom's Taxonomy of Educational Objectives*, New York: Longman.

Bobbitt, F. (1924), *How to Make a Curriculum*, Cambridge, MA: Riverside.

Bode, B. (1927), *Modern Educational Theories*, New York: Macmillan.

Bohleber, W. (2018), "The Use of Public and of Private Implicit Theories in the Clinical Situation," in J. Canestri (ed.), *Putting Theory to Work: How Are Theories Actually Used in Practice*, 1–22, New York: Routledge.

Bolotin Joseph, P. (2011), "Conceptualizing Curriculum," in P. Bolotin Joseph (ed.), *Cultures of Curriculum* (2nd ed.), 3–22, New York: Routledge.

Bolotin Joseph, P., E. Mikel, and M. Windschitl (2011), "Reculturing Curriculum," in P. Bolotin Joseph (ed.), *Cultures of Curriculum* (2nd ed.), 55–77, New York: Routledge.

Borelli, G. (2018), *Second Language Acquisition: A Theoretical Overview*, retrieved October 10, 2021, from: https://www.academia.edu/36688710/Second_Language_Acquisition_A_Theoretical_Overview

Borg, S. (1999), "Teachers' Theories in Grammar Teaching," *ELT Journal*, 53(3): 157–67.

Borg, S. (2003), "Teacher Cognition in Language Teaching: A Review of Research on What Language Teachers Think, Know, Believe, and Do," *Language Teaching*, 36: 81–109.

Borg, S. (2006), "The Distinctive Characteristics of Foreign Language Teachers," *Language Teaching Research*, 10: 3–31.

Boring, E. G. (1955), "Dual Role of the Zeitgeist in Scientific Creativity," *Scientific Monthly*, 80(2): 101–6.

Boring, E. G. (1963), "The Role of Theory in Experimental Psychology," in R. I. Watson and D. T. Campbell (eds.), *History, Psychology, and Science: Selected Papers by E. G. Boring*, 210–25, New York: John Wiley.

Botts, D., A. Losardo, C. Tillery, and M. Werts (2014), "A Comparison of Activity-Based Intervention and Embedded Direct Instruction When Teaching Emergent Literacy Skills," *Journal of Special Education*, 48(2): 120–34.

Bourns, B. (2013), *Contextualized French Grammar*, Boston, MA: Heinle.

Brandt, M., and J. Crawford (2016), "Answering Unresolved Questions about the Relationship between Cognitive Ability and Prejudice," *Social Psychological and Personality Science*, 7(8), 884–92. doi: 10.1177/1948550616660592

Breen, M. (1991), "Understanding the Language Teacher," in R. Phillipson, E. Kellerman, L. Selinker, M. Sharwood Smith, and M. Swain (eds.), *Foreign/*

Second Language Pedagogy Research, 213–33, Clevedon: Multilingual Matters.

Breen, M., C. Candlin, L. Dam and G. Gabrielson (1989), "The Evolution of a Teacher Training Programme," in R. K. Johnson (ed.), *The Second Language Curriculum*, 111–36, Cambridge: Cambridge University Press.

Breen, M. P. (1985), "Authenticity in the Language Classroom," *Applied Linguistics*, 6(1): 60–70.

Breen, M. P., and C. N. Candlin (1980), "The Essentials of a Communicative Curriculum in Language Teaching," *Applied Linguistics*, 1(2): 89–112.

Brehe, S. (2018), *Brahe's Grammar Anatomy*, Dahlonega, GA: University of North Georgia Press.

Brisard, E., and I. Menter (2008), "Compulsory Education in the United Kingdom," in D. Matheson (ed.), *An Introduction to the Study of Education* (3rd ed.), 240–65, London: Routledge.

Brown, A. (1987), "Metacognition, Executive Control, Self-regulation, and Other More Mysterious Mechanisms," in F. Weinert and R. Kluwe (eds.), *Metacognition, Motivation, and Understanding*, 65–116, Hillsdale, NJ: Lawrence Erlbaum.

Brown, J. D. (1994), *Elements of Language Curriculum: A Systematic Approach to Program Development*, Boston, MA: Cengage Heinle.

Brown, J. D. (1995), "Language Program Evaluation: Decisions, Problems and Solutions," *Annual Review of Applied Linguistics*, 15: 227–48.

Brown, J. S., A. Collins, and P. Duguid (1989), "Situated Cognition and the Culture of Learning," *Educational Researcher*, 18(1): 32–42.

Brown, L. (ed.) (1993), *The New Shorter Oxford English Dictionary*, Oxford: Clarendon.

Brown, S. (2011), *Listening Myths: Applying Second Language Research to Classroom Teaching*, Ann Arbor: University of Michigan Press.

Brown, V. L. (1985), "Two Perspectives on Engelmann and Carnine's Theory of Instruction," *Remedial and Special Education*, 6(2): 56–60.

Brumfit, C. (1984), *Communicative Methodologies in Language Teaching*. Cambridge: Cambridge University Press.

Brumfit, C. (2001), *Individual Freedom in Language Teaching*, Oxford: Oxford University Press.

Bruner, J. (2009), "Culture, Mind and Education," in K. Illeris (ed.), *Contemporary Theories of Learning: Learning Theorists in Their Own Words*, 179–88, Abingdon: Routledge.

Burgin, X., and M. Daniel (2021), "Examining Current and Future Ecuadorian Educators' Experiences Using Action Research in the English as a Second Language Classroom," *Profile*, 23(1): 41–55.

Burke, B. (2011), "Rituals and Beliefs Ingrained in World Language Pedagogy," *Journal of Language Teaching and Research*, 2(1): 1–12.

Burns, A. (1996), "Starting All over Again: From Teaching Adults to Teaching Beginners," in D. Freeman and J. C. Richards (eds.), *Teacher Learning in Language Teaching*, 154–77, Cambridge: Cambridge University Press.

Burns, A. (1990), "Focus on Language in the Communicative Classroom," in G. Brindley (ed.), *The Second Language Curriculum in Action*, 36–58, Sydney: National Centre for English Language Teaching and Research.

Bush, T., and D. Glover (2012), "Distributed Leadership in Action: Leading High-Performing Leadership Teams in English Schools," *School Leadership and Management*, 32(1): 21–36.

Butterworth, B. (1980), "Evidence from Pauses in Speech," in B. Butterworth (ed.), *Language Production: Speech and Talk*, 155–76, London: Academic.

Bygate, M. (1999), "Task as Context for the Framing, Reframing and Unframing of Language," *System*, 27: 33–48.

Bygate, M. (2001), "Effects of Task Repetition on the Structure and Control of Oral Language," in M. Bygate, P. Skehan, and M. Swain (eds.), *Researching Pedagogic Tasks: Second Language Learning, Teaching and Testing*, 23–48, Harlow, England: Longman.

Bygate, M., P. Skehan, and M. Swain (2001), "Introduction," in M. Bygate, P. Skehan, and M. Swain (eds.), *Researching Pedagogic Tasks: Second Language Learning, Teaching and Testing*, 1–20, Harlow: Longman.

Çakir, I. (2018), "Is Listening Instruction Neglected Intentionally or Incidentally in Foreign Language Teaching Contexts?" *Journal of Language and Linguistic Studies*, 14(2): 154–72.

Calhoon, S., and A. Becker (2008), "How Students Use the Course Syllabus," *International Journal for the Scholarship of Teaching and Learning*, 2(1): 1–12.

Canagarajah, A. S. (1999), "Interrogating the 'Native Speaker Fallacy': Non-linguistic Roots, Non-pedagogical Results," in G. Braine (ed.), *Non-native Educators in English Language Teaching*, 77–92, Mahwah, NJ: Lawrence Erlbaum.

Canale, M. (1983), "From Communicative Competence to Language Pedagogy," in J. C. Richards and R. Schmidt (eds.), *Language and Communication*, 2–25, London: Longman.

Canale, M., and M. Swain (1980), "Theoretical Bases of Communicative Approaches to Second Language Teaching and Testing," *Applied Linguistics*, 1(1): 1–47.

Candlin, C. N. (1980), "Discoursal Patterning and the Equalizing of Interpretive Opportunity," in I. Smith (ed.), *English for Cross-Cultural Communication*, 166–99, New York: Macmillan.

Candlin, C. N. (1987), "Towards Task-Based Language Learning," in C. N. Candlin and D. Murphy (eds.), *Language Learning Tasks*, 5–22, Englewood Cliffs, NJ: Prentice Hall.

Celce-Murcia, M., S. Dornyei, and S. Thurrell (1995), "Communicative Competence: A Pedagogically Motivated Model with Content Specifications," *Issues in Applied Linguistics*, 6(2): 5–35.

Celce-Murcia, M., S. Dornyei, and S. Thurrell (1997), "Direct Approaches in L2 Instruction: A Turning Point in Communicative Language Teaching?" *TESOL Quarterly*, 31(1): 141–52.

Center for Open Educational Resources and Language Learning (2010), "Foreign Language Teaching Methods," retrieved January 1, 2021, from: https://coerll.ute xas.edu/methods/

Chang, A. (2010), "The Effect of a Timed Reading Activity on EFL Readers: Speed, Comprehension, and Perceptions," *Reading in a Foreign Language*, 22(2): 284–303.

Chomsky, N. (1965), *Aspects of the Theory of Syntax*, Cambridge, MA: MIT Press.

Chung, S. F. (2006), "A Communicative Approach to Teaching Grammar: Theory and Practice," *English Teacher*, 34: 33–50.

Constantinou, F. (2019), "The Construct of Language Competence over Time: Using High-Stakes Tests to Gain Insight into the History of L1 Education in England," *Language and Education*, 33(6): 491–505.

Cook, G., and Y. Rutson-Griffiths (2022), "Learner Perspectives: Familiarization, Knowledge, and Perceptions of the CEFR," *CEFR Journal: Research and Practice*, 3: 44–58.

Coombe, C. (2022), "Research Questions in Language Education and Applied Linguistics: Strategies and Their Conceptualization and Development," in C. Coombe and H. Mohebbi (eds.), *Research Questions in Language Education and Applied Linguistics*, 1–8, Cham, Switzerland: Springer.

Cooper, K., B. Haney, A. Krieg, and S. Brownell (2017), "What's in a Name? The Importance of Students Perceiving That an Instructor Knows Their Names in a High-Enrollment Biology Classroom," *CBE Life Science Education*, 16(1): doi: 10.1187/cbe.16-08-0265

Council of Europe (2001), "Common European Framework of Reference for Languages: Learning, Teaching, Assessment," Cambridge: Cambridge University Press, retrieved October 24, 2018, from: https://rm.coe.int/1680459f97

Council of Europe (2018), "Common European Framework of Reference for Languages: Learning, Teaching, Assessment Companion Volume with New Descriptors," retrieved December 25, 2018, from: https://rm.coe.int/cefr-compan ion-volume-with-new-descriptors-2018/1680787989

Council of Europe (2020), "Common European Framework of Reference for Languages: Learning, Teaching, Assessment Companion Volume," retrieved April 5, 2022, from: https://rm.coe.int/common-european-framework-of-refere nce-for-languages-learning-teaching/16809ea0d4

Council of Europe (2021), "Qualitative Aspects of Spoken Language Use— Table 3," retrieved January 1, 2022, from: https://www.coe.int/en/web/common- european-framework-reference-languages/table-3-cefr-3.3-common-reference-lev els-qualitative-aspects-of-spoken-language-use

Council of Europe (2022), "Self-Assessment Grids," retrieved April 6, 2022, from: https://www.coe.int/en/web/portfolio/self-assessment-grid

Cozby, P. C., and S. C. Bates (2018), *Methods in Behavioral Research* (13th ed.), New York: McGraw-Hill.

Creswell, J. (2009), *Research Design: Qualitative, Quantitative, and Mixed Methods Approaches* (3rd ed.), Thousand Oaks, CA: Sage.

Cronbach, L. (2000), "Course Improvement through Evaluation," in D. Stufflebeam, G. Madaus, and T. Kellaghan (eds.), *Evaluation Models*, 235–47, Norwell, MA: Kluwer Academic.

Cross, J. (2011), "Comprehending News Videotexts: The Influence of the Visual Content," *Language Learning and Technology*, 15 (2): 44–68.

Cross, J. (2014), "Promoting Autonomous Listening to Podcasts: A Case Study," *Language Teaching Research*, 18(1): 8–32.

Csizer, K., and E. Kontra (2012), "ELF, ESP, ENL and Their Effects on Students' Aims and Beliefs," *System*, 40(1): 1–10.

Davies, A. (1990), *Principles of Language Testing*, Oxford: Blackwell.

Denham, K., and A. Lobeck (2009), "Introduction," in K. Denham and A. Lobeck (eds.), *Linguistics at School*, 1–6, Cambridge: Cambridge University Press.

Denzau, A. D., and D. C. North ([1994] 2000), "Shared Mental Models: Ideologies and Institutions," in A. Lupia, M. C. McCubbins, and S. L. Popkin (eds.), *Elements of Reason: Cognition, Choice, and the Bounds of Rationality*, 23–46, New York: Cambridge University Press.

Department for Education (2021), "MFL GCSE Subject Content," retrieved February 26, 2021, from: https://consult.education.gov.uk/ebacc-and-arts-and-humanities-team/gcse-mfl-subject-content-review/supporting_documents/GCSE%20MFL%20subject%20content%20document.pdf

Department of French and Italian (2019), *Français Interactif* (4th ed.), Austin: University of Texas at Austin.

DeKeyser, R. (2007), *Practice in a Second Language*, Cambridge: Cambridge University Press.

Dervin, B. (2003), "Sense-Making's Journey from Metatheory to Methodology to Method: An Example Using Information Seeking and Use as Research Focus," in B. Dervin, L. Foreman-Wernet, and E. Launterbach (eds.), *Sense-Making Methodology Readers: Selected Writings of Brenda Dervin*, 133–63, Cresskill, NJ: Hampton.

Deygers, B., B. Zeidler, D. Vilcu, and C. Carlsen (2018), "One Framework to Unite Them All? Use of the CEFR in European University Entrance Policies," *Language Assessment Quarterly*, 15(1): 3–15.

Dickinson, L. (1987), *Self-Instruction in Language Learning*, Cambridge: Cambridge University Press.

Diez-Bedmar, M., and M. Byram (2019), "The Current Influence of the CEFR in Secondary Education: Teachers' Perceptions," *Language, Culture and Curriculum*, 32(1): 1–15, retrieved January 1, 2021, from: https://doi.org/10.1080/07908318.2018.1493492

Donaldson, M. (2010), "No More Valentines," *Educational Leadership*, 67(8): 54–8.

Donaldson, M. (2013), "Principals' Approaches to Cultivating Teacher Effectiveness: Constraints and Opportunities in Hiring, Assigning, Evaluating, and Developing Teachers," *Educational Administration Quarterly*, 49(5): 838–82.

Dooremalen, H., and D. Borshoom (2010), "Metaphors in Psychological Conceptualization and Explanation," in A. Toomela and J. Valsiner (eds.), *Methodological Thinking in Psychology: 60 Years Gone Astray?*, 121–44, Charlotte, NC: Information Age.

Dougherty, K., and J. Johnston (1996), "Overlearning, Fluency, and Automaticity," *Behavior Analyst*, 9: 289–92.

Dubin, F., and E. Olshtain (1986), *Course Design: Developing Programs and Materials for Language Learning*, Cambridge: Cambridge University Press.

Dunkerly, D., and W. Wong (2001), "Introduction," in D. Dunkerley and W. Wong (eds.), *Global Perspectives on Quality in Higher Education*, 1–10, Aldershot: Ashgate.

Dunn, L. (2002), "Theories of Learning," *Learning and Teaching Briefing Papers Series: Oxford Centre for Staff Learning Development (OCSLD)*, Oxford: Oxford Brookes University.

Dupuy, B., and H. Willis Allen (2012), "Appropriating Conceptual and Pedagogical Tools of Literacy: A Qualitative Study of Two Novice Foreign Language

Teaching Assistants," in G. Gorsuch (ed.), *Working Theories for Teaching Assistant Development*, 275–315, Stillwater, OK: New Forums.

Dusek, J. B. (1975), "Do Teachers Bias Children's Learning?" *Review of Educational Research*, 45(4): 661–84.

Educational Testing Service (2019), "TOEFL," retrieved January 29, 2019, from: https://www.ets.org/toefl

Eisner, E. (2013), "What Does It Mean to Say a School Is Doing Well?" in D. Flinders and S. Thornton (eds.), *The Curriculum Studies Reader* (4th ed.), 279–87, New York: Routledge.

Ellis, R. (1997), "SLA and Language Pedagogy: An Educational Perspective," *Studies in Second Language Acquisition*, 20: 69–92.

Ellis, R. (2001), "Non-reciprocal Tasks, Comprehension and Second Language Acquisition," in M. Bygate, P. Skehan, and M. Swain (eds.), *Researching Pedagogic Tasks: Second Language Learning, Teaching and Testing*, 49–74, Harlow: Longman.

Ellis, R. (2003), *Task-Based Language Learning and Teaching*, Oxford: Oxford University Press.

Ellis, R., R. Rosszell, and H. Takashima (1994), "Down the Garden Path: Another Look at Negative Feedback," *JALT Journal*, 16(1): 9–24.

Elyas, T., and O. Badawood (2017), "English Language Educational Policy in Saudi Arabia Post 21st Century," *Forum for International Research in Education*, 3(3): 70–81.

Engelmann, K. (2020), "Origins and Elements of Authentic Direct Instruction," retrieved May 25, 2022, from: https://www.nifdi.org/what-is-di/origins-of-authentic-di.html

Engelmann, S., and D. Carnine (2016), *Theory of Instruction: Principles and Applications* (rev ed.), Eugene, OR: NIFDI (National Institute for Direct Instruction).

Erikson, R. S., and K. L. Tedin (2003), *American Public Opinion* (6th ed.), New York: Longman.

Eva, K., and G. Regehr (2005), "Self-Assessment in the Health Professions," *Journal of the Association of American Medical Colleges*, 80(10): 46–54.

Fan, M. (2003), "Frequency of Use, Perceived Usefulness, and Actual Usefulness of Second Language Vocabulary Strategies," *Modern Language Journal*, 87(2): 222–41.

Fanselow, J. (1988), "'Let's See': A Contrasting Conversation about Teaching," *TESOL Quarterly*, 22(1): 113–30.

Fanselow, J. (2019), "My Quest to Understanding Teaching and Learning," in A. Maley (ed.), *Developing Expertise through Experience: Ideas for Continuing Professional Development*, 26–31, London: British Council.

Figueras, N. (2012), "The Impact of the CEFR," *ELT Journal*, 66(4): 477–85.

Fillmore, C. J. (1979), "On Fluency," in C. J. Filmore, D. Kempler, and W. S.-Y. Wang (eds.), *Individual Differences in Language Ability and Language Behavior*, 85–101, New York: Academic.

Finn, J. D. (1972), "Expectations and the Educational Environment," *Review of Educational Research*, 42(3): 387–410.

Flavell, J. (1979), "Metacognition and Cognitive Monitoring," *American Psychologist*, 34(12): 906–11.

Flavell, J. (1987), "Speculations about the Nature and Development of Metacognition," in F. Weinert and R. Kluwe (eds.), *Metacognition, Motivation, and Understanding*, 21–9, Hillsdale, NJ: Lawrence Erlbaum.

Flinders, D., and S. Thornton (2013a), "Introduction to Part One," in D. Flinders and S. Thornton (eds.), *The Curriculum Studies Reader* (4th ed.), 3–10, New York: Routledge.

Flinders, D., and S. Thornton (2013b), "Introduction to Part Three," in D. Flinders and S. Thornton (eds.), *The Curriculum Studies Reader* (4th ed.), 143–7, New York: Routledge.

Fox, C. (1993), "Communicative Competence and Beliefs about Language among Graduate Teaching Assistants in French," *Modern Language Journal*, 77: 313–24.

Fukkink, R., J. Hulstijn, and A. Simis (2006), "Does Training in Second-Language Word Recognition Skills Affect Reading Comprehension?" *Modern Language Journal*, 89: 54–75.

Fulcher, G. (1996), "Invalidating Validity Claims for the ACTFL Oral Rating Scale," *System*, 24(2): 163–72.

Fulcher, G., and F. Davidson (2007), *Language Testing and Assessment*, London: Routledge.

Garinger, D. (2002), "Textbook Selection for the ESL Classroom," *ERIC Digest*, 1–2.

Gaspar, B., and M. Berti (2019), "A Multiliteracies-Oriented Project-Based Assessment for Intermediate Foreign Language Italian Classes," in G. Gorsuch (ed.), *Tests That Second Language Teachers Make and Use*, 276–304, Newcastle upon Tyne: Cambridge Scholars.

Gebhard, J., and R. Oprandy (1999), *Language Teaching Awareness*, Cambridge: Cambridge University Press.

Gee, J. (1990), *Social Linguistics and Literacies: Ideology in Discourses*, London: Falmer.

Gee, J. (1997), "Thinking, Learning, and Reading: The Situated Sociocultural Mind," in D. Kirshner and J. Whitson (eds.), *Situated Cognition*, 235–60, Abingdon: Routledge.

Gee, J. (2021), "Academic Language and New Literacies," in M. Kalantzis and B. Cope (eds.), *Works and Days*, retrieved May 16, 2021, from: https://newlearningonline.com/literacies/chapter-14/gee-on-academic-language-and-new-literacies

Gelso, C. J. (2006), "Applying Theories to Research: The Interplay of Theory and Research in Science," in F. T. Leong and J. T. Austin (eds.), *The Psychology Research Handbook*, 455–64, Thousand Oaks, CA: Sage.

Genesee, F., and J. A. Upshur (1996), *Classroom-Based Evaluation in Second Language Education*, Cambridge: Cambridge University Press.

Gersten, R., J. Woodward, and C. Darch (1986), "Direct Instruction Research: The Third Decade," *Remedial and Special Education*, 8(6): 48–56.

Gevara, J. R., G. Gorsuch, H. Almekdash, and W. Jiang (2015), Native and Non-native English Speaking ITA Performance Test Raters: Do they Rate ITA Candidates Differently?" in G. Gorsuch (ed.), *Talking Matters: Research on Talk and Communication of International Teaching Assistants*, 313–46, Stillwater, OK: New Forums.

Glazier, J. D., and R. Grover (2002), "A Multidisciplinary Framework for Theory Building," *Library Trends*, 50(3): 317–32.

Glick-Cuenot, S. (2014), "Predictors of Undergraduate Academic Success," unpublished doctoral dissertation, Florida Atlantic University, Boca Raton, Florida.

Glick Garcia, B. (2019), "An Oral Voice Thread Test for First-Semester French Language Learners in a U.S. University," in G. Gorsuch (ed.), *Tests That Second Language Teachers Make and Use*, 244–56, Newcastle upon Tyne: Cambridge Scholars.

Goeke, J. L. (2009), *Explicit Instruction: A Framework for Meaningful Direct Teaching*, Upper Saddle River, NJ: Pearson.

Goethe, J. (1902), *Goethes Samtliche Werke*, Stuttgart, German: J.G. Cotta.

Gorsuch, G. (2001), "Japanese EFL Teachers' Perceptions of Communicative, Audiolingual and Yakudoku Activities: The Plan versus the Reality," *Education Policy Analysis Archives*, 9(10): 2–26, retrieved August 14, 2002, from: http://doi.org/10.14507/epaa.v9n10.2001

Gorsuch, G. (2009), "Investigating Second Language Learning Self-Efficacy and Future Expectancy of Second Language Use for High-Stakes Program Evaluation," *Foreign Language Annals*, 42(3): 505–40.

Gorsuch, G. J. (2011), "Improving Speaking Fluency for International Teaching Assistants by Increasing Input," *TESL-EJ (Teaching English as a second or foreign language-Electronic Journal)*, 14(4): 1–25.

Gorsuch, G. (2012), "The Roles of Teacher Theory and Domain Theory in Materials and Research in International Teaching Assistant Education," in G. Gorsuch (ed.), *Working Theories for Teaching Assistant Development*, 429–82, Stillwater, OK: New Forums.

Gorsuch, G. (2019a), "Communicative Competence and Language Use Description Frameworks and Second Language Tests," in G. Gorsuch (ed.), *Tests That Second Language Teachers Make and Use*, 412–64, Cambridge: Cambridge Scholars.

Gorsuch, G. (2019b), "Using Course Logic to Describe Outcomes and Instruction for an ITA Course," in S. Looney and S. Bhalla (eds.), *A Transdisciplinary Approach to ITA Research: Perspectives from Applied Linguistics*, 154–77, Bristol: Multilingual Matters.

Gorsuch, G., and D. T. Griffee (2018), *Second Language Testing for Student Evaluation and Classroom Research*, Charlotte, NC: Information Age.

Gorsuch, G., E. Taguchi, and H. Umehara (2015), "Repeated Reading for Japanese Language Learners: Effects on Reading Speed, Comprehension, and Comprehension Strategies," *Reading Matrix*, 15(2): 18–44, retrieved February 9, 2016, from: http://readingmatrix.com/files/13-l624by2v.pdf

Gorsuch, G. J. (2013), "Helping International Teaching Assistants Acquire Discourse Intonation: Explicit and Implicit Knowledge," *Journal of Teaching English for Specific and Academic Purposes*, 1(2): 67–92.

Gorsuch, G. J., and E. Taguchi (2008), "Repeated Reading for Developing Reading Fluency and Reading Comprehension: The Case of EFL Learners in Vietnam," *System*, 36(2): 253–78.

Gorsuch, G. J., and E. Taguchi (2009), "Repeated Reading and Its Role in an Extensive Reading Programme," in A. Cirocki (ed.), *Extensive Reading in English Language Teaching*, 249–71, Munich: Lincom.

Gorsuch, G. J., and E. Taguchi (2010), "Developing Reading Fluency and Comprehension Using Repeated Reading: Evidence from Longitudinal Student Reports," *Language Teaching Research*, 14(1): 27–59.

Goullier, F. (2006), "Council of Europe Tools for Language Teaching," retrieved April 20, 2022, from: https://rm.coe.int/168069ce6e

Graham, S. (2006), "Listening Comprehension: The Learners' Perspective," *System*, 34: 165–82.

Graham, S. (2011), "Self-Efficacy and Academic Listening," *Journal of English for Academic Purposes*, 10: 113–17.

Graham, S. (2021), "Findings: Effects of the Proposed Changes on Teaching and Learning," *Creative Multilingualism*, retrieved March 28, 2022, from: https://creativeml.ox.ac.uk/blog/exploring-multilingualism/teacher-survey-dfes-proposal-new-gcse-content-modern-foreign/

Gravells, A., and S. Simpson (2014), *The Certificate in Education and Training*, London: Learning Matters/Sage.

Graves, K. (1996), *Teachers as Course Developers*, Cambridge: Cambridge University Press.

Gravetter, F. J., and L.-A.B Forzano (2003), *Research Methods for the Behavioral Sciences*, Belmont, CA: Wadsworth/Thomson.

Grenfell, M., and V. Harris (2014), "Learning Strategies, Autonomy and Self-regulated Learning," in P. Driscoll, E. Macaro, and A. Swarbrick (eds.), *Debates in Modern Languages Education*, 186–99, London: Routledge.

Griffee, D. T. (2012a), "Using Grounded Theory to Develop Emergent Explanations on How Second and Foreign Language TAs Construct Their Teacher Theory," in G. Gorsuch (ed.), *Working Theories for Teaching Assistant Development*, 201–30, Stillwater, OK: New Forums.

Griffee, D. T. (2012b), "The Role of Theory in TA and ITA Research," in G. Gorsuch (ed.), *Working Theories for Teaching Assistant Development: Time-Tested and Robust Theories, Frameworks, and Models for TA and ITA Learning*, 39–61, Stillwater, OK: New Forums.

Griffee, D. T. (2018), *An Introduction to Second Language Research Methods Design and Data* (2nd ed.), Berkeley, CA: TESL-EJ.

Griffee, D. T., and J. R. Gevara (2011), "Standard Setting in the Post-Modern Era for an ITA Performance Test," *Texas Papers in Foreign Language Education*, 15(1): 3–16.

Griffee, D. T., and G. Gorsuch (2016), *Second Language Course Evaluation*, Charlotte, NC: Information Age.

Hagger-Vaughan, L. (2020), "Is the English Baccalaureate (EBacc) Helping Participation in Language Learning in Secondary Schools in England?" *Language Learning Journal*, 48(5): 519–33.

Hai, L., and P. Nhung (2019), "Implementing and CEFR at a Vietnamese University: General English Teachers' Perceptions," *CEFR Journal: Research and Practice*, 1: 41–57.

Hall, J., A. Cheng, and M. Carlson (2006), "Reconceptalizing Multicompetence as a Theory of Language Knowledge," *Applied Linguistics*, 27(2): 220–40.

Halliday, M. A. K., and R. Hasan (1976), *Cohesion in English*, London: Longman.

Harari, Y. (2015), *Sapiens*, New York: HarperCollins.

Hardy, T. (2007), "MEXT-Authorized English Textbooks: Designing a Junior High School Text Series," in *Second Language Acquisition Theory and*

Pedagogy: Proceedings of the 6th Annual JALT Pan-SIG Conference, Sendai, Japan, 12–20.

Harris, J. (2014, February 24), "A Brief Overview of Four Learning Theories," [Video], YouTube, retrieved October 6, 2022, from: https://youtu.be/ACow HxGEAUg

Harsch, C. (2018), "How Suitable Is the CEFR for Setting University Entrance Standards?" *Language Assessment Quarterly*, 15(1): 102–8.

Hattie, J., and G. Donoghue (2018), "A Model of Learning," in K. Illeris (ed.), *Contemporary Theories of Learning: Learning Theorists in the Their Own Words* (2nd ed.), 97–113, London: Routledge.

Hawkes, M. (2012), "Using Task Repetition to Direct Learner Attention and Focus on Form," *ELT Journal*, 66(3): 327–36.

Hawkins, E. (2005), "Out of This Nettle, Drop-Out, We Pluck This Flower, Opportunity: Re-thinking the School Foreign Language Apprenticeship," *Language Learning Journal*, 32(1): 4–17.

Hedge, T. (1993), "Key Concepts in ELT (Fluency)," *ELT Journal*, 47(3): 275–6.

Henry, A. (2018), "Online Media Creation and L2 Motivation: A Socially Situated Perspective," *System*, 53(2): 372–404.

Heriansyah, H., P. Darni, R. Fajri, and R. Sahardin (2021), "Competency-Based Curriculum, Relevant Second Language Learning Theories, and Its Language Assessment," *English Education Journal*, 12(3): 416–27, retrieved January 1, 2021, from: https://doi.org/10.24815/eej.v12i3.21631

Hjørland, B. (1998), "Theory and Metatheory of Information Science: A New Interpretation," *Journal of Documentation*, 54(5): 606–21.

Hjørland, B. (2000), "Library and Information Science: Practice, Theory, and Philosophical Basis," *Information Processing and Management*, 36(3): 501–31.

Hoenigswald, H. (1966), "A Proposal for the Study of Folk Linguistics," in W. Bright (ed.), *Sociolinguistics*, 16–26, The Hague: Mouton.

Holliday, A. (1992), "Tissue Rejection and Informal Orders in ELT Projects," *Applied Linguistics*, 13(4): 403–24.

Holliday, A. (1994), *Appropriate Methodology and Social Context*, Cambridge: Cambridge University Press.

Hollingsworth, J., and S. Ybarra (2009), *Explicit Direct Instruction*, Thousand Oaks, CA: Corwin.

Honda, M., W. O'Neil, and D. Pippin (2009), "On Promoting Linguistics Literacy," in K. Denham and A. Lobeck (eds.), *Linguistics at School*, 175–88, Cambridge: Cambridge University Press.

House, E. R. (1993), *Professional Evaluation: Social Impact and Political Consequences*, Newbury Park, CA: Sage.

Howatt, A. P. R. (1984), *A History of English Language Teaching*, Oxford: Oxford University Press.

Huang, Y. P. (2018), "Learner Resistance to English-Medium Instruction Practices: A Qualitative Case Study," *Teaching in Higher Education*, 23(4): 435–49.

Hulstijn, J. H. (2011), "Language Proficiency in Native and Nonnative Speakers: An Agenda for Research and Suggestions for Second-Language Assessment," *Language Assessment Quarterly*, 8(3), 229–49.

Hume, D. ([1772] 2004), *An Inquiry Concerning Human Understanding*, New York: Barnes and Noble.

Hunke, M., and N. Saville (2019), "Jumping through Hoops and Keeping the Human-in-the-loop: Interview with Dr. Nick Saville," *CEFR Journal: Research and Practice*, 1: 58–65.

Hymes, D. (1972), "On Communicative Competence," in J. B. Pride and J. Holmes (eds.), *Sociolinguistics: Selected Readings*, 269–93, Harmondsworth: Penguin.

IELTS (2018), "International English Language Testing System," retrieved January 29, 2019, from: https://www.ielts.org/en-us

Isaacson, W. (2007), *Einstein*, New York: Simon and Schuster.

Ivins, T., K. Copenhaver, and A. Koclanes (2017), "Adult Transitional Theory and Transfer Shock in Higher Education," *Reference Services Review*, 45(2): 244–57.

Jack, A. (2021), "Global Britain Needs to Improve Its Language Learning," *Financial Times*, retrieved October 6, 2022, from: https://www.ft.com/cont ent/1cbc1c1e-1173-4086-a54d-bc9c34b5c986

Jarvis, P., and G. Creasey (2012), "A Theoretical and Empirical Basis for Studying Student-Instructor/Teaching Assistant Relationships," in G. Gorsuch (ed.), *Working Theories for Teaching Assistant Development*, 83–111, Stillwater, OK: New Forums.

Jin, L., and M. Cortazzi (2011), "Re-evaluating Traditional Approaches to Second Language Teaching and Learning," in E. Hinkel (ed.), *Handbook of Research in Second Language Teaching and Learning*, 558–75, New York: Routledge.

John, R. (1980), "Theory Construction in Sociology: The Competing Approaches," *Mid-American Review of Sociology*, 5(1): 15–36.

Johnson, K. (1982), *Communicative Syllabus Design and Methodology*, Oxford: Pergamon.

Johnson, K. (2009), *Second Language Teacher Education: A Sociocultural Perspective*, New York: Routledge.

Johnson, R. K. (1989a), "Overview," in R. K. Johnson (ed.), *The Second Language Curriculum*, xi–xxii, Cambridge: Cambridge University Press.

Johnson, R. K. (1989b), "A Decision-Making Framework for the Coherent Language Curriculum," in R. K. Johnson (ed.), *The Second Language Curriculum*, 1–23, Cambridge: Cambridge University Press.

Johnson, S., and A. Chalmers (eds.) ([1843] 1994), *Samuel Johnson's Dictionary of the English Language*, London: Studio Edition.

Johnstone, R. (2014), "Languages over the Past 40 Years," in P. Driscoll, E. Macaro, and A. Swarbrick (eds.), *Debates in Modern Languages Education*, 9–21, London: Routledge.

Jones, N., and N. Saville (2009), "European Language Policy: Assessment, Learning, and the CEFR," *Annual Review of Applied Linguistics*, 29: 51–63.

Jost, J. T., C. M. Federico., and J. L. Napier. (2009), "Political Ideology: Its Structure, Functions, and Elective Affinities," *Annual Review of Psychology*, 60(1): 307–37.

Kahneman, D. (2011), *Thinking, Fast and Slow*, New York: Farrar, Strauss and Giroux.

Keller, M. S. (2007), "Why Is Music so Ideological, and Why Do Totalitarian States Take It so Seriously? A Personal View from History and the Social Sciences," *Journal of Musicological Research*, 26 (2–3): 91–122.

Kelly, L. G. (1976), *25 Centuries of Language Teaching*, Rowley, MA: Newbury House.

Kerlinger, F. N. (1979), *Behavioral Research: A Conceptual Approach*, New York: Holt, Rinehart and Winston.

Kerlinger, F. N. (1984), *Liberalism and Conservatism: The Nature and Structure of Social Attitudes*, Hillsdale, NJ: Erlbaum.

Kern, R. (2008), "Literacy as a New Organizing Principle for Foreign Language Education," in P. Petrakis (ed.), *Reading between the Lines*, 40–59, New Haven, CT: Yale University Press.

Kiely, R., and P. Rea-Dickins (2005), *Program Evaluation in Language Education*, Houndmills: Palgrave.

King Abdul Aziz English Language Institute (2021), "ELI Faculty Handbook 2021," retrieved May 8, 2021, from: https://eli.kau.edu.sa/Files/126/Files/1594 55_FacultyHandbook26Feb2021.pdf

King Abdul Aziz University (2021), "ELI Programs," retrieved June 21, 2022, from: https://eli.kau.edu.sa/Pages-preparatory-year-program-en.aspx

Kissling, E., and M. O'Donnell (2015), "Increasing Language Awareness and Self-efficacy of FL Students Using Self-assessment and the ACTFL Proficiency Guidelines," *Language Awareness*, 24(4): 283–302.

Klapper, J. (2003), "Taking Communication to Task? A Critical Review of Recent Trends in Language Teaching," *Language Learning Journal*, 27: 33–42.

Kobayashi, A. (2011), "Teachers' Perceived Use and Importance of Metacognitive Instruction Techniques in Japanese EFL Classrooms," *ARELE*, 22: 185–200, retrieved March 21, 2022, from: https://www.jstage.jst.go.jp/article/ arele/22/0/22_KJ00007977417/_pdf/-char/en

Koponen, M., and H. Riggenbach (2000), "Overview: Varying Perspectives on Fluency," in H. Riggenbach (ed.), *Perspectives on Fluency*, 5–24, Ann Arbor: University of Michigan Press.

Korean National Standards Task Force (2022), *Standards for Korean Language Learning*, retrieved November 18, 2022, from: http://www.ikeneducate.org/ wp-content/uploads/2019/03/NSP1-FINAL-COPY405-455-2012-1.pdf

Krashen, S. (1982), *Principles and Practice in Second Language Acquisition*, Oxford: Pergamon.

Kress, G., and van Leeuwen, T. (2021), "Kress and van Leeuwen on Multimodality," in M. Kalantzis and B. Cope (eds.), *Works and Days*, retrieved May 16, 2021, from: https://newlearningonline.com/literacies/chapter-8/kress-and-van-leeu wen-on-multimodality

Kuhn, T. S. (1970), *The Structure of Scientific Revolutions* (2nd ed.), Chicago: University of Chicago Press.

Kumaravadivelu, B. (2006), *Understanding Language Teaching: From Method to Postmethod*, Mahwah, NJ: Lawrence Erlbaum.

Kunnan, J. (1998), *Validation in Language Assessment*, Mahwah, NJ: Lawrence Erlbaum.

LaBerge, D., and S. Samuels (1974), "Toward a Theory of Automatic Information Processing in Reading," *Cognitive Psychology*, 6: 293–323.

Lakoff, G. (1987), *Women, Fire, and Dangerous Things*, Chicago: University of Chicago Press.

Lakoff, G. (1992), *Multiple Selves: The Metaphorical Models of the Self Inherent in Our Conceptual System*, Berkeley: University of California, retrieved January 1, 2022, from: https://escholarship.org/content/qt53g1n5b2/qt53g1n5b2.pdf

Lakoff, G., and M. Johnson (1980), *Metaphors We Live By*, Chicago: University of Chicago Press.

Language Training and Testing Center (2016), "About the General English Proficiency Test," retrieved June 21, 2021, from: https://www.lttc.ntu.edu.tw/e_lttc/e_gept.htm

Lantolf, J., and W. Frawley (1988), "Proficiency: Understanding the Construct," *Studies in Second Language Acquisition*, 10: 181–95.

Lantolf, J., and M. Poehner (2011), "Dynamic Assessment in the Classroom: Vygotskian Praxis for Language Development," *Language Teaching Research*, 15(1): 11–33.

Larsen-Freeman, D. (1986), *Techniques and Principles in Language Teaching*, Oxford: Oxford University Press.

Larsen-Freeman, D. (1990), "On the Need for a Theory of Language Teaching," in J. E. Alatis (ed.), *Georgetown University Round Table on Languages and Linguistics 1990*, 261–70, Washington, DC: Georgetown University Press.

Larsen-Freeman, D. (2012), "On the Roles of Repetition in Language Teaching and Learning," *Applied Linguistics Review*, 3(2): 195–210.

Larsen-Freeman, D. (2015), "Research into Practice: Grammar Learning and Teaching," *Language Teaching*, 48(2): 263–80.

Larsen-Freeman, D., and M. Anderson (2011), *Techniques and Principles in Language Teaching* (3rd ed.), Oxford: Oxford University Press.

Lavasani, M., and F. Faryadres (2011), "Language Learning Strategies and Suggestion Model in Adults Processes of Learning Second Language," *Procedia*, 15: 191–7.

Lee, C. (2010), "An Overview of Language Learning Strategies," *ARECLS (Annual Review of Education, Communication, and Language Sciences)*, 7: 132–52.

Lee, E., and S. Canagarajah (2018), "The Connection between Transcultural Dispositions and Translingual Practices in Academic Writing," *Journal of Multicultural Discourses*, doi: 10.1080/17447143.2018.1501375

Lee, I., and S. Ramsey (2000), *The Korean Language*, Albany: State University of New York Press.

Leith, P. M. (1977), "Great Expectations: A Consideration of the Self-Fulfilling Prophecy in the Context of Educability," *Educational Review*, 29(4): 317–24.

Lennon, P. (2000), "The Lexical Element in Spoken Second Language Fluency," in H. Riggenbach (ed.), *Perspectives on Fluency*, 25–42, Ann Arbor: University of Michigan Press.

LET (Licensure Examination for Teachers) Reviewer (2020, May 2), "Prominent Theorists and Their Contributions to Education," [Video], YouTube, retrieved October 10, 2022, from: https://youtu.be/TZdIvroEKPA

Leung, C., and J. Lewkowicz (2013), "Language Communication and Communicative Competence: A View from Contemporary Classrooms," *Language and Education*, 27(5): 398–414.

Liskin-Gasparro, J. (2003), "The ACTFL Proficiency Guidelines and the Oral Proficiency Interview: A Brief History and Analysis of their Survival," *Foreign Language Annals*, 36(4): 483–90.

Little, D. (2006), "The Common European Framework of Reference for Languages: Content, Purpose, Origin, Reception and Impact," *Language Teaching*, 39: 167–90.

Littlejohn, A., and S. Windeatt (1989), "Beyond Language Learning: Perspectives on Materials Design," in R. K. Johnson (ed.), *The Second Language Curriculum*, 155–75, Cambridge: Cambridge University Press.

Liviero, S. (2017), "Grammar Teaching in Secondary School Foreign Language Learning in England: Teachers' Reported Beliefs and Observed Practices," *Language Learning Journal*, 45(1): 26–50.

Long, M. (1993), "Assessment Strategies for Second Language Acquisition Theories," *Applied Linguistics*, 14(3): 225–49.

Long, R., S. Danechi, and P. Loft (2020), *Language Teaching in Schools (England)*, House of Commons Library Briefing Paper Number 07388, retrieved March 15, 2022, from: http://intranet.parliament.uk/commons-library

Lor, P. J. (2019), *International and Comparative Librarianship: Concepts and Methods for Global Studies*, Berlin: De Gruyter Saur.

Lowie, W. (2012), "The CEFR and the Dynamics of Second Language Learning: Trends and Challenges," *CercleS*, 2(1): 17–34.

Lutz, R. (1990), "Classroom Shock," in J. Alatis (ed.), *Georgetown University Round Table on Languages and Linguistics 1990'*, 144–56, Washington, DC: Georgetown University Press.

Macaro, E., S. Graham, and R. Vanderplank (2007), "A Review of Listening Strategies: Focus on Sources of Knowledge and on Success," in A. D. Cohen and E. Macaro (eds.), *Language Learner Strategies: 30 Years of Research and Practice*, 165–85, Oxford: Oxford University Press.

MacDonald, M., R. Badger, and G. White (2001), "Changing Values: What Use Are Theories of Language Learning and Teaching?" *Teaching and Teacher Education*, 17: 949–63.

Mackey, A. (1999), "Input, Interaction, and Second Language Development: An Empirical Study of Question Formation in ESL," *Studies in Second Language Acquisition*, 21(4): 557–83.

Macnamara, J. (1973), "Nurseries, Streets and Classrooms: Some Comparisons and Deductions," *Modern Language Journal*, 57(5–6) (September–October): 250–4.

Madaus, G., and D. Stufflebeam (2000), "Program Evaluation: A Historical Overview," in D. Stufflebeam, G. Madaus, and T. Kellaghan (eds.), *Evaluation Models*, 3–18, Norwell, MA: Kluwer Academic.

Mahmood, K. (2011), "Conformity to Quality Characteristics of Textbooks: The Illusion of Textbook Evaluation in Pakistan," retrieved from: https://www.sema nticscholar.org/paper/Conformity-to-Quality-Characteristics-of-Textbooks%3A-Mahmood/9783ebe6928688017fbd4cd289ebab1816a829bb

Manley, J. (1995), "Assessing Students' Oral Language: One School District's Response," *Foreign Language Annals*, 28(1): 93–102.

Markee, N. (1997), *Managing Curricular Innovation*, Cambridge: Cambridge University Press.

Marquardt, M., and S. Banks (2010), "Theory to Practice: Action Learning," *Advances in Developing Human Resources*, 12(2): 159–62.

Martin, P. (2005), "'Safe' Language Practices in Two Rural Schools in Malaysia: Tensions between Policy and Practice," in P. A. Lin and P. Martin (eds.), *Decolonisation, Globalisation: Language-in-Education Policy and Practice*, 74–97, Bristol: Multilingual Matters.

Maxim, H. (2006), "Integrating Textual Thinking into the Introductory College-Level Foreign Language Classroom," *Modern Language Journal*, 90(1): 19–32.

McDavid, J., and L. Hawthorn (2006), *Program Evaluation and Performance Measurement*, Thousand Oaks, CA: Sage.

McGlone, M. (2007), "What Is the Explanatory Value of a Conceptual Metaphor?" *Language and Communication*, 27: 109–26.

McIntosh, P. (2013), "Gender Perspectives on Educating for Global Citizenship," in D. Flinders and S. Thornton (eds.), *The Curriculum Studies Reader* (4th ed.), 339–52, New York: Routledge.

McLelland, N. (2018), "The History of Language Learning and Teaching in Britain," *Language Learning Journal*, 46(1): 6–16.

McLeod, S. A. (2018, August 10), "What Is a Hypothesis'? *Simply Psychology*, retrieved August 14, 2021, from: https://www.simplypsychology.org/what-is-a-hypotheses.html

Meijer, J., M. V. J. Veenman, and B. H. A. M. van Hout-Wolters (2006), "Metacognitive Activities in Text-Studying and Problem-Solving: Development of a Taxonomy," *Educational Research and Evaluation*, 12(3): 209–37.

Meredith, P. (2002), "England," in L. Gearon (ed.), *Education in the United Kingdom*, 1–15, London: David Fulton.

Merton, R. K. (1968), *Social Theory and Social Structure*, New York: Free Press.

Meyer, B. J. F. (1977), "What Is Remembered from Prose: A Function of Passage Structure," in R. O. Freedle (ed.), *Discourse Production and Comprehension*, 307–36, Norwood, NJ: Ablex.

Michelson, K. (2019), "Global Stimulation as a Mediating Tool for Teaching and Learning Language and Culture as Discourse," *Foreign Language Annals*, 52: 284–313.

Michelson, K., and A. Anderson (2021), "Ideological Views of Reading in Contemporary Commercial French Textbooks: A Content Analysis," *Second Language Research and Practice*, 3(1): 34–61, retrieved December 24, 2022, from: https://doi.org/10125/69867

Minar, D. W. (1961), "Ideology and Political Behavior," *Midwest Journal of Political Science*, 5(4): 317–31. doi: 10.2307/2108991

Ministry of Education, Culture, Sport, Science and Technology (2022), "The National Curriculum Standards in Junior High School Section 9 Foreign Languages," retrieved December 18, 2022, from: https://www.mext.go.jp/content/20220607-mxt_kyoiku01-000011246_1.pdf

Mitchell, B., and A. Alfuraih (2017), "English Language Teaching in the Kingdom of Saudi Arabia: Past, Present and Beyond," *Mediterranean Journal of Social Sciences*, 8(2): 317–25.

Mitchell, R. (1992), "The 'Independent' Evaluation of Bilingual Primary Education: A Narrative Account," in J. C. Alderson and A. Berette (eds.), *Evaluating Second Language Education*, 100–40, Cambridge: Cambridge University Press.

Mitchell, R., C. Brumfit, and J. Hooper (1994), "Perceptions of Language and Language Learning in English and Foreign Language Classrooms," in M. Hughes (ed.), *Perceptions of Teaching and Learning*, 53–65, Clevedon: Multilingual Matters.

Mitchell, R., F. Myles, and E. Marsden (2013), *Second Language Learning Theories* (3rd ed.), New York: Routledge.

Miyazato, K. (2011), "Team Teaching from Administrators' Perspectives," in A. Stewart (ed.), *JALT 2010 Conference Proceedings*, 643–53, Tokyo: Japan Association for Language Teaching.

Moloney, R., and H. Xu (2015), "Transitioning Beliefs in Teachers of Chinese as a Foreign Language: An Australian Case Study," *Cogent Education*, 2(1): 1–15, retrieved January 7, 2021, from: https://www.tandfonline.com/doi/full/10.1080/2331186X.2015.1024960

Montgomery, C., and J. Beal (2011), "Perceptual Dialectology," in A. McMahon and W. Maguire (eds.), *Analysing Variation in English*, 121–48, Cambridge: Cambridge University Press.

Montgomery, C., and L. Smith (2015), "Bridging the Gap between Researchers and Practitioners," *Die Unterrichtpraxis/Teaching German*, 48(1): 100–13.

Moonen, M., E. Stoutjedijk, R. de Graaff, and A. Corda (2013), "Implementing CEFR in Secondary Education: Impact on FL Teachers' Educational and Assessment Practice," *International Journal of Applied Linguistics*, 23(2): 226–46.

Morrow, K. (1981), "Principles of Communicative Methodology," in K. Johnson and K. Morrow (eds.), *Communication in the Classroom: Applications and Methods for a Communicative Approach*, 59–66, New York: Longman.

Mouton, J. (1996), *Understanding Social Research*, Pretoria: Van Schaik.

Mukudan, J., and V. Nimehchisalem (2012), "Evaluating the Validity and Economy of the English Language Evaluation Checklist," *World Applied Sciences Journal*, 20(3): 458–63.

Munby, J. (1978), *Communicative Syllabus Design*, Cambridge: Cambridge University Press.

Muranoi, H. (2007). "Output Practice in the L2 Classroom," in R. DeKeyser (ed.), *Practice in a Second Language*, 51–84. Cambridge: Cambridge University Press.

Nash, H. (1963), "The Role of Metaphor in Psychological Theory," *Behavioral Science*, 8(4): 336–45.

Nation, I. S. P., and J. Macalister (2010), *Language Curriculum Design*, New York: Routledge.

Nation, P. (ed.) (1994), *New Ways in Teaching Vocabulary*, Alexandria, VA: Teachers of English to Speakers of Other Languages (TESOL).

Negretti, R., and M. Kuteeva (2011), "Fostering Metacognitive Genre Awareness in L2 Academic Reading and Writing: A Case Study of Pre-service English Teachers," *Journal of Second Language Writing*, 20: 95–110.

The New London Group (1996), "A Pedagogy of Multiliteracies: Designing Social Futures," *Harvard Educational Review*, 66(1): 60–92.

Newnham, S. (2013), "Text Complexity in Graded Readers: A Systemic Functional Look," unpublished master's thesis, Huntington, WV: Marshall University, retrieved December 24, 2017, from: http://mds.marshall.edu/etd

Newton, J., and G. Kennedy (1996), "Effects of Communication Tasks on the Grammatical Relations Marked by Second Language Learners," *System*, 24(3): 309–22.

Nicol, D., and D. MacFarlane-Dick (2006), "Formative Assessment and Self-regulated Learning: A Model and Seven Principles of Good Feedback Practice," *Studies in Higher Education*, 31(2): 199–18.

Niedzielski, N., and D. Preston (2003), *Folk Linguistics*, Berlin: Mouton de Gruyter.

Nimehchisalem, V., and J. Mukudan (2015), "Refinements of the English Language Textbook Evaluation Checklist," *Pertanika Journal of Social Science and Humanities*, 23(4): 761–80.

Noro, T. (2004), "A Study of the Metacognitive Development of Japanese EFL Writers: The Validity of Written Feedback and Correction in Response to Learners' Self-Analyses of Their Writing," *ARELE*, 15: 179–88, retrieved March 21, 2021, from: https://www.jstage.jst.go.jp/article/arele/15/0/15_KJ00007108 401/_pdf/-char/en

Norris, J. (2008), *Validity Evaluation in Language Assessment*, New York: Peter Lang.

Nunan, D. (1989), *Designing Tasks for the Communicative Classroom*, Cambridge: Cambridge University Press.

Nunan, D. (1999), *Second Language Teaching and Learning*, New York: Heinle and Heinle.

Ofori-Attah, K. (2008), *Going to School in the Middle East and North Africa*, Westport, CT: Greenwood.

Ohio Department of Education (2014), "Using Ohio's Learning Standards for K-12 World Languages," retrieved April 6, 2022, from: https://education.ohio. gov/getattachment/Topics/Learning-in-Ohio/Foreign-Language/World-Langua ges-Model-Curriculum/World-Languages-Model-Curriculum-Framework/Instru ctional-Strategies/7-Packet_2-Hedstrom_Blooms_FL.pdf.aspx

Ohio Department of Education (2017), "Standards for English Language Arts K-12," retrieved March 21, 2021, from: http://education.ohio.gov/getattachm ent/Topics/Learning-in-Ohio/English-Language-Art/English-Language-Arts-Standards/ELA-Learning-Standards-2017.pdf.aspx?lang=en-US

Oliver, R., M. Sato, S. Ballinger, and L. Pan (2019), "Content and Language Integrated Learning Classes for Child Mandarin L2 Learners: A Longitudinal Observational Study," in M. Sato and S. Loewen (eds.), *Evidence-Based Second Language Pedagogy*, 81–102, New York: Routledge.

O'Malley, J., and A. Chamot (1990), *Learning Strategies in Second Language Acquisition*, Cambridge: Cambridge University Press.

Ornstein, A., and F. Hunkins (2012), *Curriculum: Foundations, Principles and Issues* (6th ed.), New York: Pearson.

Ortheguy, R., O. Garcia, and W. Reid (2015), "Clarifying Translanguaging and Deconstructing Named Languages," *Applied Linguistics Review*, 6(3): 281–307.

Ostrowska, S. (2014), *Unlock Reading and Writing Skills 1*, Cambridge: Cambridge University Press.

Oxford, R. (1990), *Language Learning Strategies*, New York: Newbury House.

Oxford, R. (1994), "Language Learning Strategies: An Update," *CAL Online Resources*, 1–5, retrieved March 21, 2021, from: https://eric. ed.gov/?id=ED376707

Ozaki, S. (2010), "High-Stakes Tests and Educational Language Policy in Japan: An Analysis of the National Center English Test from the Viewpoint of Education for International Understanding," *TESOL Journal*, 2: 175–88.

Padron, Y. (1992), "The Effect of Strategy Instruction on Bilingual Students' Cognitive. Strategy Use in Reading," *Bilingual Research Journal*, 16(3 and 4): 35–51.

Palmer, H. E. ([1917] 1968), *The Scientific Study and Teaching of Languages*, London: Oxford University Press.

Palmer, H. E. (1921), *The Principles of Language Study*, London: George G. Harrap.

Paris, S., and P. Winograd (1990), "How Metacognition Can Promote Academic Learning and Instruction," in B. Jones and L. Idol (eds.), *Dimensions of Thinking and Cognitive Instruction*, 15–51, Hillsdale, NJ: Erlbaum.

Parsons T. (1951), *The Social System*, New York: Free Press.

Pavlovskaya, I., and O. Lankina (2019), "How New CEFR Mediation Descriptors can Help to Assessment the Discussion Skills of Management Students—Global and Analytic Scales," *CEFR Journal: Research and Practice*, 1: 33–40.

Pawley, A., and F. H. Syder (1983), "The One-Clause-at-a-Time Hypothesis," in H. Riggenbach (ed.), *Perspectives on Fluency*, 163–99, Ann Arbor: University of Michigan Press.

Perfetti, C. (1985), *Reading Ability*, New York: Oxford University Press.

Phillips, J. L. (2000), *How to Think about Statistics* (6th ed.), New York: Freeman.

Pica, T., H. Kang, and S. Sauro (2006), "Information Gap Tasks: Their Multiple Roles and Contributions to Interaction Research Methodology," *Studies in Second Language Acquisition*, 28: 301–38.

Piccardo, E., B. North, and T. Goodier (2019), "Broadening the Scope of Language Education: Mediation, Plurilingualism, and Collaborative Learning—the CEFR Companion Volume," *Journal of e-Learning and Knowledge Society*, 15(1): 17–36.

Pikulski, J., and D. Chard (2005), "Fluency: Bridge between Decoding and Reading Comprehension," *Reading Teacher*, 58: 510–19.

Pinar, W. (2012), *What Is Curriculum Theory?* (2nd ed.), New York: Routledge.

Pintrich, P., and E. DeGroot (1990), "Motivational and Self-regulated Learning Components of Classroom Performance," *Journal of Educational Psychology*, 82(1): 33–40.

Prabhu, N. S. (1987), *Second Language Pedagogy: A Perspective*, Oxford: Oxford University Press.

Prabhu, N. S. (1990), "There Is No Best Method—Why?" *TESOL Quarterly*, 24(2): 161–76.

Prabhu, N. S. (1992), "The Dynamics of the Language Lesson," *TESOL Quarterly*, 26(2): 225–41.

Pratt, M., M. Geisler, C. Kramsch, S. McGinnis, R. Patrikis, K. Ryding, and H. Saussy (2008), "Transforming College and University Foreign Language Departments," *Modern Language Journal*, 92(2): 287–92.

Preston, D. (2005), "What Is Folk Linguistics? Why Should You Care?" *Lingua Posnaniensis*, 47: 143–62, retrieved November 30, 2020, from: https://english.okstate.edu/images/Documents/Preston/Perceptual_Dialectology/Preston_What_is_FL_2005.pdf

Price, H. (2012), "Principal-Teacher Interactions: How Affective Relationships Shape Principal and Teacher Attitudes," *Educational Administration Quarterly*, 48(1): 39–85.

Printy, S., and Y. Liu (2020), "Distributed Leadership Globally: The Interactive Nature of Principal and Teacher Leadership in 32 Countries," *Educational*

Administration Quarterly, 57(2): 1–36, retrieved December 24, 2021, from: https://doi.org/10.1177%2F0013161X20926548

Rahimpour, M., and R. Hashemi (2011), "Textbook Selection and Evaluation in EFL Context," *World Journal of Education*, 1(2): 62–8, retrieved June 2021 from: http://dx.doi.org/10.5430/wje.v1n2p62

Rankin, J., and F. Becker (2006), "Does Reading the Research Make a Difference? A Case Study of Teacher Growth in FL German," *Modern Language Journal*, 90: 353–79.

Ranta, L., and R. Lyster (2007), "A Cognitive Approach to Improving Immersion Students' Oral Language Abilities: The Awareness-Practice-Feedback Sequence," in R. M. DeKeyser (ed.), *Practice in a Second Language: Perspectives from Applied Linguistics and Cognitive Psychology*, 141–60, Cambridge: Cambridge University Press.

Ravitch, S., and M. Riggan (2017), *How Conceptual Frameworks Guide Research* (2nd ed.), Thousand Oaks, CA: Sage.

Rea-Dickins, P., and K. Germaine (1998), "The Price of Everything and the Value of Nothing," in P. Rea-Dickins and K. Germaine (eds.), *Managing Evaluation and Innovation in Language Teaching*, 3–19, London: Longman.

Reid, W. (1999), *Curriculum as Institution and Practice*, Mahwah, NJ: Lawrence Erlbaum.

Renandya, W. A., and T. S. C. Farrell (2011), "Teacher, the Tape Is Too Fast!: Extensive Listening in ELT," *ELT Journal*, 65(1): 52–9.

Riazi, A. M. (2016), *The Routledge Encyclopedia of Research Methods in Applied Linguistics*, New York: Routledge.

Riazi, A. M., and N. Mosalanejad (2010), "Evaluation of Learning Objectives in Iranian High-School and Pre-university English Textbooks Using Bloom's Taxonomy," *TESL-EJ*, 13(4): 1–16.

Richards, I. A. (1936), *The Philosophy of Rhetoric*, Oxford: Oxford University Press.

Richards, J. C. (1990), *The Language Teaching Matrix*, Cambridge: Cambridge University Press.

Richards, J. C. (2001), *Curriculum Development in Language Teaching*, Cambridge: Cambridge University Press.

Richards, J. C., and T. S. Rodgers (1986), *Approaches and Methods in Language Teaching: A Description and Analysis*, Cambridge: Cambridge University Press.

Richards, J. C., and T. S. Rodgers (2014), *Approaches and Methods in Language Teaching* (3rd ed.), Cambridge: Cambridge University Press.

Richards, J. C., and R. Schmidt (2002), *Longman Dictionary of Language Teaching and Applied Linguistics*, New York: Pearson.

Ringvald, V. (2006), "Proficiency-Based Instruction," *Journal of Jewish Education*, 69: 5–8.

Rivera-Mills, S., and L. Plonsky (2007), "Empowering Students with Language Learning Strategies: A Critical Review of Current Issues," *Foreign Language Annals*, 40(3): 535–48.

Robins, R. H. (1997), *A Short History of Linguistics* (4th ed.), London: Longman.

Rodgers, T. (1989), "Syllabus Design, Curriculum Development and Polity Determinations," in R. K. Johnson (ed.), *The Second Language Curriculum*, 24–34, Cambridge: Cambridge University Press.

Roehr, K. (2007), "Metalinguistic Knowledge and Language Ability in University-Level L2 Learners," *Applied Linguistics*, 29(2): 173–99.

Rogers, J., L. LeCompte, and V. Plumly (2012), "Articulating the Curriculum Through Cultural Themes: A Literacy and Genre Approach to Teaching Protest, Rebellion, and the Reevaluation of the Past," *Die Unterrichtspraxis*, 45(1): 40–52.

Rogers, P. (2000), "Program Theory: Not Whether Programs Work, but How They Work," in D. Stufflebeam, G. Madaus, and T. Kellaghan (eds.), *Evaluation Models*, 209–32, Norwell, MA: Kluwer Academic.

Rose, H. (2012), "Language Learning Strategy Research: Where Do We Go from Here?" *Studies in Self-access Learning Journal*, 3(2): 137–48.

Rosenthal, R., and L. Jacobson ([1968] 1992), *Pygmalion in the Classroom: Teacher Expectation and Pupils' Intellectual Development* (expanded ed.), New York: Irvington.

Rossi, P., H. Freeman, and M. Lipsey (1999), *Evaluation: A Systematic Approach* (6th ed.), Thousand Oaks, CA: Sage.

Rossi, P., M. Lipsey, and H. Freeman (2004*), Evaluation: A Systematic Approach* (7th ed.), Thousand Oaks, CA: Sage.

Rost, M. (2005), "L2 Listening," in E. Hinkel (ed.), *Handbook of Research in Second Language Teaching and Learning*, 503–27, London: Lawrence Erlbaum.

Rumore, M. (2016), "The Course Syllabus: Legal Contract or Operator's Manual?" *American Journal of Pharmaceutical Education*, 80(10), retrieved December 17, 2020, from: https://www.ncbi.nlm.nih.gov/pmc/articles/PMC5289733/

Runnels, J., and V. Runnels (2019), "Impact of the Common European Framework of Reference," *CEFR Journal: Research and Practice*, 1: 18–32.

Rupley, W. H., T. R. Blair, and W. D. Nichols (2009), "Effective Reading Instruction for Struggling Readers: The Role of Direct/Explicit Teaching," *Reading and Writing Quarterly*, 25(2): 125–38. doi: 10.1080/10573560802683523

Saito, Y. (2006), "Consequences of High-Stakes Testing on the Family and Schools in Japan," *KEDI Educational Development Institute Journal of Educational Policy*, 3(1): 101–12.

Samuda, V. (2001), "Guiding Relationships between Form and Meaning during Task Performance: The Role of the Teacher," in M. Bygate, P. Skehan, and M. Swain (eds.), *Researching Pedagogic Tasks: Second Language Learning, Teaching and Testing*, 119–40, Harlow: Longman.

Samuda, V., and M. Bygate (2008), *Tasks in Second Language Learning*, Houndmills: Palgrave Macmillan.

Samuels, S., and R. Flor (1997), "The Importance of Automaticity for Developing Expertise in Reading," *Reading and Writing Quarterly*, 13(2): 107–21.

Samuels, S. J. (2006), "Reading Fluency: Its Past, Present, and Future," in T. Rasinski, C. Blachowicz, and K. Lems (eds.), *Fluency Instruction: Research-Based Best Practices*, 7–20, New York: Guilford.

Sato, M., and S. Loewen (2018), "Metacognitive Instruction Enhances the Effectiveness of Corrective Feedback: Variable Effects of Feedback Types and Linguistic Targets," *Language Learning*, 68(2): 507–45.

Sato, M., and S. Loewen (2019), "Toward Evidence-Based Second Language Pedagogy," in M. Sato and S. Loewen (eds.), *Evidence-Based Second Language Pedagogy*, 1–23, New York: Routledge.

Schechtman, R., and J. Koser (2008), "Foreign Languages and Higher Education: A Pragmatic Approach to Change," *Modern Language Journal*, 92(2): 309–12.

Schmidt, R. (1990), "The Role of Consciousness in Second Language Learning," *Applied Linguistics*, 11(2): 129–58.

Scrimgeour, A., and P. Wilson (2009), "International Curriculum for Chinese Language Education," *Babel*, 43(2): 35–8.

Scriven, M. (2000), "Evaluation Ideologies," in D. Stufflebeam, G. Madaus, and T. Kellaghan (eds.), *Evaluation Models*, 249–78, Norwell, MA: Kluwer Academic.

Searle, J. R. (1969), *Speech Acts: An Essay in the Philosophy of Language*, Cambridge: Cambridge University Press.

Seo, K. (2000), "Intervening in Tertiary Students' Strategic Listening in Japanese as a Foreign Language," unpublished doctoral dissertation, Griffith University, Queensland, Australia.

Shackleton, C. (2018), "Developing CEFR-Related Language Proficiency Tests: A Focus on the Role of Piloting," *CercleS*, 8(2): 333–52.

Shehadeh, A. (2002), "Comprehensible Output, from Occurrence to Acquisition: An Agenda for Acquisitional Research," *Language Learning*, 52(3): 597–647.

Shimono, T. (2018), "L2 Reading Fluency Progression Using Timed Reading and Repeated Oral Reading," *Reading in a Foreign Language*, 30(1): 152–79.

Sidhu, G., S. Kaur, and L. Chi (2018), "CEFR-Aligned School-Based Assessment in the Malaysian Primary ESL Classroom," *Indonesian Journal of Applied Linguistics*, 8(2): 452–63.

Siegle, D. (2000), "An Introduction to Self-Efficacy," retrieved October 24, 2018, from: https://nrcgt.uconn.edu/underachievement_study/self-efficacy/se_section1/

Skehan, P. (1998), *A Cognitive Approach to Language Learning*, Oxford: Oxford University Press.

Skierso, A. (1991), "Textbook Selection and Evaluation," in M. Celce-Murcia (ed.), *Teaching English as a Second or Foreign Language* (2nd ed.), 432–53, Boston, MA: Heinle and Heinle.

Snow, R. E. (1973), "Theory Construction for Research on Teaching," in R. M. Travers (ed.), *Second Handbook of Research on Teaching*, 77–12, Chicago: Rand McNally.

Sousa, F. J. (2010), "Metatheories in Research: Positivism, Postmodernism, and Critical Realism," in A. G. Woodside (ed.), *Organizational Culture, Business-to-Business Relationships, and Interfirm Networks*, 455–503, Bingley: Emerald Group.

Stake, R. (2000), "Program Evaluation, Particularly Responsive Evaluation," in D. Stufflebeam, G. Madaus, and T. Kellaghan (eds.), *Evaluation Models*, 343–62, Norwell, MA: Kluwer Academic.

Stanovich, K. (1987), "The Impact of Automaticity Theory," *Journal of Learning Disabilities*, 20(3): 167–8.

Stein, M., D. Carnine, and R. Dixon (1998), "Direct Instruction: Integrating Curriculum Design and Effective Teaching Practice," *Intervention in School and Clinic*, 33(4): 227–33. doi: 10.1177/105345129803300405

Stern, H. H. (1981), "Communicative Language Teaching and Learning: Toward a Synthesis," in J. E. Alatis, H. B. Altman, and P. M. Alatis (eds.), *The Second Language Classroom: Directions for the 1980s*, 131–48, Oxford: Oxford University Press.

Stern, H. H. (1983), *Fundamental Concepts of Language Teaching*, New York: Oxford University Press.

Stevick, E. (1982), *Teaching and Learning Languages*, Cambridge: Cambridge University Press.

Stevick, E. (1986), *Images and Options in the Language Classroom*, Cambridge: Cambridge University Press.

Strevens, P. (1987), "The Nature of Language Teaching," in M. Long and J. C. Richards (eds.), *Methodology in TESOL*, 10–25, Boston, MA: Heinle and Heinle.

Stufflebeam, D. (2000), "Foundational Models for 21st Century Program Evaluation," in D. Stufflebeam, G. Madaus, and T. Kellaghan (eds.), *Evaluation Models*, 33–83, Norwell, MA: Kluwer Academic.

Stufflebeam, D., and A. Shinkfield (2007), *Evaluation Theory, Models, and Applications*, San Francisco, CA: Jossey-Bass.

Suemori, S. (2020), "Motivators and Demotivators to Teach English in Japanese Secondary Schools," *JALT Journal*, 42(1): 51–65.

Sutton, R. S., and A. G. Barto (2018), *Reinforcement Learning* (2nd ed.), Cambridge, MA: MIT Press.

Swaffar, J., and K. Arens (2005), *Remapping the Foreign Language Curriculum*, New York: Modern Language Association of America.

Swain, M., and S. Lapkin (1995), "Problems in Output and the Cognitive Processes they Generate," *Applied Linguistics*, 16: 371–91.

Swan, M. (2005), "Legislation by Hypothesis: The Case of Task-Based Instruction," *Applied Linguistics*, 26(3): 376–401.

Taguchi, E., G. Gorsuch, and K. Mitani (2021), "Using Repeated Reading for Reading Fluency Development in a Small Japanese Foreign Language Program," *Pedagogies*, doi: https://doi.org/10.1080/1554480X.2021.1944866

Taipei Economic and Cultural Office (2011), *TOCFL*, Los Angeles, CA: Author, retrieved January 29, 2019, from: http://www.tw.org/tocfl/

Tarver, S. (1985), "Review of Theory of Instruction by Siegfried Engelmann and Douglas Carnine," *Remedial and Special Education*, 6(2): 57, 59.

Tavakoli, P., and A.-M. Hunter (2018), "Is Fluency Being 'Neglected' in the Classroom? Teacher Understanding of Fluency and Related Classroom Practices," *Language Teaching Research*, 22(3): 330–49.

Taylor, B. P. (1987) "Teaching ESL: Incorporating a Communicative, Student-centered Component," in M. H. Long and J. C. Richards (eds.), *Methodology in TESOL*, 45–60, Boston, MA: Heinle and Heinle.

Taylor, F., and E. Marsden (2014), "Perceptions, Attitudes, and Choosing to Study Foreign Languages in England: An Experimental Intervention," *Modern Language Journal*, 98(4): 902–20.

Tedick, D. (2009), "K-12 Language Teacher Preparation: Problems and Possibilities," *Modern Language Journal*, 93: 263–7.

Tedick, D., and C. Walker (1994), "Second Language Teacher Education: The Problems that Plague Us," *Modern Language Journal*, 94: 300–12.

Tedick, D., and C. Walker (1995), "From Theory to Practice: How Do We Prepare Teachers for Second Language Classrooms?" *Foreign Language Annals*, 28(4): 499–517.

Teng, L., and L. Zhang (2016), "A Questionnaire-Based Validation of Multidimensional Models of Self-Regulated Learning Strategies," *Modern Language Journal*, 100(3): 674–701.

Texas Education Agency (2020), "Texas Essential Knowledge and Skills," retrieved December 2, 2020, from: https://tea.texas.gov/academics/curriculum-standards/teks/texas-essential-knowledge-and-skills

Thibodeau, P. H., T. Matlock, and S. J. Flusberg (2019), "The Role of Metaphor in Communication and Thought," *Language and Linguists Compass*, e12327, retrieved October 6, 2018, from: https://doi.org/10.1111/lnc3.12327

Thomas, M. (2013), "History of the Study of Second Language Acquisition," in J. Herschensohn and M. Young-Scholten (eds.), *The Cambridge Handbook of Second Language Acquisition*, 26–45, Cambridge: Cambridge University Press.

Thomas, N. J. (1928), *The Child in America*, New York: Knopf.

Thompson, I., and J. Rubin (1996), "Can Strategy Instruction Improve Listening Comprehension?" *Foreign Language Annals*, 29(3): 331–42.

Thoonen, E., P. Sleegers, F. Oort, T. Peetsma, and F. Geijsel (2011), "How to Improve Teaching Practices: The Role of Teacher Motivation, Organizational Factors, and Leadership Practices," *Educational Administration Quarterly*, 47(3): 496–536.

Tilbury, A., T. Clementson, L. Hendra, and D. Rea (2010), *English Unlimited Elementary*, Cambridge: Cambridge University Press.

Tobin, K., and M. Calhoon (2009), "A Comparison of Two Reading Programs on the Reading Outcomes of First-Grade Students," *Journal of Direct Instruction*, 9(1): 35–46.

Tolman, A., A. Sechler, and S. Smart (2017), "Defining and Understanding Student Resistance," in A. Tolman and J. Kremling (eds.), *Why Students Resist Learning*, 1–20, Sterling, Virginia: Stylus.

Tomasello, M., and C. Herron (1988), "Down the Garden Path: Inducing and Correcting Overgeneralization Errors in the Foreign Language Classroom," *Applied Psycholinguistics*, 9: 237–46.

Tomlinson, B. (2013), "Materials Evaluation," in B. Tomlinson (ed.), *Developing Materials for Language Teaching* (2nd ed.), 21–48, London: Bloomsbury Academic.

Tono, Y. (2019), "Coming Full Circle—from CEFR to CEFR-J and Back," *CEFR Journal: Research and Practice*, 1: 5–17.

Trask, R. L. (2007), *Language and Linguistics* (2nd ed.), Abingdon: Routledge.

Tseng, W., Z. Dornyei, and N. Schmitt (2006), "A New Approach to Assessing Strategic Learning: The Case of Self-regulation in Vocabulary Acquisition," *Applied Linguistics*, 27(1): 78–102.

Tsuchiya, M. (2018), "The Effects of a Teacher's Formative Feedback on the Self-Regulated Learning of Lower-Proficiency Japanese Learners of English," *ARELE*, 29: 97–112, retrieved March 21, 2021, from: https://www.jstage.jst.go.jp/article/arele/29/0/29_97/_article/-char/ja

Tyack, D., and W. Tobin (1994), "The 'Grammar' of Schooling: Why Has It Been So Hard to Change?" *American Educational Research Journal*, 31(3): 453–79.

Ur, P. (2011), "Grammar Teaching: Research, Theory, and Practice," in E. Hinkel (ed.), *Handbook of Research in Second Language Teaching and Learning Vol II*, 507–22, New York: Routledge.

Urmston, A. W., and M. Pennington (2008), "The Beliefs and Practices of Novice Teachers in Hong Kong: Change and Resistance to Change in an Asian Teaching Context," in T. S. C. Farrell (ed.), *Novice Language Teachers: Insights and Perspectives for the First Year*, 89–103, London: Equinox.

Van den Branden, K. (1997), "Effects of Negotiation on Language Learners' Output," *Language Learning*, 47(4): 589–636.

Van Rijt, J., A. Wijnands, and P. A. Coppen (2020), "Investigating Dutch Teachers' Beliefs on Working with Linguistic Metaconcepts to Improve Students' L1 Grammatical Understanding," Research Papers in Education, 37(2): 1–19.

Vandergrift, L. (2002), "It Was Nice to See That Our Predictions Were Right: Developing Metacognition in L2 Listening in Grades 4–6," *Canadian Modern Language Review*, 58(4): 555–75.

Vandergrift, L. (2005), "Relationships among Motivation Orientations, Metacognitive Awareness and Proficiency in L2 Listening," *Applied Linguistics*, 26(1): 70–89.

Vandergrift, L., and S. Baker (2015), "Learner Variables in Second Language Listening Comprehension: An Exploratory Path Analysis," *Language Learning*, 65(2): 390–416.

Vandergrift, L., and C. Goh (2012), *Teaching and Learning Second Language Listening: Metacognition in Action*, New York: Routledge.

VanPatten, B., and J. Williams (2007), "Introduction: The Nature of Theories," in B. VanPatten and J. Williams (eds.), *Theories in Second Language Acquisition: An Introduction*, 1–16, Mahwah, NJ: Lawrence Erlbaum.

Veenman, M., B. Van Hout-Wolters, and P. Afflerbach (2006), "Metacognition and Learning: Conceptual and Methodological Considerations," *Metacognition and Learning*, 1: 3–14.

Vogt, W. P., D. C. Gardner, and L. M. Haeffele (2012), *When to Use What Research Design*, New York: Guilford.

Vygotsky, L. (1962) *Thinking and Speaking*, translated by E. Hanfmann, G. Vakar, and N. Minnick, Cambridge, MA: MIT Press.

Vygotsky, L., M. Cole, and V. John-Steiner (1979), *Development of Higher Psychological Processes*, Cambridge, MA: Harvard University Press.

Wajnryb, R. (2012), *Grammar Dictation*, Oxford: Oxford University Press.

Walczyk, J. (2000), "The Interplay between Automatic and Control Processes in Reading," *Reading Research Quarterly*, 35: 554–66.

Wang, Y. (2008), "Influence of Planning on Students' Language Performance in Task-based Language Teaching," *English Language Teaching*, 1(1): 83–6.

Webster's Student Dictionary (1999), P. H. Collin (ed.), New York: Barnes and Nobel.

Wenden, A. (1998), "Metacognitive Knowledge and Language Learning," *Applied Linguistics*, 19(4): 515–37.

Wilkins, D. A. (1976), *Notional Syllabuses*, Oxford: Oxford University Press.

Willis, D., and J. Willis (2007), *Doing Task-Based Teaching*, Oxford: Oxford University Press.

Winchester, S. (2004), *Krakatoa*, New York: Penguin.

Wong, J., and H. Zhang Waring (2020), *Conversation Analysis and Second Language Pedagogy* (2nd ed.), New York: Routledge.

Wong, K. F. (2010), "Breaking Boundaries, Building Bridges: Reconceptualizing and Integrating the Cultural Dimension into Chinese Language Pedagogy," unpublished doctoral dissertation, University of Hawaii at Manoa, Honolulu, Hawaii.

Woore, R., S. Graham, K. Kohl, L. Courtney, and C. Savory (2020), "Consolidating the Evidence Base for MFL Curriculum, Pedagogy and Assessment Reform at GCSE: An Investigation of Teachers' Views," retrieved March 28, 2022, from: https://ora.ox.ac.uk/objects/uuid:1f797d25-98b4-4b89-863a-779b2 348ae20/download_file?safe_filename=Woore-et-al-01nov20.pdf&type_of_ work=Report

World Institute for Action Learning (WIAL) (2021, May 6), "What Is Action Learning?" [Video], YouTube, retrieved November 18, 2022, from: https:// youtu.be/x8gjjN0pu5o

Wright, A., D. Betteridge, and M. Buckby (1979), *Games for Language Learning*, Cambridge: Cambridge University Press.

Yang, N. D. (1992), "Second Language Learners' Belief about Language Learning and Their Use of Learning Strategies," unpublished doctoral dissertation, Austin: University of Texas.

Young, A., P. Bowers, and G. MacKinnon (1996), "Effects of Prosodic Modeling and Repeated Reading on Poor Readers' Fluency and Comprehension," *Applied Psycholinguistics*, 17: 59–84.

Yuan, F., and R. Ellis (2003), "The Effects of Pre-task Planning and On-line Planning on Fluency, Complexity and Accuracy in L2 Monologic Oral Production," *Applied Linguistics*, 24(1): 1–27.

Zakaria, F. (2020), *Ten Lessons for a Post-pandemic World*, New York: Norton.

Zhu, W., and J. Flaitz (2005), "Using Focus Group Methodology to Understand International Students' Academic Language Needs: A Comparison of Perspectives," *TESL-EJ*, 8(4), retrieved April 1, 2021, from: http://www.tesl-ej. org/wordpress/issues/volume8/ej32/ej32a3/

INDEX